SECURITY MANAGEMENT
Readings from
Security Management
Magazine

Edited by

Shari Mendelson Gallery
Director of Publications
American Society of Industrial Security

BUTTERWORTH PUBLISHERS
Boston • London
Sydney • Wellington • Durban • Toronto

Individual chapters reprinted with permission of American Society for Industrial Security, from *Security Management*.

Library of Congress Cataloging in Publication Data
Main entry under title:

Security Management.

  Includes index.
    1. Industry—Security measures—United States—Manage-
ment—Addresses, essays, lectures.   I. Gallery, Shari
Mendelson.   II. Security management (Arlington, Va.)
HV8290.S375   1984   658.4'7   84–3218
ISBN 0–409–95099–8

Butterworth Publisher
80 Montvale Avenue
Stoneham, MA 02180

10 9 8 7 6 5 4 3 2 1

Printed in the United States of America

CONTENTS

ASIS

The American Society for Industrial Security is a worldwide organization of management specialists dedicated to protecting corporate and institutional assets. Founded in 1955, the Society is comprised of directors, managers, and supervisors responsible for security and asset protection programs in government, public institutions, and every field of business.

For large and small organizations from New York to New Delhi, ASIS members develop and administer programs to thwart every conceivable crime—from pirating trade secrets to shoplifting. They are also responsible for minimizing losses from natural and man-caused disasters.

ASIS disseminates information and tailors instructional programs to meet the rapidly expanding responsibilities of security professionals. Through more than 160 chapters in the US and abroad, and through frequent educational programs and publications, ASIS enables members to keep posted on developments in security and to share their specialized knowledge and skills.

ASIS has standing committees whose efforts focus on security functions common to most types of organizations such as physical security, disaster planning, computer security, proprietary information, fire prevention, and terrorism. A second group of committees concentrates on security concerns of specific types of organizations, such as government installations, retailers, financial institutions, health care facilities, and energy firms.

Security Management

Security Management is a monthly magazine published by the American Society for Industrial Security (ASIS). Written for the benefit of practicing security professionals, *Security Management (SM)* covers all aspects of the diverse field of security. Every kind of organization—from large defense contract manufacturers to hotel and motel chains to transportation companies—has assets that need protection. In some cases the assets are costly physical equipment, in other cases the assets take the form of critical information or the specialized knowledge of a top executive. Each month *SM* presents articles that help security managers, in all kinds of organizations, learn ways to better protect their employers' assets.

INTRODUCTION

Security is a delicate balancing act. Ideally, it protects and preserves freedom—the freedom of individuals, organizations, and society as a whole. By their very nature, however, the measures adopted to achieve security threaten to reduce freedom. This fact often poses a dilemma to those responsible for providing security. Achieving the appropriate balance between protection and accessibility is essentially what security management is all about.

Most security pros would agree that anything can be made secure against all but the direct threat. As soon as access is required to what is being protected, however, the ability to protect is impinged upon. The degree to which access is needed has a direct, inverse correlation to the extent protection can be provided. The more people who need to be able to use an item, the harder safeguarding it becomes. The more a person to be protected must be able to travel about, the tougher the security assignment is.

Clearly, protection to the extent of total inaccessibility is of little value on a day-to-day basis. Security that incapacitates an organization, its employees, or clientele might be considered worse than losing whatever the organization hopes to protect. Take, for example, the contents of a museum. If every visitor is permitted to handle the artworks, the risk of their being damaged, either from wear or vandalism, seems quite high. Given the value of many artworks, the likelihood of thefts is also significant. In contrast, if the artworks must be locked away in a vault to protect them, the purpose of the museum is defeated altogether.

Similarly, if critical proprietary information is stolen or leaked from an organization that depends on it for a competitive edge, then that organization may not be able to survive. However, having the information is of little value if employees cannot be allowed to work with it. If employees are unable to use the information or tools they need to perform their jobs, their employer will surely go out of business. Whether the needed materials are unavailable due to theft or excessive security precautions makes little difference; either will result in an undesirable situation.

In many instances, finding the fine line between what preserves freedom and what violates it is difficult and subject to much debate. The people inconvenienced by security measures are likely to view them as excessive and unnecessary. Likewise, persons who are feeling the pinch of budgetary constraints may eye expenditures on security jealously or see them as being wasteful; yet those same individuals, if attacked in the company parking lot or laid off because a piece of equipment crucial to their job has disappeared or been vandalized, no doubt would rail against their employer for poor security.

The decision to expend resources for security is inherently conjectural. Like preventive health care or insurance, effective security sometimes gives rise to insidious doubts that the effort is worthwhile—after all, we can never be sure that the event being protected against would ever come to pass. The success of security efforts cannot be measured quite as simply as increased sales or decreased production costs. The value of good security seems most apparent when it is lacking and some problem occurs. In fact, frequently security awareness is greatest in organizations that have recently experienced a significant loss, something akin to locking the barn door once the horse is out. This is not to say that locking the barn door now will not keep the next horse from escaping but is to suggest that many times the lesson of why good security is worth having is learned the hard way. Fortunately more and more organizations seem to be learning from the misfortunes of competitors, neighbors, and other organizations in their line of business.

Regardless of how the lesson is learned, once an organization recognizes the need for good security, the question of how to achieve it arises. That question is the prime focus of *Security Management* magazine, which is published by the American Society for Industrial Security (ASIS). The thousands of members of ASIS are individuals charged by their employers with identifying what assets are at risk, determining what risks can and should be addressed, and specifying how those risks can be minimized. Through ASIS and *Security Management,* they share ideas, problems, and solutions. This book offers selections from *Security Management.*

As those assigned the task of providing security have often learned, recognition on the part of management that organizational assets are worth protecting does not assure that appropriate security measures will be accepted. In essence, security decisions are no different than other business decisions; they must make sense in terms of expected benefits received as a result of the resources expended. Failure to heed that fact can spell death to security proposals. The so-called security manager who is not first a manager and second a security specialist almost invariably meets with resistance and frustration. For this reason, the selections in this book concentrate on the management aspects of security.

Security is, according to Clifford Evans, corporate security manager of International Harvester, "the only function in a company, other than the chief executive, that can affect, at one time or another, every single person, operation, product, service, and financial procedure." For this reason and because security often is most needed during times of pressure, the security manager must have professional credibility well established. Attempting to implement security policies and procedures in the midst of a crisis and expecting people to heed the direction of someone they perhaps don't know or respect is futile. The security staff must have sold the organization on the idea that security is good business and that the security staff is capable *before* a crisis arises.

This book focuses on what the job of a security manager is and how the functions performed by every professional manager (planning, organizing, staffing, directing, and controlling) are specifically applied to achieving effective security. Factors that affect security programs, such as legal considerations and the expectations of upper management and of other people security affects, are also addressed.

The experience of a wide variety of security practitioners is reflected in the contents of this book. Expertise gained over many years in the field and in many different kinds of organizations and situations is shared by the authors in hopes of promoting understanding and professionalism.

PART I

The Job of Security Management

Security manager, director of security, vice president for loss prevention, security and plant protection supervisor—the titles of the people who oversee security efforts in organizations run the gamut. Just as the titles vary widely, so do the responsibilities that accompany those titles. Perhaps more than for any other position, the duties of the security manager (by whatever title) differ from one organization to the next. The scope of responsibilities can be quite narrow or impressively broad. Seldom does the title make clear who is responsible for security decisions or what security responsibilities an individual has. The power or authority vested in security positions also differs widely despite the apparent comparability of titles.

Numerous factors influence the esteem with which the security function is viewed in an organization, as well as the extent to which security considerations are heeded. The organization's past experience plays a big part in its attitudes toward security. If a loss occurred involving thefts by employees, the organization is likely to emphasize pre-employment screening, examination of employee parcels, and perhaps even honesty testing. If, in contrast, the organization found itself outfoxed by a competitor due to a leak of crucial information, data security will probably be stressed.

Just as past experience often affects how an organization and the people within it look on security, so do the background and competence of the person(s) charged with overseeing the security function. If the security manager clearly is competent and displays professional attitudes and skills, the security function will probably be respected within the organization. If, however, the security manager perpetuates the old frustrated rent-a-cop image, security is unlikely to be viewed as important.

Many organizations, when first faced with a security problem, choose to hire retiring law enforcement or military officers, assuming such individuals have the appropriate background to handle the assignment. While many security professionals have come from these sources, neither law enforcement nor military experience necessarily prepares individuals for security responsibilities. A different perspective is required. Effective security is preventive in nature rather than reactive. Effective security management is essentially effective management of a specialized function.

Effective security managers foresee problems, identify solutions, gain acceptance for appropriate solutions and oversee the implementation of them. Acquiring needed information, analyzing it, planning, using personnel and equipment to best effect, budgeting, and communicating are all parts of the job of security management.

CHAPTER 1

Security Management: Challenge or Dilemma?

Gilbert V. Bresnick
Manager, Real Estate and Office Services
Department
Baltimore Gas and Electric Company

Your industry is on the threshold of a most exciting and rapid growth period. How well you manage your resources will be the determining factor of your success. I have been in a unique position to witness a phenomenal transition in our society over the last fifteen years. It all started when the riots of the late sixties and high unemployment caused a rapid increase in crime in most cities across the country. Radical groups multiplied. At the same time, our public law enforcement agencies were hard pressed to handle this increase in crime because of limited budgets and manpower. Private industry had to pick up a greater share of this burden.

My security dilemma began when corporate security became my responsibility. What did I find? Security people didn't understand my language and I didn't understand theirs. Planning, budgeting, and related controls seemed to be improvised. Security people tended to dramatize problems or go for the overkill, in my opinion.

At the time, I also found that personnel screening was still in its infancy, and training was non-existent. Moreover, security people had difficulty in presenting a program in concise, logical, and analytical terms. No attempt was made by security people to sell themselves to top management, yet the people who were unwilling to talk with management complained that security jobs were at the bottom of the corporate totem pole.

In March 1981, the Nuclear Regulatory Commission (NRC) published a report entitled *People-Related Problems Affecting Security in the Licensed Nuclear Industry*. The survey revealed that security managers were deficient in certain skills. The areas of deficiency included:

Reprinted with permission of the American Society for Industrial Security, from *Security Management*, April 1982, pp. 79.

- inability to establish a working rapport with corporate management;
- failure to develop subordinate supervisors;
- failure to establish effective lines of communication within the security force; and
- failure to delegate responsibility properly or to give subordinates authority commensurate with their responsibilities.

Not all of my experience with security has been negative, however. Here are some of the positive changes in security I have observed over the years:

- Many firms have added professional security specialists to their staffs to handle security-related incidents of all types.
- Security planning is now an on-going function in most large corporations.
- Comprehensive loss reports are now prepared for top management's information, the data being collected on highly sophisticated computers for analysis.
- Daily incident reports are distributed throughout organizations for immediate corrective action.
- Security control centers are being established in many large companies and manned on an around-the-clock basis for centralized reporting of security incidents and problems.
- Crisis management centers are being established to handle such bizarre events as kidnappings, hostage takings, holdups, and civil disturbances. These situations require a highly organized effort involving top management and local law enforcement agencies for quick assessment of the severity of problems.
- Sophisticated security training programs have been created to provide complex training for nuclear security officers. Security awareness programs and new employee indoctrination seminars have also become more prevalent.
- Technical units have been created to develop and coordinate corporate-wide security programs and systems. These programs include security protection and access control plans for power plants, computer centers, business complexes, and operating centers. These technical units have been responsible for developing highly sophisticated microwave and TV perimeter surveillance and computer alarm systems to control access to protected and vital areas.
- Emergency response planning involving comprehensive security operations have been created for all nuclear power plants in the US today.

Less than ten years ago I conducted a survey of the top twenty-five utilities in the country. Not one identified security as a separate operating entity or budgetary function. Today, virtually every utility has a separate security function within its organization, clearly defined as an integral part of its corporate structure.

With this increase in corporate stature and responsibility, security people now face a new opportunity, that of cost-effective management. The instances when a "good old boy" or "untrained ex-cop" heads a corporate security operation will be rare in the future.

In addition to the normal language that security people use in their day-to-day surveillance, perimeter control, vandalism, assault, and emergency response operations, a new list of terms has been added to security vocabularies, including: cost-benefit analysis, zero-based budgeting, cash forecasting, work programs, loss trends, job descriptions, corporate sub-planning, work measurement, resource control, and a whole raft of others.

The entire set of management principles are now a part of security. Surely you have heard of such terms as planning, organizing, staffing, directing, and controlling. Perhaps a brief review of these terms is worthwhile:

- planning: determining what work must be done.
- organizing: classifying and dividing work into manageable units.
- staffing: determining the requirements for and ensuring the availability of personnel to perform work.
- directing: bringing about the human activity required to accomplish objectives.
- controlling: assuring the effective accomplishment of objectives.

Basically, each of the functions identified here is performed by every professional manager at every level.

Most of us have had exposure to organizing, staffing, and directing management functions. Few managers, however, place enough emphasis on the planning and controlling aspects of management. Too few understand these concepts. If I may expand, for example, on the planning function. This step involves:

- defining roles and missions: determining the nature and scope of work to be performed.
- forecasting: estimating the future.
- setting objectives: determining results to be achieved.
- programming: establishing a plan of action to follow in reaching objectives.
- scheduling: establishing time requirements for objectives and programs.
- budgeting: determining and assigning resources to reach objectives.
- policy-making: establishing rules, regulations, or predetermined decisions.
- establishing procedures: determining consistent and systematic methods of handling work.

The organizing, staffing, and directing functions are the ones we know about and generally do well. The tasks involved in these steps are straight-forward:

- organizing: structuring and integrating effective productive teamwork among organizational units.
- staffing: determining personnel needs, selecting personnel, and developing personnel in line with organizational needs.
- directing: assigning, motivating, communicating, and coordinating group efforts to accomplish individual and group objectives.

The fifth management function, controlling, is the true test of management, and the one we tend to ignore. Remember, controlling is assuring the effective accomplishment of objectives. This encompasses the following:

- establishing standards: devising a gauge for successful performance in achieving objectives.
- measuring performance: assuring actual—versus planned—performance.
- taking corrective action: bringing about performance improvement toward objectives.

LOOKING AHEAD

What is our dilemma for the future? Most security professionals are not qualified or trained to handle the array of problems associated with being a manager in the business or the private sectors of industry today. Universities have only now begun to recognize the need to incorporate business management principles into their law enforcement and criminal justice curriculums.

Corporate management does not always understand security, nor have those involved in security recognized the effect of this lack of understanding by top corporate management.

The top professional security designation, that of Certified Protection Professional (CPP), has not really identified the need for an in-depth knowledge of fundamental management principles for security professionals.

Interaction with existing law enforcement organizations has only been successful in rare instances. Think of the power you could generate if you could mobilize the talent within local law enforcement organizations, the FBI and other federal agencies, and the private business and private security sectors. Interaction with these groups should take place regularly.

Technical surveillance systems such as television, microwave, radio, and computer systems are in the embryonic stage. Most of these systems have been designed by computer firms or engineers who know little or nothing about security.

WHAT CAN WE DO?

We must take advantage of the entrepreneurial zeal that is so lacking in many large corporations if security is to reach the organizational stature it truly deserves. How can we accomplish this? By:

- working with local community colleges and universities to include management and supervisory training as an integral part of the criminal justice program.
- encouraging membership in professional societies and including basic principles of business, statistics, and finance as part of educational requirements.
- closely identifying with local law enforcement agencies and capitalizing on each other's skills and knowledge. We have to actively seek each other's counsel.
- expanding our skills into other diverse activities to better understand the new technology that is quickly changing our profession.
- mixing disciplines to expose non-security people to security operations and to expose security people to non-security related management functions.
- recognizing that it takes different skills, experiences, and knowledge to manage an operation effectively.
- designing technical or electronic systems alongside engineers.
- actively seeking out ways to participate in corporate planning activities.
- selling security at every opportunity to top management in a professional manner.
- attending business and management seminars.
- encouraging graduate studies in business and finance.
- encouraging treatment of management subjects at association meetings.
- practicing what you learn, above all! Take it from young Pam Shriver, our local tennis sensation, who recently said, "The most difficult thing I had to learn was to be a true professional; you have to practice a little every day."

I have frequently been asked to list those factors that I believe a sound manager must possess. Simply, stated, these are:

- Be a team player. This sometimes requires that we subordinate self interest to the needs of the corporation.
- Have a high energy level. Be enthusiastic. This inspires enthusiasm in others. Don't be afraid of hard work.
- Exude confidence. Believe in yourself and have enough guts to do what you believe to be right.

Lastly, and most difficult:

- Develop "people sense". Put your self in the other guy's shoes, know what to say and how to say it, be tuned into people, and know how to pick the right people and how to give them room to do their job. Be a good listener!

As I said in my introduction, the security industry is on the threshold of a most exciting and rapid growth period. How well you manage your resources will determine your success or your dilemma.

CHAPTER 2

What Is a Security Manager?
Mary Alice Kmet
ASIS Staff Writer

The president of a west coast company contacted ASIS headquarters recently asking for advice on what title to give the newly-appointed head of security in his firm. He wanted a label which would accurately describe the position and corresponding responsibilities.

A quick glance through the ASIS membership roster revealed that the titles for top security people are as diverse as the persons who hold them. A random selection from one page listed at least five suggestions: Director of Loss Prevention, Chief of Security, Chief of Plant Security, Corporate Security Director, and Director—Safety & Security.

If people within the industry cannot agree on what to call the person charged with the security function, then can they agree on the duties they should perform? Obviously, a security expert must be technically qualified to secure the personnel and assets of a company. But other skills, management skills, have helped to elevate them to this position of responsibility. Just what does a security *manager* do?

To answer that question, six top ranking security directors and managers were asked about the management of their companies, the management of their security function, and their personal management styles. At the end of this article, background information on each person is given as a framework for their specific responses.

Each of these security professionals works in a different environment with different responsibilities. They assume different roles in their organizations and bring different credentials to their positions. Nonetheless, they all confront similar management problems as a regular part of their jobs. Their solutions, based on experience, provide an interesting array of management expertise. Each was asked the following questions.

Reprinted with permission of the American Society for Industrial Security, from *Security Management,* May 1979, pp. 6.

HOW WOULD YOU CHARACTERIZE YOUR
"MANAGEMENT STYLE?"

"I manage by participation and coordination," says Darlene Sherwood, Manager of Security Administrative Services at SRI International. She trys to anticipate and thus avoid problems, but when they occur, she makes sure everyone affected understands the problem and then participates in the solution. She attempts to be "flexible in problem solving" while projecting a "positive attitude that a solution can be found."

Effective supervision for Sherwood means keeping people informed, asking for input, explaining decisions, and working as a team to solve problems. She also encourages her subordinates to look for ways to improve their own jobs and recognizes their contributions. She strives to provide an environment where "people will enjoy coming to work."

"Responsive" is the word Donald L. Perkins uses to characterize his management style. As Director of Security and Safety at Central National Bank, he encourages communication and feels that many problems arise because people are reluctant to address the issues. He prefers to recognize a problem and then "get on with it rather than imagine or avoid the conflict."

Perkins trys to supervise "as little as possible" and encourages decision making on the part of his staff. He feels he motivates and is motivated by those in his department and looks for ways other than "short term satisfiers" to bolster his staff. He would like to provide a constant awareness and recognition of performance, a feeling that each one "does make a difference."

Joseph F. Doherty, Director-Corporate Security, AT&T Corporation, thinks that management style is formed at both a conscious and unconscious level. He delegates authority and does not believe in unnecessary, close supervision. His philosophy of "participative management" encourages people to work on a problem together when a change is needed. "Everyone's input is better than only one person's ideas," he says. At the same time, Doherty feels he is demanding. "I won't tolerate sloppy work."

Doherty motivates his staff by giving them an opportunity to develop through "initiative," and by welcoming new ideas.

Frederick A. Bornhofen's goal as Director of Security for the Sun Company, Inc. is to "strive for perfection—to provide the best service we can." He sees his job as "sales oriented," selling rather than dictating changes through an explanation of the reasons. Cost effectiveness is an important part of this sales approach.

He supervises through "guidance and inspiration" although he feels his staff is largely self-motivated. Bornhofen reviews their work through biweekly progress reports and motivates by example. He adds that bonuses, salaries, and "the courteous treatment of people" are other important motivators.

William L. Miller, Manager of Government Security and Plant Protection at Martin Marietta Corporation, calls his staff "professionals who don't need day-to-day supervision." "Training is my responsibility," says Miller, and his people complete a six-month training course in government regulations and how they apply to the work at Martin Marietta.

While his supervision is "loose," Miller has confidence in the ability of his staff. "If they are not competent people, they don't stay," he comments.

Performance evaluations are required annually by the company although special evaluations can be done at any time. Miller feels these "one-on-one" sessions help to motivate his staff.

Texas Instruments uses Objectives, Strategies, and Tactics (OST), which Floyd E. Purvis, Manager of Site Services, calls more a framework for management than an actual management style. The process is tied into the setting of departmental goals. The system takes "a lot of communication" by Purvis during weekly security staff meetings, monthly meetings with all salaried staff, and quarterly meetings with all employees. In these sessions, goals are "refined, redirected, and reported on."

Purvis motivates people by recognizing their achievements, by giving them responsibility and authority, and by providing a "way to grow financially and professionally." He also feels he must be willing to listen when problems do occur.

HOW DO YOU HANDLE PERSONNEL MATTERS?

Purvis makes his own hiring decisions although they are subject to review by the Personnel Department. If a person is to be terminated, the steps of "progressive discipline" must be followed. In these cases, Purvis collects facts and the employee has the right of appeal. "I'm a fact finder, not judge and jury," he says.

Sherwood might discuss a candidate for employment with the Director of Security, but the final decision would be hers. Involuntary terminations have to be approved by a Termination Review Board. Sherwood presents the case to the Director of Security who in turn consults his reporting Vice President.

Sherwood handles personnel problems by being honest. "If something is bothering me I'll tell the person how I feel about it," at the same time showing how the action affects others. She feels this explanation of the "why" is especially important.

Bornhofen acts as an advisor in the hiring of security staff at the other companies that are a part of Sun. He will recruit and then negotiate with applicants, presenting the best candidate in his opinion to the management of the hiring company. The final decision rests with that division.

Bornhofen spends three to four months training a new security manager for a new corporate assignment. He maintains a "sustaining interface" with that person on security matters although the management direction comes from the division.

While Perkins seeks the expertise of the Personnel Department on employment matters, he makes the final hiring decisions. Any increases in staff are cleared through appropriate budget channels. How does he solve personnel problems? "Immediately!" he replies.

Miller handles personnel problems on a "one-on-one basis." He chooses to solve employee problems at the lowest level possible, "and cry wolf as a last resort." Firing decisions can be overridden by the Employee Relations Department but Miller has not experienced this action.

When an opening occurs at AT&T, Doherty canvasses the operating companies for candidates. This company policy rotates employees into new positions although they can return to their original company after three to five years. Doherty makes final hiring decisions but a number of people at various levels would be contacted in a firing decision. Rather than being terminated, an employee often is sent back to his operating company or given another assignment.

Doherty feels this rotating policy benefits security because persons with security experience are later placed in other functions in the company.

WHAT MAJOR ISSUES DO YOU FACE AS A SECURITY MANAGER? WHAT IS THE IMAGE OF SECURITY IN YOUR COMPANY?

"Ninety percent of my time is spent preventing outsiders from defrauding the company," says Doherty. Toll fraud and theft of property are constant problems because the company is so large. "We deal with all the American people," he explains.

To combat these problems, Doherty advocates prevention. "We're not an after-the-fact organization." In the last year, the security departments in the Bell System have averaged five thousand arrests, of which four thousand were prosecuted. AT&T security people are "career telephone people" who think in terms of prevention. Doherty is invited to speak at conferences of other employee groups where he emphasizes that "everyone is responsible for the protection of property, revenue and assets of the company—especially supervisors and managers." His department also contributes material to in-house publications to promote security.

Budget is a major issue for Miller at Martin Marietta. "In the business of security, there is never enough money," he laments. Miller feels the budgeting process in his company is fair, however, and says "if you can justify something you will get it."

Miller does not find the company cop image a problem, "although some employees always think of you as the fuzz." He works to relay the image that "we're here to help the employee and to help keep the company out of trouble."

Miller attends staff meetings in product divisions and is open for questions from the group. A recent article in the house organ on the emergency medical service "is one of the best PR projects we've done in years." His department has also made five films, the latest of which describes "security as good business." It was shown to all employees and also has been sold outside of the company.

Problems arise for Sherwood at SRI in arranging priorities for serving the entire staff, particularly the "timeliness of clearances" for people who must travel. These issues are related to personnel problems in Sherwood's opinion, and she often reminds her staff "why we're here."

Sherwood does not face a negative image although she feels her role constantly needs to be explained. "People don't understand what is involved in security—that it's more than guards." Sherwood finds herself defining security not only to other staff members but also to outsiders, especially applicants for employment.

"Awareness" is the largest concern faced by Perkins at Central National Bank. He wants employees to see security as "preventive not reactive" and as the persons in the bank who provide a "worksite free of hazards to personal safety." The idea of a company cop image "hits a nerve" with Perkins. He has taken "great strides to reduce that image" mainly through training and by showing that "security is a business management function not a quasi-police department." He spends time talking to people and assisting outside the security realm to promote the corporate image.

The Sun Company had a company cop image of security and Bornhofen is trying to shift that thinking. He feels successful in instances when he has been able to solve management problems through investigative techniques. The paraprofessional on his staff recently presented a session on personal awareness at one company where some criminal incidents had occurred.

Any employee of the Sun Company can attend an internal college in which fifty to sixty courses are offered three to four times a year. Bornhofen has been involved in presenting the security viewpoint at several of these courses.

Purvis at Texas International feels that people who accept the company cop tag are "a little naive" but knows it exists. His people are involved in patroling parking lots and traffic patterns which can cause employee friction. To counteract any negative feelings, Purvis emphasizes the service side of his operation especially in emergencies.

HOW DO YOU PERSUADE UPPER MANAGEMENT TO SUPPORT YOUR IDEAS?

"Justify them on a cost/benefit basis through data," says Doherty. Whenever possible, he shows how the suggestion can be integrated into an existing program with a minimum of cost. Doherty has found that an interdepartmental task force which can present a consensus opinion helps gain support for a solution because the details are worked out ahead of time.

Miller visits with upper level management to talk about the problem and show how his solution is "achievable, beneficial and cost effective."

"Credibility" has been the key for Bornhofen. As the security successes compound, he finds management at all levels more willing to accept his proposals and seek his advice.

Both Purvis and Sherwood use facts as their ally. Purvis spells out alternatives, shows the consequences (both of action and inaction) and estimates the cost. If he loses, Purvis makes sure he adequately researched the issues and has fully developed the solution. Then he finds a new pitch, or decides the project really should not be done.

Sherwood shows exactly what steps need to be taken to further the company goals keeping cost effectiveness in mind. If she is turned down, Sherwood often will present the idea again, adding new information. She sometimes feels success is a matter of timing. "I presented the exact same proposal three times," she recalls, "and the third time they bought it."

HOW DO YOU MANAGE YOUR TIME?

Time management has not been a real problem for Perkins. He sets priorities although those rankings change routinely. He tries to stick with his daily objectives, avoids paper shuffling, and attempts to spend his time wisely. "It's valuable and expensive," he says.

Perkins refers to his calendar at the beginning and end of each day and is "not crazy about meetings or committees." If he has to attend a meeting, he tries to make his presence worthwhile. He has cut down on the amount of time he spends traveling, finding that trips were a "major time waster."

Sherwood sets priorities by examining "the trend of the problem." She handles those issues that "will be worse later" while saving those that can wait. Her assistant divides the mail into four categories: action, signature only, ASIS, and general. She often restates her overall goals to keep a clear sight of the most important items in her day.

Bornhofen has taken many courses on time management and feels that as a result he is "very efficient." He sets priorities "based on gravity and impact on customers or the company." He consciously sets aside time to learn more about security in the company and time to communicate with his peers at professional meetings.

Both Purvis and Miller feel they manage time "poorly." Purvis comments that "there is a lot a manager can do and should do but there is never enough time to accomplish what there is to do." He has tried many methods such as lists and pocket recorders but is "very dissatisfied" with his success so far.

Miller prepares a list of daily goals while driving to work in the morning. But, "the first phone call throws that out." He tries to set aside some time each day to communicate with employees and upper management and some time for ASIS. (Miller served as a Regional Vice President at the time he was interviewed.)

HOW DO YOU COPE WITH STRESS?

Miller thinks of himself as a "calm individual" but does find stress building up on occasion. At those times, he enjoys working on his stamp collection "and then I'm in good shape." He feels that coping with stress is a part of managing time and tries to work the two out together.

Bornhofen exercises regularly and enjoys canoeing, but he really doesn't feel that he works under stress. "When you work in an environment where you don't want to be—that's stress," he comments. Boredom and a feeling of no hope are also contributing factors in Bornhofen's opinion. "There's always hope here," he says, and he especially likes the freedom and intellectual stimulation in his job. "I'm enjoying myself," he notes.

Perkins enjoys being with his family and likes to think he can leave work problems "behind the desk." He watches his weight and tries to avoid situations which add to stress, "like putting off decisions."

Sherwood attempts to work at a controlled pace and to match her energy levels to the functions she must perform. While that pairing is not always possible, she limits the time she allows herself to dwell on or be concerned about any problem. She considers all setbacks as temporary and tries to give herself and her staff credit for what they do accomplish in a day even if it wasn't what they had planned.

"I haven't cracked up yet," says Doherty. He exercises when he can and enjoys working on the garden and landscaping around his home. "I was in combat in World War II," he comments, "and if you can cope with that you can cope with anything!"

Security management is not easily defined. As each of the persons interviewed testified, management is very much an individual style developed through experience tempered by familiarity with one's company. While top security positions on the one hand require certain technical expertise, top management positions require certain interpersonal skills which are often hard to quantify.

What can a person with this combination of skills be called? How about *"professional!"*

PROFILE—FREDERICK A. BORNHOFEN

Frederick A. Bornhofen, CPP, is director of security for The Sun Company, Incorporated, Radnor, PA, the twenty-third largest company in the Fortune

500. Fourteen major companies, including such diverse oil interests as pipelines, refineries, oil wells, gas wells, exploration, and ship building, comprise the parent company.

Bornhofen provides "functional guidance" in security for all fourteen companies. At least one representative from each division reports to him on a dotted line basis. Three individuals at Sun report directly to Bornhofen—a paraprofessional and two managers. Bornhofen reports to a vice president of administration along with seven other directors of such functions as materials control, general administration, and aviation.

Bornhofen thinks of his position as having three parts: he acts as an expert consultant; he provides a sustaining force (offering guidance as needs arise); and he performs an auditing function (making comments and recommendations to management). He feels that support by upper management for his department is "excellent" although "security at Sun is new."

Before Bornhofen joined the company, security was viewed as compliance with the requirements of government contracts. In the year and a half that he has been with the company, Bornhofen has recovered $1 million for the company.

PROFILE—JOSEPH F. DOHERTY

Joseph F. Doherty, CPP, holds the title of director-corporate security for the largest private company in the world—AT&T. Twenty-two other directors or assistant vice presidents of such departments as accounting, budget, and taxes report with Doherty to a vice president and controller. Doherty feels he is correctly placed on the financial side of the corporation because of his responsibility for the protection of the revenue and assets of the business. "We work closely with auditing on internal matters," he comments. If auditing finds security irregularities, they refer the case to Doherty for investigation.

Both staff and line responsibilities are handled by Doherty at AT&T. In his staff function, he sets corporate policy for the twenty-three companies plus Western Electric and the Bell Laboratories which join to make AT&T. Each of these companies has its own security organization. Doherty develops new preventive procedures to be used by all the companies as well and coordinates major investigations which cross company lines.

Doherty has direct, or line responsibility for the nearly 12,000 employees who work for AT&T Corporation in Basking Ridge, NY. Within this structure, nine employees report to him, including five supervisors who have responsibility for such security concerns as electronic toll fraud, protecting proprietary information, toll message fraud, and secrecy of communication. Each of these positions requires specific technical expertise and experience with the company as well as security knowledge.

Doherty holds a degree in law and feels this degree is a "necessary prerequisite" for his job because of the many state and federal laws which regulate and affect the company. Investigation and the collection of evidence are also important aspects of his position and his law degree serves him well in both capacities.

With AT&T for twenty-five years, Doherty started at the Bell Lab in methods and procedures—"which has nothing to do with security." One year later he became involved in security through government work and then branched out into the protection of assets and revenue.

Over the years, Doherty has seen an increasing support for security within the company until today it is "very well established." Written statements of security policy have been "approved and supported at the highest levels."

PROFILE—WILLIAM L. MILLER

The manager of government security and plant protection at Martin Marietta Corporation, Denver, CO, is William L. Miller. Miller reports along with a manager of program security to a director of security.

Miller oversees the work of fifty-eight persons in three departments: operations, administration and plant protection. The operations department conducts general security business such as personnel clearances, visitor control, classification management, education and audits. Administration includes four special security officers who handle the security requirements of special contracts given to Martin Marietta. Plant protection, with forty-six people, is the largest department and includes guards, fire fighters, and paramedics. Miller calls his department, "strictly a special services organization" prepared to provide guidance in the protection of assets, proprietary information and personnel."

Miller calls the management support for security a "mixed bag" because he does not work directly with all phases of the company. Of those departments that he works with on a routine basis, Miller feels security receives "quite a bit of respect. They support us and we support them."

Miller began at Martin Marietta twenty-three years ago as a security officer, a position much like the job of the special officers in his department today.

PROFILE—DONALD L. PERKINS*

Central National Bank is the largest of the banks assigned to Centran Corporation in Cleveland, OH, a trust organization of $3 billion in assets. Fifty-two branch operations in one county comprise the bank, a figure which is expected to grow due to new state banking regulations.

Reporting to the senior vice president for personnel are four vice pres-

---

*Since this article was published, Mr. Perkins has become Corporate Director of Loss Prevention for The Sherwin-Williams Company.

idents: the director of personnel, the director of research and development, the director of employee and personnel services, and the director of security & safety. This last position is held by Donald L. Perkins, CPP.

With a staff of thirty-five, Perkins is responsible for all bank protection and physical security including investigations, credit card fraud, and new security design. Twenty-nine members of his staff are uniformed protection personnel who report through a staff officer to Perkins.

Perkins has been with Central Bank since January 1978 and provides consulting services to all the banks included in Centran Corporation.

PROFILE—FLOYD E. PURVIS*

Texas Instruments in Dallas, TX, has a "highly decentralized structure," according to Floyd E. Purvis, CPP, manager of site services. The company includes 78,000 people worldwide in nearly thirty facilities. While Purvis has corporate responsibility for policy and procedures for safety and security at all sites, he also maintains line responsibility in the Dallas headquarters.

Purvis reports to an executive vice president who is a member of an operating committee headed by the president of the company. Between forty and fifty corporate managers are at his level. Six persons report directly to Purvis: the managers of safety and security in the Far East and in Europe and four people in Dallas. Of those four, two are in safety, one is in security, and one is in transportation.

Purvis has worked for Texas Instruments for nearly twenty years. He began there as security administrator in a product division. As the company grew, Purvis's responsibilities evolved into his current position.

PROFILE—DARLENE SHERWOOD†

Darlene Sherwood is manager of security administrative services at SRI International, a research and development company in Menlo Park, CA, largely involved in classified government work. She reports to a director of security and telecommunications and oversees a staff of twenty-five. Among the duties performed by her staff are security clearances, visitor control, personnel administration and business office services for the six departments under the director of security and telecommunications.

One-third of the income for SRI comes from the national security community. When a contract is awarded, the company agrees to abide by

---

*Since this article was published, Mr. Purvis has retired and now operates a consulting business.

†Ms. Sherwood is the 1984 Senior Vice President of The American Society for Industrial Security.

the security requirements of that proposal. Therefore, management recognizes security as an integral part of the total organization and, according to Sherwood, supports it accordingly. She feels the staff is "very professional" and if she needs management support, "they are always there to back us up."

In turn, Sherwood feels a "strong responsibility to management and all of SRI" and views her role as one of service. Cost effectiveness is always an important consideration, and while she thinks her department "could do better with more people," she tries to work realistically within her budget.

Sherwood has been with SRI for fifteen years. She started in the security department as the secretary to the manager, was promoted to secretary to the director, and then became administrative aide to the director. She has held her current position for five years.

CHAPTER 3

Security Management in Transition

Kenneth T. Derr
President
Chevron USA, Inc., and
Director and Vice President,
Standard Oil Company of California

It might seem to many of you that management is most often aware of breaches of security, events that result in reported losses for the company. It is impossible, after all, to estimate the losses that don't occur thanks to effective security.

But those prevented losses, those events that never happened, do get reported in one sense. They show up in the bottom line as part of the profits that any business earns.

The connection between security and profitability grows more apparent and more important each year.

It used to be that industrial security meant simply the physical means of preventing crime. It meant guards and gates, lights and locks. A security specialist was most likely an elderly guard patroling a beat armed with a flashlight and a thermos of coffee.

But over the years, crimes against businesses have grown in frequency, in complexity, and in value of losses. According to the estimates of the US Chamber of Commerce, they now represent an annual forty billion dollar bite out of business profits.

In order to meet this growing threat, industry has come to depend on a new breed of highly trained professionals who have helped to develop new concepts for security. Industrial security is no longer a matter of simply locking up company property. Now it means a systematic approach to pro-

This was presented as a speech to the San Francisco Bay Area Chapter of ASIS at their July, 1982 meeting.
Reprinted with permission of the American Society for Industrial Security, from *Security Management*, October 1982, pp. 27.

tecting all forms of corporate assets, including those intangible but precious assets—a company's reputation and ethics.

The modern security specialist is less like a policeman and more like a safety engineer. Both are really in the business of managing risks.

As you know, these changes in corporate security—both philosophical and technological—have meant new responsibilities for the company managers charged with overseeing the security function. What I want to focus on today is what management can do to provide the best possible framework for an effective security program.

The first step is to come to grips with the problem. Managers have to be aware of the vulnerabilities in their business operations and the potential threats facing the company.

Obviously, every company has a unique situation when it comes to security. But if you wanted to get a quick survey of the different ways any business might be vulnerable, it could help to look at the operations of a major oil company. Standard Oil Company of California and its various subsidiaries is to a security chief what Everest is to a mountaineer.

We deal in products that are volatile, toxic, and potentially very hazardous if abused. They are very valuable and yet very difficult to identify without complex laboratory analysis. What's more, we transport these products through pipelines or on barges where precise measurement of volume or flow is difficult.

All of these characteristics have attracted thieves in the past. In one widely publicized case, a group in Southern California used an abandoned fruit stand as a cover to tap into our pipelines and steal gasoline. In another recent instance, we discovered a well-organized ring had been preying on fuel barges in the Mississippi River. Employees of a New Orleans barging service were stealing and selling our diesel fuel to shrimp boat operators in the area.

Theft of oil field equipment is an old problem that has grown much more severe in recent years with the increase in drilling activity and in costs and the corresponding shortage of necessary materials. Drill bits, valves, lengths of pipe, coils of wire, anything and everything used in the oil patch is liable to disappear in a "midnight requisition" to be resold to some unscrupulous contractor. We're not talking about petty pilfering here. One major equipment supplier estimates the oil industry suffered losses exceeding 100 million dollars from this type of theft in 1980.

We also have to worry about industrial espionage. For instance, the data we gather in the process of exploring for oil and gas is very valuable and very sensitive. We go to great lengths to guard that information.

To give you an example, early last year we started drilling three wells offshore in a new area off Point Conception in Southern California. We thought the wells would be significant in their own right, but they would also tell us whether to bid on neighboring tracts in a big lease sale coming up later in the year. While the drilling was going on, we made sure not one scrap of information leaked out. We kept the daily well-logging results under lock and key. When we sent used drillbits back to the shore, we first scrubbed them clean of tell-tale cuttings. We kept the oil samples we obtained in special locked tanks, under security guard.

As it happened, we made a very exciting discovery with those wells, but we had to restrain that excitement and maintain very strict security right up until the morning of the next lease sale. Our great success in that sale will give you an idea of what that classified information was worth. Along with our partners, we made winning bids totalling 1.2 billion dollars for twenty-three offshore tracts, including ten parcels located just north and west of our discovery site. One of these bids set an all-time record for a single tract—333 million dollars. The story might have had a very different ending if there had been any security breach.

* * *

We've learned about new vulnerabilities in automation technology. Computers have opened a world of new opportunities for criminals today. The computer time is valuable, the information in the computer is valuable, and the computer equipment itself is very valuable. As operators of one of the largest computer networks in the country, we at Standard Oil have had to take extensive precautions to ensure the security of our system.

Credit card abuse, especially fraudulent use of lost or stolen cards, has been another chronic headache for the retail end of our business. Last year, our losses due to credit card fraud came to about 3.2 million dollars. Credit card verification is complicated by the sheer size of our system. We have roughly eight million cards out representing more than five million separate accounts.

Over the years, we've had to deal with hijackers, counterfeiters, extortionists, even pirates. We've learned the value of risk analysis, and when our security people inform us of some new possible threat we listen.

Once you've surveyed the vulnerable points in your operations, you have to set up the security policies and procedures that seem most likely to give you protection in those areas. I'm not really thinking of physical measures here, although such measures should naturally be a part of your security planning. What I mean is that management must set up a code of conduct for company employees. This code should be published and made available to all employees. It's a big mistake to trust such important matters to the office grapevine.

In our company, we maintain extensive policy manuals, but we also try to highlight important aspects of our policy through special employee bulletins or other publications. For instance, in 1979 our company published a handy pocket-sized pamphlet entitled "Our Business Conduct . . . Principles and Practices." It spells out company policy on a number of vital topics, including conflict of interest, antitrust laws, multinational operations, government relations, and environmental protection.

To my mind, the most important part of the guide is our board chairman's introductory statement to all employees making clear the underlying principle of our company policy. He writes, "It is of course the policy of the company for all employees to comply fully with the law at all times in their conduct of the company's business. However, the policy of the company goes beyond this. Our business should be conducted not only in compliance with the legal rules, but voluntarily in accordance with the highest standards of business integrity and honest dealing. While community standards of ethics may vary at different times and different places, the strict standards of honesty and integrity are a basic and continuing cornerstone of our business in all areas and functions and at all times."

I should add that such high principles don't mean much unless you make every effort to put them into practice. And in the matter of compliance with the law that can sometimes be difficult. Innumerable laws regulate business in this country and not all of them are clear. Some become fuzzy through inconsistent enforcement and some were never clear to begin with.

The outpouring in recent years of new laws aimed at protecting the environment or the health and safety of employees has given us many problems in correct interpretation and compliance. It's been a test of our principles, but I think we've measured up.

A few years ago, for instance, we issued a policy statement to all operating companies on compliance with environmental, health, and safety regulations. We required our managers in the field to comply with all such laws, regardless of the degree of enforcement, and to document that compliance. We had special teams perform selective audits of our facilities, in effect playing the role of enforcement authorities.

This effort has cost us significant amounts of money, but we feel it's been worth the expense. And it's been well received by our people. They know what's expected, and they know where they stand.

One real benefit of a written policy, by the way, is that it brings employees into the security process.

Obviously, the specifics of each company's security policy will vary, but you should be prepared to spell out your company's posture on compliance with the law; treatment of company property, including proprietary information; and on-the-job behavior. You also need to explain what the penalties are for any violations of that code.

Most people will think of obtaining legal advice in drawing up such a policy statement, but it's a good idea to get the input of the security manager as well. After all, the security manager will be charged with enforcing the policies.

Enforcement is one area in which the actions of management can make or break the effectiveness of a corporate security program. Management has to give security specialists the authority they need to carry out their responsibilities.

Management must make it very clear that company policies apply to *everyone,* without exception. If you are willing to tolerate the possibility of corruption in the executive suite, you can forget about trying to prevent it in the plant.

In that vein, management should be wary of placing its security manager far down in the reporting structure. Security has to have quick access to top management when the need arises.

Security problems are almost by definition extraordinary events, which often require a quick decision. If the problem has to work its way slowly up and back down the reporting structure, the opportunity to take action may be lost. In our case, our corporate security manager reports directly to a corporate vice president.

Security measures aren't always popular. When first implemented, they tend to upset the normal working routine. No matter how well you communicate the necessity for such measures, you can expect a certain amount of grumbling. But management has to stick to its guns and support the security staff. There's a story from our company that illustrates my point.

Before the era of radical disturbances, our office buildings were open. People could come and go freely. But a series of incidents, culminating in a bomb explosion in one of our buildings, convinced us we would have to restrict that freedom of access. We then installed a system of electronic locks operated by employee badges.

The new system was a trauma for many employees, and there was a great deal of muttering and grumbling when it was first installed. Employee complaints were eventually brought to the attention of Bill Haynes, then chairman of the board.

"Mr. Haynes," a staff member said, "we've really got to make some adjustment in this new badge system. Do you realize that if an employee forgets his badge, he can't even get into the bathroom?" Mr. Haynes thought about that for a moment and then said, "I guess he won't forget it twice, will he?"

* * *

I've talked about our approach to security as if it were a sequential process. First, analyze the problem. Then, choose policies and procedures to solve the problem. Then, see to it that those policies are enforced.

I should make clear that these steps are part of a dynamic, ongoing process, and the key to that process is communication.

Security planning, like any other kind of business planning, can't be cast in concrete. It has to be adaptable to changing conditions. To give you an example, consider the many security considerations involved in the recent development of self-service gas stations. Obviously, the self-service design saves on labor, which allows the dealer to be more competitive in pricing. But there's a trade-off. That station, with perhaps a lone attendant, becomes a more tempting target for robbery.

With the help of security specialists, our industry has developed special booths, safes, and pump controls to protect the employee in the self-service location. We've found it's very important to communicate with our security people about new developments in our business operations and to get their recommendations early in the planning stage.

*　　*　　*

Before I conclude, I want to make one last point—to my mind, the most important point.

The best security people in the world can't be effective if they have to function in a climate where integrity and honesty are the exception rather than the rule. It's up to management to establish the highest ethical standards for business conduct and to see that those standards are adopted throughout the company. You can't establish such standards in proclamations, only in practice.

I'm very proud of the record our employees have established over the years for doing business in a fair and honest way. I've always thought the real security of our company rests on that foundation.

CHAPTER 4

Expect Pigeons

James L. Hayes
President and Chief Executive Officer, AMA

My purpose today is to try to convey a message to you who are what I would term "growing professionals." Not personally growing, because you may be as significant to your organizations today as you will ever be. I hope not, but I really mean that as a tribute, because you do some great work. But, primarily because you are entering the mainstream of management, the kind of task you've assumed professionally may not have its full recognition at this point.

Now, the title of my talk, "Management in the Eighties," reminds me of a topic I've been talking about recently: When I was given this topic, including what the people who want to be pros in the future should be thinking about, I went back and looked in my notes (as is my inclination) to see if I'd ever addressed a similar topic. And my notes revealed these topics I have spoken about in my lifetime: "Management in the Forties," "Management in the Fifties," "Management in the Sixties," "Management in the Seventies," and now "in the Eighties." Probably the most astounding thing about my outlines for these topics is that they haven't changed much in all those years.

Many of us do not recognize what has happened in the United States, particularly, but it's true throughout the world that we have grown from very small, family-type organizations to very large organizations. And even in small organizations, we've become very complex. People over here sometimes don't know the people over there, and I know this has contributed dramatically to your problems. We've been through the research on the internal and external security problems that we have—pilferage, the protection of citizens, the protection of workers, a sense of security where we work.

But what I am more concerned about is that we are losing a quality of major importance in our industrial society when *we deprive people of the time to be creative.* And where is the time going? It's going into worrying

Reprinted with permission of the American Society for Industrial Security, from *Security Management,* November 1980, pp. 12.

about personal security on the job. It's going into worrying about the security of the company as a total financial investment because of some things that are being drained off for unlawful purposes. And it's going into areas that have to do with attitudinal change. .

A QUESTION OF ATTITUDE

Quickly, if I were to go back several years ago to when I was a young man, and I don't want to, but if I were to go back, I can remember the day when if you worked in our organization and I saw you walking out with a set of tools in your hand, I could look at you and say, "You're stealing." Most of us had ten rules that we had memorized. In our society, no matter what your religious persuasion was, and this was true in many countries in the world—the Ten Commandments were fundamental. Stealing was something we could identify. You didn't want to get caught; I was really kind of embarrassed catching you. You knew you were wrong, there was punishment, and so it went. That was a *simple* society to deal with.

Today, if I catch you walking out with that set of tools and I say "You're stealing," you say, "No, this is adjusted compensation." In other words, "You know those guys upstairs don't pay me enough, so I have to take it in kind." This has tremendously complicated the picture today. It isn't just a question of who's taking what, who's checking what, how do we keep people from getting something—but it's a question of ATTITUDE. We are doing more of our own thinking today than ever before in history, and we have a great need for some understanding of principles.

I'd like to see security personnel as members of the management team. I think you can be of the greatest help to management as respected members of that team contributing to the *total* management of the organization, rather than just saying "Here's what we need in the security department. Let me tell you about it from our point of view." That's isolationism.

Suppose you're in a security situation and you're the manager or director . . . I'd like to know where you'd like to have your group five years from now. What are the things you'd like to have in place? And if you say "Gee, I just sit here and react. They kind of tell me what to do," then you're a menace to security.

A *REAL* MANAGER

If you're *really* a manager, regardless of what anyone else is doing, you have a little dream that you're trying to fulfill, and that's the thing that holds the team together. We call it *management by objective,* management by results. The whole idea is for you and your people to get your heads together and say, "here's where *we* want to be," and stop being just a response mechanism to a management that may be shunting you off to the side because *you* aren't practicing management in your organization. I used to think years ago that *everyone* believed in planning. I don't think so anymore. I'd be surprised if half the people in this room really believe in planning.

But the thing I'm talking to you about is—are you ready to be a professional manager? I do not doubt that you are a professional security persons. But are you ready to be a professional *manager*? I think the answer to this question is going to be the critical element in the way you gain recognition in the years to come.

Coming back to planning—how many of you recognize that the basis for planning in your group is preventive medicine. Good professional managers are problem preventers—not problem solvers. Years ago when I was in the university, a professor would bounce in and say "Dean, I know you're working on this problem, would you let me take a crack at it?" I wasn't really confident that he could help me, but I thought, what is there to lose? So I said, "Go ahead, give it a try." And by golly, he solved the problem. It was only upon mature reflection that I found out he *should have been able* to solve the problem—he *created* it.

While you as managers are planning for what you want to do, plan to *lead* the corporation in its security activities rather than simply responding to what some other manager believes you ought to be doing to protect what *they* are doing. That's not a conflict—that's the place of the pro, because planning basically prevents or works on four things. Planning is a preventive mechanism in budgetary control, cost control, morale, and productivity.

But how often do we ignore the fact that our fine employees, who are trying to realize satisfactions out of jobs in your company and mine, depend upon *your* activities to be comfortable in achieving what they believe is an important part of their lives? And finally, we talk today in every quarter about productivity, and so often we forget that productivity starts with good management. Indeed, I have seldom found an organization that could not exist with 15 percent fewer managers, if only they put their minds to doing what we know can be done today.

ORGANIZATIONAL FILTERS

If I take you through years of management we'll find that every management system has a decision-making system, it has a communication system, it has a supervisory system. And what we find is that the decision-making system up to 1980 has done remarkably well. Most decision makers are pretty good. Decision-making starts up there with the president, then moves down to the vice presidents, and finally down through the organization. But isn't it strange how we've forgotten that the nature of the message changes as it goes down through the organization? By the time that message, that decision, often a good one, moves down through four or five levels in the organization, higher management had better start supervising or the message is going to get lost. You see, every decision-making organization has filters.

If I came into this wonderful ballroom as president of the American Management Associations, and let us say we owned it, and I look around and say, "Very attractive, I like this very much. Beautiful room. When we were putting it together," I say to some vice president, "did we think about in place of these green drapes, maybe a beige drape?" And someone says, "Oh, yes sir, we thought about it, but we thought the green would be more practical." And I say, "very nice," and walk out. The vice president picks up the telephone, calls down one level, and says, "When we were doing that room, what did we say about beige drapes?" Someone says, "Well, we thought about it, but we didn't think they were very practical, why do you ask?" "Well, Hayes was just asking." And they call down one more level and they say, "Guess what—Hayes is interested in changing those drapes from green to beige." Down one more level they say, "I don't give a damn, put them on overtime and change them tonight!"

Now, don't applaud, because that happens in my organization. I know it doesn't happen in yours . . . but nevertheless, this is the way the filters work. Now watch what happens on the way back up. The workers get in here tonight and they say, "If Hayes wanted beige drapes, why didn't he make the decision in the first place? Why do we have time to do it over but we never have time to do it right?" Up one more level they say, "Look, workers always squawk. They got paid overtime for doing it, what are they yelling about? You know, it doesn't make any difference to them. They got their money." It goes up one more level and they say, "Well, it lightens up the place a little bit, but we're going to have problems. We're going to have to change them." It goes up one more level, and they say, "Kind of interesting isn't it, how it highlights the stage?" And finally, they come to me and they say, "Hayes, people admire your taste.

Now what I'm saying to you is that if you and I don't realize this filtering is happening, we may be following the direction of someone four or five levels down who has filtered the message out incorrectly, causing things to happen that are directly opposed to what you think professionally ought to happen. But if you *know* the system, then you're the person who ought to be making the suggestions.

GET OUT OF THE OFFICE

Why don't we have better supervision? In the United States we have lost the sense of supervision as we have grown. In any organization, people at the top ought to be getting out of their offices regularly. Not all the time, but on a regular basis, sort of erratic, wandering down through the organization, visiting with people, asking questions. Observing, seeing, and being seen. We've lost this some place. As a consequence, your job is much tougher.

But *you're* the ones who ought to be saying, "Hey, let's get someone down on the floor once in a while. Why can't we get some recognition from the top that this is good and that is bad? Why don't you get down here and see the way we have to work out here in the parking lot, or why that instrument won't work if they don't push the switch, or why we need that item in our budget?" The people who can make that decision often aren't getting down there. And so, what do we find? We find that people at the bottom are no longer listening, they become indifferent.

I can walk into organization after organization as the president maybe one day goes through. He sees a guy down there working, and says, "Good morning." The guy says, "Who are you?" He says, "I work topside." This exchange shows the employee really comes in the back door. If he came in the front door, he'd see the president's picture and know who he is. But nevertheless, he says, "Who are you?" You see, they don't *know* the president, so the attitude develops that nobody cares. *The* management of this organization is that guy I report to, or that gal I report to, and this is the XYZ Company. And often you are faced with an attitude of complete indifference to the totality of the organization.

But down there there are two groups who listen, and listen very well. *Unions* listen. Unions represent what the people are saying down at the bottom. It may not always be the way it really is, but that's what they hear. Also, *politicians* listen. The dumbest politician I ever met knows there are more votes at the bottom of the pile than on the top.

Communicating in a circle is good so the decisions going through and being filtered are reinforced by people at the top. A company is too large when the people at the top no longer have the time to show up periodically at the lower level. In this situation we develop an indifference down the line. I'm sure people look at you from time to time and say "What are *you* worried about, it's not *yours?*" This is what you have to tell management— that they ought to be down there to reinforce these wonderful decisions.

Some of us can remember the old manufacturing concept where, if I took some water and I poured it into this glass and it kept right on running through, I'd come to the conclusion that it's a defective glass—that didn't take great brains. But now, I come to the point where I have to deal with people who have a different point of view. They are cheating a little bit on time—being a little late, leaving a little early, taking a little longer coffee break, being careless with company property—all of this is a breakdown which will not be solved by *catching* people, as you well know, but by a general policy that says, *"We* are a team, and *we* have to work together, because *we* have this company in our hands, one way or another."

Let me give you an illustration. A hundred years ago, my wife bought this stand. She asked the merchant, "How much?" "A hundred dollars." "I'll take it." That's known as an economic exchange. And that's an exchange in which each party to the transaction feels that more is being gained than is being lost. My wife wants the stand rather than her one hundred dollars. The merchant wants the one hundred dollars rather than the stand. Beautiful.

Now, if you remember, there was another class down the hall being taught called salesmanship. And that was the snap course that only the dummies took in order to get good marks. And most of us thought it was about as practical as an oral examination in penmanship. But down there they were telling a very important thing: that every exchange a company makes is on a satisfaction curve. It looks like the arch in St. Louis. And the place where the exchange trades off is right up there at the peak—that red hot moment when both parties think they win.

In 1980, we have a whole new phenomenon. We say, "When will you deliver it?" "Thursday." I come home, my wife says, "Jim, no stand. Call them up." I call them up and they say, "Sorry Mr. Hayes, but we've had a strike of our delivery people. We think we can straighten it out this week-end. You ought to get your stand some day next week." I come back and tell my wife, presuming the problem is solved. She says, "I'm not going to sit around this apartment every day next week until *they* decide when they're going to deliver my stand. You ask them when they're going to deliver it, and I'll be here. But I'm not sitting around waiting for them."

Now that's the way *my* wife reacts at least. While she's waiting, what's happening to the satisfaction curve? It's dropping off. And by the time the stand is delivered, there isn't a man, woman, or child in the United States that can't find something wrong with it. Why? Basically, they don't want it any more. . . . And for *your* purposes it no longer has the value that it had when it was purchased. Therefore, to not pay for it, to mar it in such a way that we don't have to pay for it, to find a fault that makes it less than useful, all these attitudes begin to develop.

Such attitudes are things we depend on *you* people to point out to us, because a lot of managers don't sense this.

You are the ones we depend upon as professionals to say, "If you want attitudinal changes, *deliver* on time," because that is not a peculiar problem of marketing, it isn't a peculiar problem of transportation—it's a management principle that's very old. And if *you* would tell us that, we might listen a lot more sharply as to how to solve our problems. But probably more importantly, you may be the voice that comes through and shows us how to prevent problems, which is really where we'd like to get some day in the future.

USE THE TALENT YOU HAVE
TO CHANGE ATTITUDES

A final point I'd like to emphasize is that social change is very important. It's very easy for people in your position, and indeed for every manager in this country, to stand back and say, "Well, you know, we didn't have these problems twenty-five years ago. You know—a different moral code, and we didn't have all those people coming into this country, and the blacks weren't coming up—*They've* caused all the problems. . . ." That's *nonsense!* Our problems today go far deeper than that. We have had a kind of breakdown that has made your job possible, and given you the opportunity to become professional.

I think it's very important that we get the attitudinal change that says, "Look, we live in a society together. Let's not try to exclude some people." I find managers every day who say, "Gee, if we could only get good people. . . ." Please. If you only had good people, you'd only need half as many managers to start with so they'd be out of work—which isn't all bad.

But the thing that's important is that we're not going to have businesses if we don't use all the people in our society. The trick of management is to use the talent you have, not the talent you'd rather have. And if society says, "We're going to move in this way," then I think you can be a very important part of saying, "Hey, why don't we think this thing through and see how we can use the people in our community and give them opportunity?"

Let me talk to you of what I see. The president goes off to a beautiful luncheon like this and finds that the National Alliance of Businessmen have a speaker. And let's say I come in to the Miami area. We look around and say, "We have some problems to straighten out here, with the Puerto Ricans, the Cubans, the blacks . . . and one of the ways we can solve them," the speaker says, "is to give more of these people jobs. If they get jobs, with a little time they'll want more education. With more education, they'll then grow and want greater education. And some day, we'll all have the problem solved—but most of us will be dead at that point."

So Mr. President sits down there in the audience and says, "Gee, that makes sense." He comes back to the plant, he calls in the vice president and he says, "I was at an interesting meeting this noon, and the speaker was talking about how we have to help the minorities in our community, particularly the blacks. We want to help them, so I volunteered to take five. See what you can do with them." The vice president offers an exclamation that in another setting would be described as a prayer, goes down to a plant manager, and says, "I don't know where the boss was this noon, but guess what he brought back? You get three." The plant manager goes down to the foreman and says, "You know that job you wanted filled? You got a man—lots of luck."

Now what I want you to sense is the rise in the level of bias as you go down the decision-making tree—for different reasons, because the president is the only person in the organization who has no future. Most of the others would like a little better job, a little more money, a little better position . . . so how do they protect themselves? Throughout history, man has protected himself by *excluding* people, whatever the reason may be. So, as we go down, we find the level of bias rising. Ah, but I know all about those laws . . . I know all about those things we *have* to do. I go to church (at Christmas time), I've heard some of those things. We have EEOC people who keep the pressure on us to get the statistics right, we know how to move them around.

TEACHING THE ART VERSUS KNOWLEDGE

That isn't the spirit of what we're trying to do. If we're pros, we say, "This is something that *has* to be corrected." And so, what we find all of a sudden is that we have some subtle attitudes that affect security that I think you're missing at this point. Watch what the foreman does. The foreman says to the black man, "Come on over here and let me show you how to use this machine." "Naw, that's a reject, take your time, it's very simple . . . Naw, now concentrate, we've got kids in here who can do it, you can do it. Try it." "Nope."

Then the foreman goes over to the plant manager and says, "That black man can't learn. They don't have the background for this complex machinery." So the plant manager, only one level higher in bias, says "Yeah, I've been watching. So we'll get him a job pushing boxes around, or running the elevator. But we need someone on that machine—any suggestions?" The foreman says, "I have a brother. . . ." "Well, bring your brother in and see if you can teach him the machine."

The foreman brings him in and says, "All right, brother, let me show you how to use this machine. You put the piece on the machine like this. Slap it with the side of your hand to make sure its tight with the form. Press down on the foot lever, and on this particular machine, if you'll bounce it just about one inch off the floor as you quickly yank the handle, it'll come out neatly. Try it, brother." "Beautiful."

What just happened? I'm going to use a word that our younger generation has mangled, but it comes back to ATTITUDE—a management attitude. When I love you, I teach you the *art* of the job. When I tolerate you, I teach the *technology*. Attitudinally, we are throttling ourselves in the nobility of tolerance.

Have any of you had the wonderful experience on Christmas Eve of assembling toys, guided by the "easy-to-follow" directions? You take the red wire in your left hand, the green wire in your right hand, you put them together and the light will come on. No light. I used to go to my neighbor and say, "Andy, help me." He'd say, "Oh yeah, Jim. You take the red wire in your left hand and the green wire in your right hand, you put them together and then, just a little spit, and there's the light!" Now I went back and read those instructions and the word spit did not appear once. And even on the expensive toys it didn't say saliva! Where did that come from? That's the little *art* of the job.

We can take people in our organization, we can send them to training courses on the assumption that if we only throw enough knowledge at them, *eventually* they'll become good workers, *eventually* they will become good managers, *eventually* they'll become moral. What a fantastic thing we're doing. Our ethics aren't very high, why don't we send them to a course on ethics. . . . The people who are unethical already know *more* ethics than some who are behaving correctly. It isn't knowledge, the correlation is very low. But what I want to do for you, if you work with me, if I'm the leader of a team, is to teach you the art of management. You won't get that through knowledge. And if I *don't* transmit this to you, I can kill your attitude, and I can make a thief of you. I can make you, at best, indifferent.

Probably all the combined brains in this audience, with all the exhibits you have out there in the hall, cannot outdo the ingenuity that will be exercised by employees made indifferent. But if somehow I can change and teach you the little art, so that you *know* that I gave you something you couldn't get otherwise, I can take you on the road to being a citizen. And we're not *doing* this.

Men, when you go home from this meeting, a little exercise for you—try making a cake. Now if you're a normal man, you'll walk into a kitchen (I'll assume you're married), and you'll get a cookbook and you'll say, "Honey, where's the big pan?" And she gives you the big pan. And then she'll probably say to you, "Honey, do you *really* want to bake a cake?" And you say, "Well, that's what the man said." She says, "All right, number one, put down the book." Do you realize there isn't a cookbook throughout the *entire* world that says first, put down the book. No there are only two ways to learn to put down the book: Trial and error, like millions of people before you, or having someone who cares enough to pass on that little trick of leaving you with one hand free.

Throughout organizations today, we are getting into elaborate programs, elaborate technologies, elaborate education, and we're forgetting the fundamentals. And ladies and gentlemen, you people in this profession might be the greatest inspiration that sophisticated management has, if somehow you sharpen your management knowledge to the point where you say, "As a member of the *management* team, let me help you think through what we *should* be doing five years from now to get our statistics where we want them in these particular fields."

I'm on the board of a rather large department store, and every once in a while we get to talking about shrinkage. I have a favorite line; I keep pumping at it over and over again. I say, "Look, I walk into the store, and I can't seem to get waited on. If you can't wait on me, I can steal it." It's *attitudinal*. In other words, I want it. I'd like to do the right thing, but you won't give me the opportunity.

Coming back, what can we do to make social changes? In your company, right now, what are the plans for people over 65? Amazing how many companies say, "We have no plan," or worse yet, "We're waiting for the regulations." Let me predict something. If we don't make a conscious social effort to do something with the people over 65, we're going to have an amazing new rash of problems with people who for years have had marvelous records with the company but are now getting a little older. It must be recognized that some people ought to be retired at 65, indeed there are some people who ought to be retired at 35, but those who can do the job, have the *right* in our society to work as long as they are productive and are members of the team. When you're pros as *managers,* you're the people who can deliver a message on attitudinal changes that other managers could effect to help *you* do your job.

EXPECT PIGEONS

I feel a little privileged at being here. It's kind of a culmination of part of my life, because my father was a policeman. And I lived with him working three shifts a day, and a third of the year I didn't see him. I'm just happy that I'm here because I was able to go to college and get a good education (and how I did it on a policeman's salary I will never figure out, but thank God that problem's been taken care of and all law enforcement people are now justly compensated).

But be that as it may, one thing I admired my Dad for, (he died when he was 42 years old—I thought he was pretty old at the time)—he had three sayings I remember well. The first two aren't quite applicable, but they're interesting.

He said, "If you want to get hit by lightning, be sure to climb the hill." If you really want to be a pro at management, I think you have to keep struggling to get up there to where you're a recognized member of the team. If you want to get hit by lightning, if that's where you want to be, keep climbing the hill.

The second one was a little more interesting. He said, "If you want to be a statue in the park, expect pigeons." So if you want to be a manager, there are going to be pigeons around. It isn't always going to be pleasant. There are some nasty things you have to do.

And I think the third one was by far more prosaic. I used to say to him, "Dad, what do you do?" And he'd say, "I *help* people." He didn't say, "I arrest people." In fact, I remember one of those little incidents in any married life, when my mother chewed him out because he had given a few dollars to someone to take a cab home and loaded him into the cab to get him off the streets.

I think that's what we're trying to do as pros: develop attitudes to the point where we are problem *preventers,* while facing the fact that every day we'll have to be skilled in *solving* problems. So I try to leave you with one serious message in these noontime meetings, one that may be a little more prosaic than those you've had historically. BE A PRO. Don't be satisfied with being a director or a manager, unless you're willing to test your knowledge of MANAGEMENT, so that you're accepted by those other pros as an equal. It does no good for you to have a title, if you're still recognized just as *that* security guy or gal. You *must* know as much as they do, and the wonderful thing about aspiring, as most of you people are doing, you have the opportunity to learn it right, rather than simply gaining an appointment because of other circumstances.

I think there are marvelous opportunities for our system, but it depends on *management*. My appeal today is: *Your* position in management is one that's gaining a great deal of ground, so sharpen up your management know-how, and become a member of the team. Until then, you simply *respond* to what the team wants. Your opportunities are absolutely outstanding. Thank you.

CHAPTER 5

Translating Security Into Business Terminology

Richard J. Healy, CPP
Department Head, Security & Safety
Aerospace Corporation, and
Timothy J. Walsh, CPP
President
Harris & Walsh Management Consultants

Security is both a process of activity and a condition resulting from the activity. As a process it can be considered as "the use and application of personnel, equipment and procedures to reduce or eliminate risks of loss of enterprise assets, tangible and intangible, from causes and events not considered to be within the boundaries of conventional speculative or profit/loss activities." As a condition, security may be considered as: "The result of emplacing appropriate countermeasures at selected points in the enterprise at which it can be reliably determined that substantial reductions will be achieved in exposures to risks of asset losses."

Operationally, recognizing the distinction between security as a state and security as an activity is important. Management's aim is to keep the company secure, and it approves investment and expenditures to that end. If security is not achieved, then security activity is pointless, if not worse, since it may induce a false sense of protection when, in fact, there is none.

To help non-security management (particularly those in industrial relations and personnel capacities) avoid this false confidence trap, security managers should try to give their counterparts a clear perspective on the objective of security measures. Doing so will aid professional relations between security and the rest of the organization. The remainder of this article is intended to foster this clear perspective by discussing some practical tests,

Reprinted with permission of the American Society for Industrial Security, from *Security Management*, June 1979, pp. 30.
Article adapted from *Security Policies, Programs, and Problems* by Richard J. Healy and Timothy J. Walsh, copyright © 1978 by The Bureau of National Affairs, Inc., Washington, DC 20037.

which should be shared with non-security managers, for determining whether an organization is actually secure and how much that security costs.

Why would a security manager want other managers, especially an industrial relations and personnel professional, to be familiar with the security activity? *First,* because security necessarily affects employees, often restrictively, and thus must be considered a factor in the employment environment. *Secondly,* security will directly affect the collective bargaining situation because either the security organization itself is a bargaining unit or because its functions, chiefly its enforcement of rules and its conduct of investigations, will involve employees who are members of the unit. Even in non-union organizations, security actions can involve the enterprise in unfair labor practice litigation under state and federal labor laws.

Thirdly, security affects top management in enterprises where the security organization is part of the industrial relations management line. In these enterprises, the senior industrial relations manager may also manage the security unit. Finally, security affects the personnel selection process (and vice versa) since most of the losses of business enterprises vulnerable to theft and other crimes are caused by employees, not by strangers or outsiders. The application of effective personnel controls and selection techniques is one of the prime defenses against such losses. But federal statutes and recent high court litigation in the areas of employee rights, equal employment opportunity, and the individual right to privacy seem to militate against effective screening of applicant or control of incumbents; and, consequently, in many organizations the inclination to deemphasize security controls is understandable.

On the other hand, what may not be understandable, at least to your managerial counterparts outside the security realm, is some of the terminology you use. To facilitate communication, a few key terms should be clarified. They are briefly defined here in terms non-security personnel will understand.

- *Cost-Benefit Ratio:* This is the proportion between the real cost of establishing and maintaining security countermeasures and a total security system and the probable cost of the losses which might occur without them.
- *Integrated Security System:* The coordinated combination of equipment, personnel, and procedures used to neutralize security vulnerability.
- *Protection of Assets:* A term from the security field used to describe security programs aimed at comprehensive protection for the *entire* organization—its personnel, installation, information, and material assets.
- *Pure Risk:* This is a term of art familiar to insurance underwriters. It refers to a situation in which the risk is one of *loss* only. For example, in considering exposure to fire, the risk is that a fire will occur. If there is no fire, the risk has not materialized; but there has been *no gain.*

Pure risks are "loss/no-loss" propositions. There is never gain or profit as in a speculative business risk. Among the sources of pure risk are the following:
—Crime
—Conflict of interest
—Natural disaster
—Civil disturbance
—Terrorism
—War
—Insurrection
—Fiduciary defalcation
—Employee dissatisfaction
—Industrial catastrophe (fire, structural collapse, nuclear emergency, etc.)
—Management negligence
—Disobedience to or violations of enterprise rules and regulations.

- *Security Countermeasure:* A physical device, a person, a procedure, or a combination of one or more of these intended to reduce or eliminate one or more pure-risk exposures.

Now that you've established common understanding of terms, the next step in familiarizing managerial colleagues with security is to explain some of the major basic concepts used in security.

The concept of **vulnerability-criticality** is based on the idea that every security exposure or risk is composed of two major elements: probability of occurrence and severity of impact. Probability of occurrence depends upon a number of things including (1) *physical* factors such as nature and composition of the asset, its location in time and space, and its physical environment; (2) *socio-political* factors, for example, the ethnic, economic, and political character of persons involved in any way with the asset itself or the environment of the asset; (3) *loss-history* factors indicating the kinds, frequencies, and sizes of past asset losses experienced by the enterprise; and (4) *criminal-state-of-art* factors dealing with the uses of technology by aggressors to overcome security countermeasures.

Criticality, or the severity of impact a loss would have upon the enterprise, is usually stated in terms of cost. The generally recognized costs of a security loss are: (1) cost of permanent replacement of lost or damaged assets; (2) cost of a temporary substitute, should one be needed, for an asset that has been lost or damaged; (3) related losses caused by inability to carry on normal activities as a result of the lost or damaged asset; (4) discounted investment losses or the amount of short-term income which could have been earned on the amounts of money diverted to meet the costs described in (1), (2), and (3).

Because vulnerability to loss is measured according to the degree of probability that the loss will occur, it is necessary to distinguish the various levels of probability, levels which, at best, can only be approximated. Probability may be broken into four levels: *virtually certain, highly probable, moderately probable,* and *improbable.* Based upon the available data concerning the various factors, a loss event such as a burglary, or a fire, or a violent strike can be assigned one or another level of probability. The decision to assign a possible loss to a particular level is a technical judgment and involves professional competence in the security field. How the professional weighs and evaluates various probability factors is worth outlining to non-security management.

When measuring impact, the size of possible losses may be used, and, like probability, broken down into four levels: *fatal to the enterprise, very serious, moderately serious,* and *not serious or negligible.* The criticality of a security loss is a *relative matter.* What is a non-serious loss for a large concern may be a very serious or fatal loss for a small one. A fatal loss is one which effectively halts the production of a facility or entity. A very serious loss requires recapitalization and significantly affects investment.

For the giant corporation, the loss of a single facility would probably not cause the demise of the corporation (fatal loss), but might require large infusions of capital to restore operations (very serious). A serious loss decreases profit or increases loss sufficiently to require an explanation by management. A non-serious or negligible loss is one that can be absorbed in the operating statement for the current fiscal period without significant impact on net positions.

Risk logic is the statement of security vulnerabilities in such a way as to indicate their combined vulnerability/criticality and their relationship to each other. If the level of vulnerability (probability) is designated by a letter (A = virtually certain, D = improbable) and level of criticality is designated by a numeral (1 for fatal through 4 for negligible), then the combination of the letter and the numeral signifies the weighted value of a loss. Each type of risk would be labeled with an appropriate reference symbol, and data in that risk identified by the symbol. The risks would then be ordered by rank with the more serious listed first, thus establishing a system of priorities when selecting countermeasures.

Once risk priorities have been established, another type of analysis may be undertaken for each type of loss. A loss may be thought of in terms of events or conditions leading up to the actual loss, and the process may be diagrammed in the shape of a pyramid or tree with the loss at the diagram's apex. Successive levels below the actual loss show the conditions or events necessary for the loss to occur. In plotting each risk, a pattern emerges showing a complex of events and preconditions similar to those depicted in Exhibit 5–1. Note that the various preconditions *must occur together* or *may occur independently.* That is, that they are logically related to each other by the terms "and," "not and," "or," "not or." These links indicate which

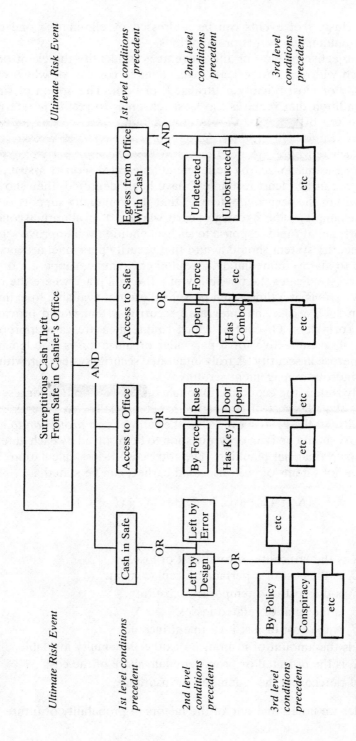

Exhibit 5–1. Risk logic diagram.

groups or clusters of events can be addressed by eliminating one of the required simultaneous events or conditions.

The objective of plotting these events is to identify the event or condition which will require the least investment to correct, or which can be most quickly or most reliably neutralized, or both. The notion of singling out the condition that requires the least resources to rectify is referred to here as the use of **leverage.** Careful application of this technique for the entire risk pyramid will *produce the optimum cost-effective security system for the enterprise whose risk exposure profile has been properly diagnosed.*

Leverage is maximized by designing an **integrated security system.** Once conditions requiring "least resources" have been identified, they should be arranged within the security system so that they mutually support one another. For example, if alarms can give early warning of an abnormal condition of some sort, and if rapid response to such a condition will improve security, then the security system should assure that security personnel are available to respond to alarms immediately. As another example, suppose a fire prevention survey indicates the possibility of a fire in a place where the risk of loss is very serious at a time when personnel are not available to extinguish the fire. In such a case, an integrated security system would provide for automatic sprinklers. Of course, which countermeasures are appropriate, reliable, and cost-effective for a particular organization is a judgment requiring expertise in security. A truly integrated security system can withstand the most rigorous management scrutiny.

Briefly stated, the economic rationale or **cost justification** for a security program is that the cost of protection is substantially less than the losses incurred without the protection. What the ratio of *cost protection to cost of probable loss* should be is an open question to be resolved by each enterprise within its own financial planning. The total cost-of-loss calculation, based upon the various items of cost discussed earlier, can be stated as:

$$K = (C_p + C_t + C_r + C_d) - (I - C_i)$$

where

> K is the criticality or total cost of loss.
> C_p is the cost of a permanent replacement.
> C_i is the cost of a temporary substitute.
> C_r is the total of related losses.
> C_d is the cost of lost investment income.
> I is the amount of insurance or other indemnity available.
> C_i is the prorated or proporationate share of the cost
> of purchasing the indemnity or insurance.

Earlier we noted that one of the factors of probability of future losses is the record of past losses. To accumulate a useful record of such losses, each enterprise must have a loss reporting policy. Such a policy should require that all losses of known or suspected pure-risk origin be reported in a standardized way, usually on a special form, to a central unit responsible for collecting and processing data. Whether or not insurance is available, the **loss data base** permits prevention planning and loss predictions when enough data have been accumulated.

Among the information that should be reported are: (1) the description of the asset(s) involved, (2) the date/time of loss or the interval during which it occurred, (3) the value of the asset and the means for valuation (depreciated book, replacement, purchase, etc.), (4) the circumstances of the loss (how it occurred), and (5) the person accountable for the lost asset(s). Proper analysis of such information can develop loss profiles which will suggest to security professionals the appropriate security measures.

In an enterprise with many tangible assets exposed to pure-risk loss, some of the losses will result from crime, especially pilferage and other forms of larceny. But it is highly probable that a careful examination of the nature of the tangible assets will indicate that only a portion are theft targets. Theft targets are marked by the following characteristics: they have universal appeal or can be easily disposed of on the criminal market; they are of high unit value; they are small enough in size to be secreted on the person or in a hand-carried container; they are on hand in large quantities at the enterprise or are used over the year in high volume.

When tangible assets are measured against these criteria, it may be found that only 20 to 30 percent will meet all of them. A company loss history will often reveal that 70 to 80 percent of the known or suspected criminal losses are from the 20 to 30 percent of the assets designated as theft targets. By **targeting** these **loss risk exposures,** countermeasures can be concentrated on a relatively small group of assets, and can result both in improved security and significant economy.

Non-security managers can probably appreciate the frustrations often faced by security professionals in the lack of clear general public policy on security. Unclear federal and local statutes, rules in regulatory agencies and varying policies at the state level are shared by security just as other facets of the organization must try to live with conflicts in public policy. Since the trend is toward increasing regulation of security personnel, the security manager might find that keeping colleagues informed of this trend is to his advantage.

Civil rights is one area in which public policy clearly affects the security operation. The well-known Title VII of the 1964 Civil Rights Act and subsequent EEOC and federal court decisions have developed a body of doctrine directly governing certain traditional security activities. In another area of civil rights, the Fair Credit Reporting Act has become a concern since it affects employers through the security operation. Making non-security managers aware of how such legal matters fit into the security picture can increase their understanding of the security function.

Just as security and civil rights have sometimes come into conflict, so too have labor relations issues become a security concern. Traditionally under the National Labor Relations Act (NLRA) (and under analogous state labor relations acts) security programs, including enforcement of rules and the conduct of investigations, have not been treated as a separate class or variety of actions but have been viewed in terms of their impact on collective bargaining—that is, they have been measured in terms of tendency to coerce or restrain collective bargaining on the basis of their specific nature, essential reasonableness, and even-handed application or use. Under this rubric, investigations which probed too deeply into labor-union affiliations or attempted to observe workers specifically engaged in protected collective bargaining activities would be found to constitute unfair labor practices. Enforcement of rules in an arbitrary or discriminatory way so as to penalize protected workers would likewise be condemned.

Because labor rulings hold important implications for employers, their effect on security procedures should be made known to other managers.

There is a noticeable trend in the law to hold employers more and more to rules of strict liability (that is, if an injury results, the employer is liable even if he was without actual fault or malice). This tendency will appear in civil litigation by aggrieved employees (and others on the business premises) who allege some physical or psychic harm as a result of security-force actions. Among charges leveled might be defamation of character as a result of remarks made by guards or investigators; assault committed by guards or others in physically touching the grievant; and invasions of privacy by searches or inspections of lockers, persons, vehicles, and work locations. This is not to say that such practices as searches, questioning, and the use of physical constraint must be abandoned but, rather, that careful review of policy and actual practice should be made by legal counsel and industrial relations executives to assure that marginal or doubtful practices are avoided or discontinued.

To be sure, any enterprise must operate within the safe boundaries of public policy. However, it must enunciate its own privacy policy if its security program is to have any real purpose. Policy declarations are needed regarding the following:

- The mission and function of the security program
- The organizational and reporting position of the security department or group
- The responsibility of individual employees, supervisors, managers, and senior executives for accomplishment of the purposes of the security program
- The requirements and techniques of security loss reporting
- The specific requirements of all major security rules, which typically

would cover, among others, the following areas: access control; property control; personnel, incident, or other types of investigations; parking and vehicular control; control of proprietary information; disaster and emergency operations.

On these major elements of security, a clear and coherent statement of policy, promulgated by the highest executive authority, should be readily available to all personnel. Once policy is established, rules and procedures may be developed by lower levels, usually by security or by systems and procedures, and issued to complement and implement policy. Experience has shown that the single biggest defect in security programs in the private sector is their lack of clear policy statements defining their purposes and goals.

PART II

The Security Program

Security programs can encompass a broad spectrum of services and responsibilities or can be relatively narrow in focus, depending upon the needs of the organization. In a comprehensive operation, the security manager might have responsibility for line supervision of corporate-level security personnel and functional oversight of all security personnel, direction and control of investigations, executive and employee protection programs, development of physical security standards, and information protection. Political and terrorism risk forecasting, crime risk forecasting for existing and planned sites, and crisis management fall within the comprehensive security program as well. The establishment and implementation of security education programs, establishment and monitoring of ethical standards, development of financial controls, and policymaking regarding each of these specialties also are responsibilities in a full-fledged security program.

In large organizations, each of these security functions may be directed at each corporate site by a specialist who reports either to a corporate-level security executive or to an on-site security or general manager. In other situations, like small concerns, the security manager may handle only physical security and security personnel responsibilities.

Regardless of the scope of a given security program, certain features are common to most. Some type of planning effort is needed; policies to guide security operations are needed; information-gathering and assessment are needed. Whether a security program is being established for a new organization or reviewed for an existing one, evaluation of environmental conditions as well as the specifics of the organization and its line(s) of business is basic to identifying vulnerabilities. Once these risks are identified and their seriousness is gauged, the relative importance and means of protecting against each one can be determined. From this assessment, the security requirements are derived, budgets and manpower requests are submitted, and procedures are defined. What is approved by the powers that be is put in place, and the whole process of assessing risks, determining security requirements, and implementing them begins again. Security needs change as an organizaiton and its environment change; therefore, security is very much an on-going process.

CHAPTER 6

Program Planning:
You've landed that new job.
Now what?
Clifford E. Evans, CPP
Corporate Security Manager
International Harvester Company

You did it! You convinced the Bauble, Bangle, and Bead Corporation (BB&B) that you are the best candidate for the position of security director.

Tomorrow is starting day, how do you feel? Confident you can handle the job, but a bit apprehensive nonetheless?

You no doubt want to give yourself the best chance for success at the new job. Where do you begin? Your initial homework has been done. You know what the company produces or what its services are, and where it operates. You've examined the financial stability of the company, annual reports, past articles in business and trade publications (thank goodness for public libraries), and the form 10-K. You have discussed the firm with people who are close to or have worked for the organization. Now you must establish credibility and work hard to earn the confidence of company management and employees. But how?

Many of us have faced this task at one time or another due to our mobile society and profession. Starting a new job may not always be easy, but it is usually exciting and challenging. The key is to establish yourself quickly, but not so fast that you are viewed as presumptuous.

This article presents a model plan for establishing yourself successfully in a new job. The model may be used by people entering either newly created or existing top security positions, and can be modified to help those entering second echelon security jobs. The model is not absolute and may be modified to fit the style of almost any company.

Reprinted with permission of the American Society for Industrial Security, from *Security Management*, June 1981, pp. 30.

THE MODEL

Step 1: Assess the company

Learn as much as you can about the company. Some of this will have been done during your research prior to accepting the position. Seek out documents that will help you learn important basics about the company.

A. Tangible things to learn about the company:

1.   *The financial position of the company:* Find out all you can about the financial condition and future growth of each entity (i.e., group, division, subsidiary, etc.). It would be poor form to recommend growth-oriented security improvements to a division that is being scaled down.

2.   *How it compares with similar companies:* How does the company stack up against it competitors? Is your company the best? The most cost-efficient? A leader? A follower? What sort of security is in effect in competitive companies?

3.   *The products or services of the company:* Discovering them all may require more research than you think. The major products or services of most companies may be well known to the casual observer, but it is essential to determine the minor ones as well. Find out all the subsidiaries and/or joint ventures and the locations of all the company's facilities.

4.   *The company structure:* Locate copies of all organizational charts. From them determine the power bases of the top managers. What is the formal managerial structure of the company (i.e., pyramidal, matrix, etc.)?

5.   *The company's mission statement:* Obtain a copy of the formal statement of mission of the company. This should be the basis for the mission statement of security. If, for instance, the company strives to be the least-cost producer, then security should assist in that goal by maintaining high effectiveness at the least possible cost.

B. Intangible things to learn about the company:

1.   *The ethical reputation of the organization:* Research the past reputation of the company in the business world. Is it viewed as having highly ethical top officers? Does a strong policy on ethics exist, and is it made known?

2.   *The management style of the firm:* Is the prevailing style in the company autocratic, laissez-faire, permissive, participative, or something else? You should be prepared to adapt your personal style to "fit in" as much as possible.

3.   *The company personality:* Every company has a unique personality.

You should identify it and make sure your personality is complementary.

Step 2: Assess the people

A. *Conduct individual interviews:* Talk to people at all levels. Arrange for individual appointments and precede each meeting with a letter identifying what you consider to be the elements of a comprehensive security program. This letter will form the basis of your discussion and should be sent to all non-security personnel you plan to interview. The security personnel will already have things on their minds and usually do not need the letter to spark their thought processes. Your schedule of interviews should include:

1. All top managers, including the chief executive.
2. A representative sample of middle and upper level managers from a wide variety of functions.
3. A representative sample of your security managers and workers.

B. *Rank the priorities:* Once these three sectors of the corporate population have been interviewed, you may consolidate the relevant concerns expressed, assign them priorities, and rank them. Several items will probably be high on the list of concerns expressed by nearly everyone in each group. These become the critical issues. Other concerns may be limited to individual personnel groups. The ranked list of priorities will be used later.

Step 3: Assess the company's problems

A. *The company's loss history:* If none exists, complete a total loss history of the company at least for the past year, or for the past three years at most. Remember to calculate the total cost of loss[1] for each incident. It will probably be a multiple of the value of the actual asset(s) lost. Coming up with a figure may involve some estimating if needed data are lacking. Some incidents will be documented, others will not.

1. Documented cases: Calculate the true cost for each loss documented. This documentation may have to be compiled from a file located in such departments as security, audit, operations, finance, personnel, etc.
2. Undocumented cases: Some losses may not have been reported in the past because no procedure was established. One method of estimating

[1]Timothy J. Walsh and Richard J. Healy, *Protection of Assets Manual,* The Merritt Company, Santa Monica, CA, 1975, Volume II, Chapter 2, pp. 2–15.

unreported losses is to interview a sample of managers of different operations. The information gathered in this way can be compiled and used as the basis of a projection for unreported losses at all locations.

B. *The company's historical reaction to losses:* How has the company reacted to losses in the past? Have the incidents merely been solved and forgotten, or have they been solved and measures implemented to prevent future recurrences? If the former has been the case, you may have to educate management in the value of learning from losses and using that information to prevent future ones.

Step 4: Make a professional assessment of the people and problems

In this vital phase, all the information compiled thus far (i.e., people's reactions, the loss history, and the past position of the company regarding losses) is analyzed from a professional security standpoint so the foundation may be laid for a program of professional assets protection. Either or both of the following resources may be used:

A. *Yourself:* You are in the best position to analyze the security needs of the company, providing you have adequate experience and have established the initial credibility needed. Compare the personal preferences of company executives and managers, the views of security personnel, and the history of losses at the company, so you can make a personal, professional assessment of the security priorities.

B. *A security management consultant:* A good consultant can provide the benefit of an outside professional viewpoint, which, in certain instances, will lend a higher level of credibility to your recommendations. Selection of the consultant is extremely important since the quality of the job he or she does is absolutely essential to your own credibility.

Step 5: Establish the direction for security efforts

At this phase you will take all the available data, which you have analyzed, and formulate the blueprint for security. A number of key issues should be addressed:

A. *Accountability:* In its purest form, accountability may be the most significant concept ever presented to the security field. The concept recognizes that security is unique in being the only entity in a company (other than the chief executive officer) that can affect, at one time or another, every single person, operation, product, service, and financial procedure. The chief executive is the only other part of the company whose impact encompasses this broad a range.

Operations' day-to-day activities have little effect on staff. Administration has little concern with financial matters. The personnel staff is concerned with people, but not buildings. Safety personnel are not concerned with accounting controls, and the finance department is not concerned directly with people.

Accountability is simply this: the top security executive in a company is accountable for security throughout the organization. This fact does not circumvent responsibility for security at the local level; rather it provides for an authority if one part of the company engages in security practices that could affect other operations. This authority gives the top security executive a greater stake in the company's security and places him in a more responsible role than the common one of in-house consultant. Preserving local responsibility avoids the conflict that tends to arise when local security managers report exclusively to the top security executive rather than to local management. In essence, clear accountability preserves the dotted line relationship, but makes the dots very heavy.

B. *The services and responsibilities of security:* You should clearly establish a wide variety of security services and responsibilities and widely publicize them. Management today generally has preconceived ideas about security duties, often recognizing only the traditional services. Since your business will frequently come from managers, it is essential that they be aware of all security responsibilities and services. A partial list of the services and responsibilities a comprehensive security operation might encompass includes:

1. Line supervision of corporate staff security personnel.
2. Functional supervision of all other security personnel.
3. Direction and control of all investigations (including authority to delegate).
4. Executive and employee protection, domestic and international.
5. Political and terrorism risk forecasting for foreign operations.
6. Crime risk forecasting for future sites, domestic and foreign.
7. Information protection, to include hard copy, data processing (hardware and software), verbal and electronic communications (i.e., telephone, teletype, data links, etc.).
8. Establishment and monitoring of ethical standards.
9. Policy-making.
10. Development of financial controls in cooperation with audit.
11. Crisis management.
12. Development of physical security standards.

13.   Establishment and implementation of security education programs for security and non-security employees.

C. *The reporting structure:*

1.   The operational reporting relationship: The level and function to which you will report is critical. If it is too low, you may be rendered powerless—buried in the organization. In large corporations you could also conceivably report to too high a level. Many middle to upper-level managers would like to report to the CEO. Since not everyone can, the CEO must be selective. In a very large company, the CEO cannot devote adequate day-to-day attention to security. A consequence of reporting to such an individual may be a security executive with high political power but no real authority. This situation is self-defeating and could render you ineffective. In most companies, the security executive should report to the first layer of management below the CEO. In very large corporations, a reporting relationship to the second layer is acceptable. Security should, in most cases, report to administration, since that function comes closest to the wide span of duties handled by security. Other functional corporate entities to which security might logically report are human resources, law, and finance. Which one makes most sense depends on the personality of the corporation. Gauge the historical power level of the respective functions and attempt to be aligned with the most influential one. Reporting to the audit entity is probably not a good idea, since the security organization and the audit organization should be of equal status so each can act as a check and balance to the other.

2.   The functional reporting relationship: If your new company has security managers for subsections of the organization (i.e., branch, group, plant, division, store, etc.) the reporting relationship those individuals have to you is important. Historically problems have developed with both dotted line (functional) and solid line (operational) reporting relationships. Functional reporting provides too little control, while operational reporting breeds conflict between you and the subsection general managers, who would have no control over the security manager in their operation. A subsection general manager's ability to control his organization should not be compromised; however, security must have complete freedom when necessary. Perhaps the optimal solution is to establish a strong functional relationship (i.e., dotted line) that becomes operational (solid line) during a major investigation. All parties that might be affected should be made aware that this change will occur and under what circumstances it will occur. One way to accomplish this arrangement is to convince the general manager of the subsection that your objective is in the best interests of the company as a whole. Doing so requires development of career path programs for the sub-

section security manager and provision of a way to gauge the technical qualifications of candidates for security management positions. In this way, you have control over the security careers of subsection security managers, which causes them to be responsive to you as well as to their operational supervisors.

Step 6: Sell the program

Convincing management to implement your program will really test your skill. Effective salesmanship is a learned ability, not a hereditary attribute. Three points are integral to making a successful presentation:

A. *Know your subject:* If you have gone through steps one through five of this article, you should have no problem with this point.

B. *Know your audience:* What are their positions in the company? What are their backgrounds? What approaches do they like? What approaches do they not like? What is their perception of you? These questions and other similar ones must be answered before you can give your audience a truly effective presentation.

C. *Use good communication skills:* Brush up on your verbal and nonverbal skills. The way you say something is equally as important as what you say. The nonverbal signals you give should complement the words.

Certainly your proposed program must be sold to top management, but remember that parts of it must also be sold to middle management and, to some extent, to company personnel at large. Top management support will ensure initial acceptance, but long-term success will depend on the support of middle management and cooperation (or at least obedience) by the rank-and-file employees.

Step 7: Perform

Once you have stated your case, justified your existence, mapped out a plan for security, and sold the program, the time for performance is at hand. You must follow through on your promises. People in the business world sometimes make grandiose proposals that look great on paper. What separates the professional manager from the amateur is the ability to perform as stated in his proposals. If you have sold the program well, you will probably be left alone and expected to perform on your own. The temptation to let other, newer projects take priority will be great. No matter how little supervision you are subject to, rest assured that at some time in the future, your performance will be judged. Your future will depend upon that evaluation.

CHAPTER 7

Fitting Security into the Management Structure

Clifford E. Evans, CPP
Manager of Corporate Security
International Harvester Company

"Why should I bother to sell management on security? I'm not a salesman and have no desire to become one. I'm a security professional. Security is self-explanatory and does not need to be sold. Everyone knows you need security in a company. Besides, it's far too much bother. Management accepts security . . . well at least most of them tolerate it. In reality, they just don't understand what I do, and I guess that causes a few problems at times. It's difficult to get additional people or money for my department. If only I had a few more people and more dollars—I could really show this company some effective loss prevention. Why do they have so much trouble seeing that? I constantly have to beat security knowledge into them."

Does this train of thought sound familiar? Management typically finds it hard to relate to security because it is a specialized function whose details are unfamiliar to most people. In addition, security is the only function in a company, other than the chief executive, that can affect, at one time or another, every single person, operation, product, service, and financial procedure.

Security departments don't just fit neatly into a box on an organizational chart. A security professional can become involved in issues or specific functions for which his or her boss has no responsibility or organizational concern. These factors of specialization, mystery, and uniqueness make it imperative that the security executive constantly strive to sell management on security.

Reprinted with permission of the American Society for Industrial Security, from *Security Management*, November 1982, pp. 15.
Based on a chapter from *Controlling Cargo Theft: A Handbook of Transportation Security*, edited by Louis A. Tyska and Lawrence J. Fennelly, published by Butterworth Publishers, 1983.

PROFESSIONAL CREDIBILITY: THE KEY

The key element in selling management on security is firmly establishing a high level of professional credibility. Professional credibility makes the job of selling security much easier; if you can sell them on yourself once, future presentations about your programs can be centered on the programs in question, not on you. Company executives must have a positive attitude about you before they will devote attention to your programs.

Professional credibility consists of credibility as a security authority and as a businessman or woman. The person who displays only security expertise will be viewed as a "company cop" or a "captain of the guard" and will never be allowed to pursue more sophisticated loss prevention activities. Conversely, the person who only has business experience will not be viewed as competent to handle the specialized functions of security. The proper image to present is that of a business manager first, with expertise in the specialized area of security.

ESTABLISHING SECURITY CREDIBILITY

Before you can begin to establish credibility, you must remove some barriers. It is an unfortunate fact that certain negative images of security personnel exist; many people view the function with apprehension and a bit of fear. Security can be frightening to employees, especially when an investigation is being conducted and people are being fired and prosecuted. At the same time, some employees view their company security department as a protector and guardian. Both viewpoints suggest that the high level of authority security has can be intimidating. Tear down these barriers by making it clear that the security department is comprised of people who work for the company, just like everyone else. In other words, show you are human. Once a little humanity is injected into security, establishing security credibility will be easier.

The many activities required to establish total security credibility can be divided into two broad categories: organizational authority and bottom line results. Organizational authority is how the security function fits into a company, the scope of its responsibility, and the authority it exercises. Although proper organizational authority is essential to effectiveness, selling security to management must frequently be accomplished first in order to correct deficiencies in organizational authority. Bottom line considerations are simply those steps that develop financial accountability for the security department. Security must show it is worth the investment by proving it can return to the company more than it costs. This is known as a positive return on investment (ROI), which a good security operation can generate through tangible recoveries that result from investigative efforts and assets protection services.

ORGANIZATIONAL AUTHORITY

Establishing organizational authority requires you to analyze your company to determine which approach to security is most acceptable. Every company has a personality, and the most successful managers are those who adapt their own style to fit in with the personality of the company. Once this assessment is completed, you should think about the following considerations:

Accountability

Accountability is simply this: the top security executive in a company is accountable for security throughout the organization. This fact does not circumvent responsibility for security at the local level; instead, it provides for an overall authority if one part of the company engages in security practices that could affect other operations. This authority gives the top security executive a greater stake in the company's security and places him or her in a more responsible position than that of in-house consultant. Preserving local responsibility avoids the conflict that tends to arise when local security managers report exclusively to the top security executive instead of to local management. In essence, clear accountability preserves the dotted line relationship but makes the dots very heavy.

Services and Responsibilities

You should clearly establish and publicize a wide variety of security services and responsibilities. Managers often have preconceived ideas about security duties, frequently recognizing only traditional services. Since your business will frequently come from managers, it is essential that they be aware of all security responsibilities and services. A partial list of the services and responsibilities a comprehensive security operation might encompass includes: line supervision of corporate staff security personnel and functional supervision of all other security personnel; direction and control of all investigations; executive and employee protection; political and terrorism risk forecasting for foreign operations; crime risk forecasting for future sites; information protection; establishment and monitoring of ethical standards; policymaking; development of financial controls; crisis management; development of physical security standards; and establishment and implementation of security education programs for security and non-security employees.

The Reporting Structure

The organizational level and function to which you report is critical. If it is too low, you can be rendered powerless, buried in the organization. In large corporations it is possible to report to too high a level. Many middle to upper level managers would like to report to the CEO. Since not everyone can, the CEO must be selective. In a very large company, the CEO cannot devote adequate day-to-day attention to security. A consequence of reporting to such an individual may be a security executive with a lot of political power but no real authority.

In most companies, the security executive should report to the first layer of management below the CEO. In very large corporations, a reporting relationship to the second layer is acceptable. Security should, in most cases, report to administration, since that function comes closest to the wide span of duties handled by security. Other functional corporate entities to which security might logically report are human resources, law, and finance. Which one makes the most sense depends on the personality of the corporation. Gauge the historical power level of the respective functions and attempt to be aligned with the most influential one. Reporting to the audit entity is probably not a good idea, since the security organization and the audit organization should be of equal status so each can act as a check to the other.

Your functional reporting relationship is also important, especially if your company has security managers for subsections of the organization (i.e., branch, group, plant, division, store, etc.). Historically, problems have developed with both dotted line (functional) and solid line (operational) reporting relationships. While functional (dotted-line) reporting provides too little control, operational (solid-line) reporting can breed conflict between you and the subsection general managers. A subsection general manager's ability to control his or her organization should not be compromised; however, security must have complete freedom when necessary.

Perhaps the optimal solution is to establish a strong functional relationship that becomes operational during a major investigation. All parties that might be affected should be made aware this change will occur and under what circumstances it will occur. One way to accomplish this arrangement is to convince the general manager of the subsection that your objective is in the best interests of the company as a whole. Doing so requires development of career path programs for the subsection security manager and the provision of a way to gauge the technical qualifications of candidates for security management positions. In this way, you have control over the security careers of subsection security managers, which causes them to be responsive to you as well as to their operational supervisors.

BOTTOM LINE CONSIDERATIONS

Establishing credibility for security at a corporation's bottom line is the true businesslike approach to making security accepted as a management discipline. When you can show that the benefits of security exceed the cost, then top management will take notice and not view security as a drain on profits. Establishing financial accountability for the security department is no small task. As a start, focus on two major security assignments, investigation and prevention.

Investigation

Figuring the bottom line for investigative operations is relatively easy since you only need to tally up the losses and the recoveries and compare them to the investigative costs. In addition, you should determine a value for preventing future losses stopped by the successful investigations. The true cost of loss[1] must encompass much more than simply the value of the item(s) lost, since many costs must be considered in replacement and investigation of the loss.

A convenient method to show the true loss is to construct a financial loss summary for each investigation. An example of this type of summary is contained in Exhibit 7–1. Each item in the exhibit is explained as follows:

Permanent replacement cost: The complete cost to replace the item(s) lost. This figure may differ significantly from the depreciated book value of the item. The replacement cost must be used no matter how much the item has depreciated because the company was not intending to buy a new item at the time of the loss.

Temporary substitute cost: Costs for any equipment that must be rented while a permanent replacement is on order.

Man hours: Standard hourly costs for the various employees involved in investigating the case. These costs include not only salary, but also benefits, office space, and all other costs that can be attributed to the employment of these persons. For example, an investigation manager who makes $52,000 per year earns $25 per hour; the cost of benefits, secretarial support, office space, and expenses easily can add another $25 to the hourly cost for a total of $50 per hour for the services of that employee. To show a precise amount for each employee involved in replacing the loss and the resulting investigation is unnecessary. Instead, develop standard approximate hourly costs for each type of employee.

Outside assistance (consultants): This figure reflects the costs of outside agencies, such as investigative firms, polygraph specialists, and hostage negotiators.

Idle man hours cost: A figure can be calculated for this category when a loss causes a halt in production, thereby idling workers. If the workers are laid off, then the cost of unemployment compensation should be included.

Value of lost production: If production ceases or slows, then the amount lost is figured here. The amount should be calculated as the total payment

---

[1]For another discussion of the cost of loss, see T. Walsh and R. Healy. *Protection of Assets Manual,* Chapter 2 (Santa Monica, CA. The Merritt Company, 1975).

Permanent Replacement Cost: _____

Temporary Substitute Cost: _____

_____ man hours at $ –/hour (top management): _____

_____ man hours at $ –/hour (management): _____

_____ man hours at $ –/hour (audit management): _____

_____ man hours at $ –/hour (audit): _____

_____ man hours at $ –/hour (investigative
     mgmt.): _____

_____ man hours at $ –/hour (investigative) _____

_____ man hours at $ –/hour (administrative): _____

Outside assistance (Consultants): _____

Idle man hours cost: _____

Value of lost production: _____

Other related costs: _____

Opportunity cost: _____

  Less: Net insurance rebate _____

       Net tax reduction _____

                    TOTAL IMPACT: _____

  Recovery: _____

  Prevention value: _____

Exhibit 7–1. Financial loss input.

a company receives for its product. If, for instance, the company manufactures trucks costing $20,000 to produce, but the company receives $25,000 from their independent dealers, then the $25,000 figure should be used.

Other related costs: Any other direct costs associated with the loss should be placed here.

Opportunity cost: If the company had not sustained the loss, then the money used to recover from the loss could have been invested back into the company. The opportunity cost is the cost of this money, which is calculated by totaling all previous costs (except man hours) and multiplying that total by the company's current cost of money. This figure can be obtained through the finance department of your company.

Less: net insurance rebate: Any amount which the insurance company pays on the loss is placed here after you have subtracted the amount of the premium for the part of the insurance applicable to the loss.

Less: net tax reduction: This figure is used when the loss qualifies as a tax deduction. The net amount of the reduction in taxes due to the loss should be placed here.

Total impact: This is the grand total of all costs associated with the loss. In many instances, it will be much larger than the replacement cost of the item lost. This figure is to help demonstrate to management the true effect of a company loss.

Recovery: If any costs are recovered as a result of the investigation, those figures should be entered here. The amount should be either the replacement cost for items not sold by the company or the total payment received by the company for finished goods.

Prevention value: In many cases, a successful investigation stops losses that are occurring and prevents future losses that would have occurred if the losses had not been discovered. The exact value of these savings is highly subjective since it involves an estimation of what might be lost. As a result, a precise formula for this calculation cannot be used successfully. Each case must be looked at individually.

For example, if a theft ring responsible for losses of $10,000 per month for 24 months is broken, then the prevention value could be estimated at one half the total or $120,000. Conversely, if a person is caught taking $100 worth of parts on an impulse, then it is best to stay conservative and omit a prevention value unless, of course, control measures were changed to prevent similar impulse thefts by others.

Once all incidents are summarized in this manner, it becomes easy to provide management with a quarterly cost summary such as the one shown in Exhibit 7–2.

A bottom line summary of the investigation activities of security will not only help to build department credibility, but will also help justify the need for additional resources.

Prevention

Calculating a bottom line for prevention activities is more subjective than investigations. The potential return on investment (ROI) must be higher

Number of investigations:	63
Total loss impact:	$8,300,000
Net recoveries:	$1,000,000
Value of future losses prevented:	$5,500,000
Investigative costs:	$ 250,000
Return on investment (ROI)*	400%

*This percent is calculated by dividing net recoveries by investigative costs, and is expressed as a percentage.

Exhibit 7–2.   Summary of losses and security investigations.

than the expense for investigation activities in order to be accepted. Consider using the following steps.

Determine the potential for loss: Many losses can occur, but some have a higher probability than others depending on the following factors:

- External infuences: These factors include the neighborhood crime rate, the desirability of the assets, the potential for government interference/overthrow, and the economic climate.
- Formal loss history: This factor includes all documented cases of loss.
- Informal loss history: At times, losses will go unreported. Interviews with local management can help uncover previously unreported losses.
- Employee morale: Losses tend to increase as morale deteriorates.

Once this data is compiled, a picture of the potential for various types of losses emerges. These losses can then be ranked from the most likely to occur to the least likely to occur.

Estimate the financial loss possible for each potential loss: The same calculations described in the section on investigation can be used (see Exhibit 7–1).

Develop countermeasures: Countermeasures should be allocated carefully so one countermeasure covers as many of the more likely losses as possible.

Compare the total cost of the countermeasures to the total impact of the more likely losses: The resulting potential return on investment should be very high, leaving room to adjust the figure if management does not buy all of your calculations.

ESTABLISHING BUSINESS CREDIBILITY

The job of establishing both security and business credibility must be tackled simultaneously. To totally neglect one for the other can cause an imbalance in management's perception of you as a manager first who also has security expertise. Business credibility separates security professionals from the "company cops." Business credibility allows you to be viewed as a manager who can be promoted into other areas of management. Without this potential, all you can hope to achieve is the top security job. In order to progress professionally, you would have to find a security job in a bigger company. A security professional who wishes to become a competent business manager must be able to grasp some basic business concepts. These concepts are essential to any corporation operating in a free world environment.

Stockholder benefits: The primary goal of any corporation is to maximize the benefit of its stockholders. This concept involves much more than the simple profit motive. Profit is absolutely necessary, of course, but the stockholders may not really benefit from a short-sighted profit motive. A company that seeks a high profit margin for only the next year may actually sacrifice subsequent years' profits. In the long run, then, this policy would not benefit stockholders. Stockholder benefit involves a commitment by the company to provide a consistently high return to the stockholders over a long period of time. To accomplish this goal, the company must strike a balance between dividend payouts and the reinvestment of profits into the company.

Employee benefits: Stockholder benefits also involve a commitment by the company to develop a satisfied and productive workforce. Employees must receive a fair wage, equitable benefits, good working conditions, and other elements of job satisfaction. In exchange, employees are expected to give eight hours of work for eight hours of pay.

Profit: In order for a corporation to survive, it must make a profit. Without a profit, a company cannot grow, nor does it stay the same size. Corporation economics in an inflationary economy are like a turntable. If no profit is made, then the company appears to stand still; but actually it goes backward because no profit is available to reinvest in the firm to keep up with the rising costs. If a company is to grow, it must make sufficient profit to finance expansion and keep up with the rising cost of existing operations.

"TURNING ON" TOP MANAGEMENT

To be accepted as a part of the management team, management must view you as a professional in all respects. The following qualities can help others be more receptive to you as a manager.

Competency: No one likes an amateur who is trying to pass as a professional. You must be competent in your profession by keeping up with the latest developments in security and combining them with the tried and proven methods. Also, you must not be afraid to admit mistakes or pretend to know an answer when you do not. Managerial aptitude is also essential to being viewed as totally competent.

Good judgment: When J. Paul Lyet, chief executive officer of Sperry Corporation, was asked what he considered the number one measure of a prospective employee, he immediately replied, "good judgment." Good judgment is a learned attribute. It involves pausing to reflect on the possible outcomes of a decision, weighing all available data, and doing the right thing. Judgment can be learned from others you admire and who display such a quality.

Personality fit: Every company has a different personality. Successful managers strive to discover that personality and then adapt their own style of management to fit and complement this personality—without compromising, of course, their own basic principles. As the personality of the company changes (usually a gradual process), your style should change right along with it.

Comunication skills: Good communication skills are essential to being understood properly. Spoken communication involves both verbal and non-verbal signals. Researchers have estimated that at least half of spoken communication is relayed through nonverbal signals.[2] It is not only what you say, but how you say it. Courses at many universities teach the techniques of nonverbal communication and public speaking. A good public speaking course will not only enhance your communication skills in front of a group, but will assist in one-on-one conversations.

Sensitivity to ROI: Top management is thinking constantly about return on investment, stockholder benefit, profit, and the other concerns in running a business. If you talk to them about security and do not relate your message to their concerns, you will lose them. You must get on their wavelength by thinking about how security will benefit the corporate bottom line. Remember, security must do what is good for the company and not what is only good for security. Without the company, security would not exist.

ACHIEVING BUSINESS ACUMEN

By using the methods discussed to "turn on" top management, security professionals can develop what is called business acumen. Once achieved, this level of business acumen will pave the way for total credibility. Security professionals can help achieve business acumen through four educational processes.

Formal outside training: College courses in business administration and related subjects can be very helpful. Consider taking a few courses, or even better, pursue a bachelors or masters degree in business administration.

Formal inside training: Many companies offer courses in management skills that can be beneficial educationally. Attending these courses also provides an opportunity for visibility in a non-security role.

Self-study: The public library is a good resource for books on management, communication, and time management. See the accompanying bibliography for suggested readings.

The security survey: This tool gives the security manager an advantage over everyone else in a company. The survey is obviously valuable for the security department, but the security manager also receives an in-depth look at the operation of the various segments of the company. Since a survey can be conducted in almost every facet of the organization, this opportunity to learn a great deal about the company is unique. The security survey is also an excellent method for continuing business education.

---

[2]S. Weitz, *Nonverbal Communication Readings With Commentary* (New York, NY, Oxford University Press, 1974).

SELLING SECURITY TO MANAGEMENT

Selling security to management is not easy and it cannot be accomplished overnight. The process is continual. It requires laying groundwork by displaying management skills and security expertise, presenting facts and figures impressively, and achieving tangible results. As a result, you will truly be viewed as a manager first and a security specialist second. Then the work really begins because even more will be expected of you. While selling security is a never-ending responsibility, it is the most exciting and challenging aspect of business life. You must always be ready to present your ideas to one person in a department or to the entire board of directors. The key to selling can be summarized in the following three rules:

- Know your subject.
- Know your audience: What are their positions in the company? What are their backgrounds? What approaches do they like? What approaches do they dislike? What is their perception of you? These questions and other similar ones must be answered before you can give your audience a truly effective presentation.
- Close the deal: Ask for some action, whether it be approval of a concept, commitment of funds, establishment of policy, or extension of authority. Never sell them any alternatives to consider. Request some kind of action and make sure your proposal has the justification to insure its acceptance.

Once your have established yourself as a business manager with security expertise, you have achieved all the necessary credibility to enable you to sell security effectively to management. Once you have sold management the first time, all subsequent efforts to establish effective security and obtain resources will be easier. If you do not sell management on security, then it will be a continual uphill battle fraught with frustration. Frustration in the business is certainly something we do not need. Happiness is an informed management sold on security.

BIBLIOGRAPHY

Bennett, E., and F. Brandt, and C. Klasson. *Administrative Policy Cases for Managerial Decision Making*. Columbus, OH: Charles E. Merrill Publishing, 1974.

Drucker, Peter F. *Management: Tasks, Responsibilities, Practices*. New York: Harper and Row, 1974.

Drucker, Peter F. *Managing for Results*. New York: Harper and Row, 1974.

Gibson, J., and J. Ivancevich, and J. Donnelly. *Organizations: Structure, Processes, Behavior*. Dallas, TX: Business Publications Inc., 1973.

Knapp, Mark L. *Nonverbal Communication in Human Interaction*. New York: Holt Rinehart and Winston, Inc., 1972.

Mackenzie, R. Alec. *The Time Trap*. New York: McGraw-Hill Book Company, 1975.

Smith, Donald K. *Man Speaking a Rhetoric of Public Speech*. New York: Dodd, Mead & Co., 1969.

Walsh, T. and R. Healy. *Protection of Assets Manual*. Chapter 2. Santa Monica, CA: The Merritt Company, 1975.

Weitz, S. *Nonverbal Communication Readings With Commentary*. New York: Oxford University Press, 1974.

CHAPTER 8

A Policy Structure Gives the Basis for an Effective Security Program

James A. Schweitzer, CDP
Manager, Electronic Information Security
Xerox Corporation

Company programs are established to accomplish an objective. The purpose may be to train employees, improve productivity, increase sales, reduce gasoline use, or improve security. Many company programs fail because poor foundations are laid. Without a firm base of documented management commitment and direction, a program seldom succeeds. Particularly vulnerable to this problem are staff-developed programs that are not perceived as profit-related. A security program is a good example.

The basis for a successful, effective program is a strong policy structure. A description of such a structure, its constituent parts, how it is developed, and how it works, follows.

What is policy? *Webster's Seventh New Collegiate Dictionary* provides an excellent definition of policy: "a course of action selected from among alternatives . . . to guide and determine present and future decisions." Note the intent of policy is to *guide* decisions. Policy doesn't specify what to do in a precise situation; rather, it guides one toward a goal. This concept of policy as a high-level guide is the basis for, and is explained by, the *policy structure*.

The *policy structure* mirrors the classic organizational structure. Broad decisions are made at the top. Increasingly detailed and variable decisions are made at lower levels. (see Exhibit 8–1). All of these decisions must support the goals set by decisions at the top, but they are not necessarily all the same because of differences in situation, function, and perception. Personality and management style also influence how the policy structure is accommodated at each successive level of the organization.

Reprinted with permission of the American Society for Industrial Security, from *Security Management,* December 1980, pp. 18.

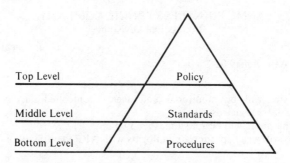

Exhibit 8–1.   The policy structure: A three level tree.

    To differentiate the levels in the policy structure, and to allow discussion of each level's role in a successful program, we can look at the policy structure as a three-level tree. The top level provides broad general guidance towards a management goal. The middle level, where standards are ideally set, establishes needed uniformity and identifies preferred methods and technology. The bottom level, where actual procedures should be determined, provides local or unit-oriented how-to-do-it direction at the working level. Exhibits 8–2, 8–3, and 8–4 demonstrate how the policy structure concept might be applied.

ACME POINTLESS PENCIL COMPANY

Policy 02-25   September 1980

Security

Scope: All Units
Effective: September 1, 1980
Policy: APP will provide adequate security measures to protect
             employees, assets, and business viability.

A. Special security programs will cover these subject areas:
   1. Physical facilities.
   2. Information in oral, paper, and electronic forms.
   3. Personal security of key employees.

B. Requirements
   1.1 Access to all APP facilities will be controlled.
   1.2 Visitors will be identified and authorization obtained from sponsor
       before entry.
   1.3 Sensitive areas (e.g. laboratories, data processing, telecommunica-
       tions) will be further segregated and access limited to identified
       employees and screened visitors only.

Exhibit 8–2.   An organization's top level might set a policy such as this partial one.

    The overall tree structure, which may encompass several functions and multiple unique requirements at lower levels, makes up the policy instru-

ACME POINTLESS PENCIL COMPANY
Inkless Pen Division

Standard A-12:   Physical Security

Reference: APP Policy 02-25

Guards

All facilities will be monitored and access controlled during working hours by contract guards.
1. Working hours will be 7:30 a.m. to 4:30 p.m.
2. Guards will wear appropriate uniforms with APP identification evident.

Exhibit 8–3. An example of a standard (partial) the company's middle level management might determine for the policy set forth in Exhibit 8–2.

ACME POINTLESS PENCIL COMPANY
Inkless Pen Plant #2
Acorn, New Hampshire

Procedure: 10   Guard Practices

References:

APP Policy 02-25
IPD Standard A-12

Reporting and Supervision

1. Guards will report to gate C at 7:45 a.m.
2. Uniforms will be inspected. APP Shield will be worn on left breast pocket.

Exhibit 8–4. An example of a procedure (partial) to implement the policy of Exhibit 8–2 in keeping with the standard set in Exhibit 8–3.

ment. As will be shown, the policy structure is the key to a successful security program.

GENERAL RULES FOR DEVELOPING GOOD POLICY

Good policy (set at the top level of the policy structure) provides general guidance for actions that lead to an expressed management goal. Policy is a decision rule; that is, policy helps managers make decisions within critical constraints and guides them towards some defined end result.

Policy does not tell managers what to do or how to do it, except in critical cases. An example of such a case would be a death on company property for which policy might properly provide detailed reporting instructions. In a critical case like this, top management intentionally removes all discretionary powers from subordinate levels. Such constraint must, however, be a rare exception if policy is to be effective.

A decision rule establishes courses of action to be taken in various circumstances. For example, "BUSINESS CONFIDENTIAL information is to be stored in a file cabinet with bar lock or equivalent." Details of the equipment—type of lock, substitutions, and make of cabinet, for instance—are left to local discretion. Similarly, the policy statement "CONFIDENTIAL information is restricted to employees requiring that information to do their assigned jobs" is a decision rule that allows management at lower levels to determine implementing procedures within an extensive set of alternatives. The end result desired is clearly stated, and local managers should be able to test results against the policy's stated goals.

A good policy will provide for:

- mandated critical actions
  Example: "Thefts of over $100,000 value will be reported immediately by telephone or telex to the corporate security department."
- limitations
  Example: "Guards at energy facilities will carry sidearms except where prohibited by local law."
- prohibitions
  Example: "Class A Business Planning Documents will not be released to general distribution."
- exceptions
  Example: "Where senior division managers determine that compliance with this policy is not justified under established cost/benefit rules, exceptions may be approved by the senior functional vice president with the concurrence of the director of security."

A good policy offers a decision rule for all foreseeable circumstances while allowing flexibility at all levels. This flexibility requirement includes the provision for exceptions to policy, with proper approvals. After all, business itself is a risk-taking endeavor. A policy that leaves no way out will not be effective.

CHARACTERISTICS OF A GOOD POLICY

A policy can be evaluated after it is written by examining it for vital characteristics. An effective policy contains:

- a brief statement of the end result desired for each major function covered.
  Example: "All information created in the course of business operations is confidential and proprietary to the Acme Company."
- clearly defined critical prohibition.
  Example: "No public statements or papers concerning plant protection

systems will be offered without prior approval of the director of security."
- decision rule frameworks allowing for local flexibility in determining compliance actions.
  Example: "Logical access control systems will provide for system user identification, authentication, and authorization to access, change, move, or operate on data."
- motivation for action.
  Example: "Corporate auditors will include security considerations in all audit reviews."
- requirements having general consensus of senior managers at lower levels.
  Example: "Policy will have been thoroughly staffed and all critical exceptions worked out before it is issued."

THE POLICY-MAKING PROCESS

Policy is an expression of the intent and purpose of executive management. While this statement may seem trite, all too often policies are published without the knowledge and support of top management. Since middle- and lower-level managers are motivated by their perceptions of higher-level managers, the specific, overt approval and support of policy and programs by top-level managers is critical. To paraphrase popular advertising, don't leave headquarters without it!

Usually, policy creation begins when line or staff managers recognize that a problem exists. A draft policy is written up by the responsible functional staff. At this point a critical decision must be made. Should the lower levels of the organization, or the operating units in a big company, be brought into the policy-making process?

Experience shows that a better policy results if lower levels of the organization are allowed to review and comment. Since the policy, by definition, is a set of decision rules, it must be relevant to real-life operating situations at all levels. Review and comment by lower echelons will uncover potential sticking points. (For example, guard dogs are impractical in some countries where dogs are used as food.) Policy statements that have been reviewed at several (if not all) levels allow more flexibility in decisions that will be made locally, a characteristic that is the hallmark of effective policy.

After the proposed policy is circulated for review and comment, differences must be reconciled as best as possible. Final policy almost never makes everyone happy, but the fact that the people who must live with the policy had an opportunity to review it in advance indicates an honest attempt to meet all perceived objections. The final policy should be circulated among the original reviewers before being released (or published). The policy should have an effective date clearly specified.

A new policy, or one supporting an important program, should be accompanied or supported by a memo from senior management. In the case of a security program, usually seen as pure overhead and a burden to business operations, the kick-off management letter is crucial. Such a letter should explain the concerns that led to the policy formulations, the participation required of managers at various levels, and the manner in which resources will be provided to the program (who provides funds, staffing, or other needs).

The policy-making process can be summarized as follows:

1. Functional staff develops a policy proposal.
2. Other functional staffs review and comment on the proposal.
3. Policy is rewritten.
4. Company operating unit managers are asked to comment.
5. Comments are reviewed and policy is rewritten.
6. Final policy proposal is reviewed by all parties affected.
7. Policy is published with a concurrent memo from executive management outlining policy and program background, purpose, and responsibilities.

The policy should now be reasonably complete, adequate, and practicable at all operating levels of the organization.

If a policy is a guide to a course of action, and allows considerable latitude of action except in instances necessitating critical limitations, how do employees know *what* to do, or how to do it? In other words, how do they select from the range of possible actions allowed by policy?

STANDARDS

The answer is provided at the next level of the policy structure, where standards are established. Standards explain in more detail how employees should do certain tasks within the intent of the policy. Standards can be used to

- establish uniformity if it is needed.
  Example: All guards will wear the Acme shield on the left shoulder of the uniform blouse.
- set minimum requirements.
  Example: Fencing will be at least eight feet from building perimeter.
- identify preferred methods and technologies
  Example: The DES encryption method will be used. Encryption will always be on a point-to-point basis, never by links within a network.
- allow flexibility where needed.
  Example: BUSINESS CONFIDENTIAL reports distributed from data

processing centers may be handled in either of two ways: specific controlled distribution to end addresses, or in bulk, sealed in cartons, to a major user for subsequent controlled redistribution.

Keep in mind that these examples would be supporting policy statements. The first example, regarding uniform patches, might support a policy statement that merely says "all guards will be neatly uniformed in line with local custom." Such a statement meets the policy goals in that it points to an objective and is flexible.

Standards may be of two types. They may describe things that must be done, and they may, as necessary to achieve consistency, explain how to do them. Standards can also be used to define actions to be taken or items or technologies to be used. For example, a policy requiring facility access control might be supported by a standard explaining the various kinds of locks, door constructions, and surveillance systems considered acceptable. The two kinds of standards should not be mixed because one (definitional) is advisory, and the other (what/how to do) is directive.

When a large company has operating units or divisions, standards may be used to define what is required to implement the policy at each operating level. Standards can be used to establish policy-driven actions suited to a particular geographic locale. For example, security standards for Europe, where practice and culture dictate certain approaches, could set practices and standardize procedures for implementing policies published by a US-based parent company.

While standards may provide instructions on necessary common methods or preferred technologies, flexibility remains important because the standards are applied widely. Can the standard be met equally in Akron, Ohio, and in Lausanne, Switzerland?

PROCEDURES

Procedures are local "how to do it" instructions, usually based on standards. Procedures should be specified only when needed. Many policies may be supported by standards, while few, if any, procedures are detailed. Experience with policy structures like the one described does show, however, that specific procedures are usually helpful.

Because no two facilities, towns, sales departments, showrooms, or factories are exactly alike, some detailed instructions on how to implement the standards are generally necessary. Procedures cover the most detailed level of employee activity. For example, a procedure might set guard reporting times or check-in procedures. This procedure would support a standard requiring that guards control access to research facilities. The standard would be implementing a policy stating that company research activities would be secured in accordance with government and industry practices for that particular technology.

Any program is more likely to succeed if a good policy structure is provided for it. Such a structure has three levels: the policy-making level, the standard-setting level, and the procedure-establishing level. The structure allows goal identification and support, standardization as needed, and flexibility at the lower levels. A policy structure is a powerful and flexible management tool, *if* applied properly and supported visibly by top management.

CHAPTER 9

Risk Management Strategies: Stacking the Odds in Your Favor

Thomas Beall
Sr. Research Associate
Washington Programs Office of
    the University City Science Center

Robert A. Bowers
Sr. Research Associate
Washington Programs Office of
    the University City Science Center

Andrea G. Lange
Assistant Director
Washington Programs Office of
    the University City Science Center

In the last ten years, managers in government and private industry have shown an increasing interest in strategies for improving internal controls. Major dollar losses, caused by flagrant abuses or poor administration, have sparked the use of cost-benefit, cost-effectiveness, and risk analyses to identify program weaknesses. But when vulnerabilities are identified, managers frequently must choose among conflicting or costly investments of limited resources to improve or upgrade security controls.

Reprinted with permission of the American Society for Industrial Security, from *Security Management,* August 1982, pp. 57.

The following information is intended to guide public and private security managers as they conduct vulnerability and risk assessments for internal control. Several models for these analyses are discussed, and the strengths and weaknesses of the various approaches are highlighted. Practical problems of data insufficiency and cost accounting are also addressed.

The conclusions in this article are based on three assumptions:

- Any investment in security measures constitutes a financial risk;
- The risks associated with security alternatives can be assessed and compared; and
- Such comparisons allow the manager to make a rational choice among alternatives (one of which is simply to change nothing at all).

VULNERABILITY ANALYSIS

Before the proposed method for comparing risks can be used, the manager must conduct a program vulnerability analysis. (Vulnerability analysis is discussed here in terms of government benefits programs only, since most of the recent work in the field has been tried in this sector. However, the assessment steps discussd are directly transferrable to private organizations.)

Vulnerability analyses can assess individual programs in business or government and identify common points of vulnerability across several different services. The technique is drawn from many sources, including the security operations of nuclear plants, computer facilities, and hospitals. The use of the process to analyze public benefit programs was pioneered by the University City Science Center in a multi-agency study of federal benefit programs.[1] Fifteen benefit programs were analyzed to identify offender categories and patterns of associated threats. Four potential offender categories were identified:

- *Recipients*—persons who receive program benefits directly.
- *Administrators*—persons charged with managing benefit programs.
- *Third Party Providers*—persons or agencies responsible for providing benefit services.
- *Auxiliary Providers*—persons or agencies that offer contracted services to third party providers and administrators. (Exhibit 9–1 depicts the relationship between these potential offender groups.)

After identifying the potential offenders, an analysis was made of the types of threats likely to be encountered in each benefit program. This assessment disclosed that several different threats perpetrated by one or more potential offenders could occur at each point in a transaction.

---

[1] Andrea G. Lange and Robert A. Bowers, *Fraud and Abuse in Government Benefit Programs* (Washington, DC: Government Printing Office, November 1979).

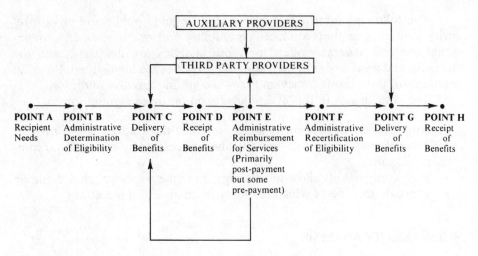

Exhibit 9–1. Program vulnerability points.

As a result of this work, a two-step approach to vulnerability analysis, useful in either government or private business settings, was identified.

The first step in this approach is the development of a program model. This should define specific activities and the flow of transactions in a business, department, or program. The model should include three elements:

- *Events*—the major points in the program or business that are related chronologically and reflect the logical sequence of the endeavor. In Exhibit 9–1, for example, the events correspond to points B through H.
- *Activities*—tasks or work conducted by various personnel to support or establish an event. Using transaction point B in Exhibit 9–1 as an illustration, an example of an activity might be the completion of the appropriate forms by an eligibility worker.
- *Actors*—the individuals who perform the activities, such as clients, customers, employees, or managers.

Once the events, activities, and actors in a program have been identified, the potential for theft, abuse, and waste to occur can be analyzed. Events should be reviewed for possible gaps in procedures. The absence of such events as quality or inventory control, for example, may suggest the need for redesign.

When studying activities, ways in which each activity helps or hinders intentional attempts to obtain benefits, merchandise, or services improperly should be reviewed.

Actors are a key component of any program or business. On the one hand, they overcome the limitations of a poorly designed program. On the other hand, they can subvert the operation of a well-designed one. All actors are potential offenders and, hence, a source of vulnerability.

The second part of a vulnerability analysis is an assessment of external conditions that may adversely influence a program or business and ultimately create security gaps. For example, depressed economic conditions may cause the number of persons eligible for unemployment insurance to increase and, consequently, the volume of work at point B in Exhibit 9–1 to increase. Because this growing caseload could strain routine operations and increase the chance of program eligibility abuse, a depressed economy should be considered as a possible threat to the effectiveness of an unemployment insurance program.

The following data should be collected on each threat and offender category:

- The percentage of cases/items/recipients (whatever the chosen unit of measurement) subject to fraud, theft, abuse, and waste.
- The range of potential dollar loss per unit of measurement.

These two figures can be based on actual or estimated data. Estimates may come from several sources: records showing the number of fraudulent cases within a specific time period divided by the total volume of cases processed in that same period (or, the number of items stolen divided by the total number of items in inventory during a specified period); the experience of recognized professionals who have dealt with similar cases; or interviews or surveys.

Data obtained in the vulnerability assessment may be used to compare the cost of security alternatives through the following risk analysis techniques.

RISK ANALYSIS

Risk analysis gives the security manager a method for ranking various threats to a program or business. It also helps substantiate the need for expenditures to combat these threats.[2] Like cost-benefit and cost-effectiveness analyses, risk analysis provides another method for selecting among competing security strategies. Risk analysis also avoids much of the precision required for cost benefit or cost effectiveness analysis, circumventing the need for assumptions about the relationship between costs and benefits over time.[3]

---

[2] Arthur E. Hutt, "Management's Role in Computer Security" in Douglas B. Hoyt, *Computer Security Handbook* (New York: MacMillan, 1973), pp. 1–3.
[3] Many of the problems associated with the conduct of a cost-benefit and cost-effectiveness analysis in public benefit programs are discussed in the appendix to a separate paper by the University City Science Center entitled "Vulnerability and Risk Analysis for Agency Internal Control: A Working Paper," July, 1981.

Risk analysis assumes that, in the absence of precise risk measures, a reasonable priority of risks can be derived by estimating the probability of occurence for various offense threats. The approach taken here is that risk analysis can prioritize the risks by determining the greatest reduction of an offense for the least cost.

To show how the calculations work, two examples will be discussed, one in a government setting and one in a retail setting.

GOVERNMENT SETTING

Consider the following hypothetical situation: the security manager of a government benefit program must decide whether to spend limited financial resources to combat either misrepresentation of eligibility by benefit recipients, or overcharges by third party providers (see Exhibit 9-2). Assume the probability that each offense might occur is ten percent.[4] Further assume the potential loss range is $100-$200 per case per year for recipient misrepresentation, and $100-$300 per case per year for provider overcharges (see Exhibit 9-3).

The following four steps will help the manager identify the seriousness of each threat, estimate the cost of implementing specific security alternatives, and determine the effectiveness of each proposed security strategy.

Step I: First, determine, a "weighted risk" (WR) value range by multiplying the probability of occurrence (a percent) by the number of cases or

Potential Threats	Recipients	Potential Offenders		
		Sponsor Agency	Third Party Providers	Auxiliary Providers
Misrepresenting Eligibility	●	●	●	
Creating "Ghost" Eligibles	●	●	●	
Improperly Using Benefits	●			
Receiving Additional Benefits	●		●	●
Overcharging for Services			●	●
Withholding Services			●	●
Offering Unneeded Services			●	
Accepting or Paying Kickbacks		●	●	●
Tampering with Records	●		●	
Embezzling or Stealing Benefits		●		
Over or Underpaying Benefits		●		
Counterfeiting Benefits	●	●		
Illegally Owning Benefit Services			●	

Exhibit 9-2. Offenders and offenses for government program.

[4]Ten percent is used in this hypothetical example for each offense threat because the majority of respondents to a previous fraud and abuse survey indicated that actual occurrence fell in the 0 to 10 percent range for both patterns (See Lange and Bowers, *op. cit.,* Appendix H, Item 22.)

Threat	Probability of Occurrence Per Case	Potential Dollar Loss Range
Recipient		
Misrepresentation	.10	$100 to $200
Third Party Provider		
Overcharging	.10	$100 to $300

Exhibit 9–3. Risk cost for government programs.

incidents in the program per year.[5] The WR in this example indicates the number of cases per year that might include a particular offense. Assuming a case load of 2,000 cases per year, the computation for misrepresenting eligibility and for overcharging by third party providers would be:

$$.10 \times 2,000 = 200$$

This value is then multiplied by the potential dollar loss range per case, giving the weighted risk loss range for misrepresenting eligibility:

$$(\$100–\$200) \times 200 = \$20,000–\$40,000$$

and for overcharging:

$$(\$100–\$300) \times 200 = \$20,000–\$60,000$$

That is, a greater WR value range is incurred with provider overcharges than with recipient misrepresentation.

Based on this information alone, the manager would probably choose to combat overcharges rather than misrepresentation, because the potential loss is greater. *However,* this risk information becomes more meaningful if the manager also determines the cost of implementing a strategy to combat each threat. If the costs of strategy implementation are higher then the WR value for an individual threat, it would not be cost effective for the manager to combat that threat. Where the implementation cost is lower than the WR value, the manager can more easily justify combatting that threat with a given security strategy. Nonetheless, other considerations must influence a straightforward decision, specifically, the effectiveness of a given security strategy at reducing fraud and abuse.

Step II: Next, determine the effectiveness of a given security strategy by estimating the rate at which the offense will continue after that strategy is implemented. For example, the manager may conclude, based on prior experience, that educating clients about eligibility tends to reduce the rate of recipient misrepresentation from ten to eight percent. Stated differently,

[5]Hutt, *op. cit.,* pp. 4–5.

two percent of those individuals who might have acted fraudulently could be deterred by the education strategy.

Step III: Using the new probability of occurrence rate, compute new WR values. The following equations are for an education strategy to combat misrepresentation, assuming a case load of 2,000 cases per year:

$$.08 \times 2,000 = 160 \text{ potential fraudulent cases per year}$$

$$(\$100 \text{ to } \$200) \times 160 = \$16,000 \text{ to } \$32,000 \text{ potential annual loss}$$

Step IV: Finally, subtract the new weighted risk (NWR) range from the old WR value to obtain "risk reduction values." These values reflect the potential dollars to be saved or recouped as a result of implementing a specific security strategy. This is expressed in the following equation, which gives a range of risk reduction values:

$$
\begin{array}{l}
\text{Low WR} \\
\underline{-\text{Low NWR}} \\
\text{Low Risk Reduction Value}
\end{array}
$$

$$
\begin{array}{l}
\text{High WR} \\
\underline{-\text{High NWR}} \\
\text{High Risk Reduction Value}
\end{array}
$$

Using the example of education as a strategy for combatting eligibility misrepresentation, the following numbers fit the equation:

$$
\begin{array}{l}
\$20,000 \\
\underline{-\ 16,000} \\
\$\ 4,000 \text{ Low Risk Reduction Value}
\end{array}
$$

$$
\begin{array}{l}
\$40,000 \\
\underline{-\ 32,000} \\
\$\ 8,000 \text{ High Risk Reduction Value}
\end{array}
$$

That is, between $4,000 and $8,000 could potentially be saved or recouped through the implementation of an education strategy to combat misrepresentation of eligibility by recipients.

Exhibit 9–4 compares hypothetical data for four security strategies (education, audit, investigation, and computer quality control) designed to combat both eligibility misrepresentation and provider overcharges. Based on the hypothetical data presented in Exhibit 9–4, investigations would appear to provide the greatest gain in combatting misrepresentation. Likewise, the use of a computer strategy is the most cost-effective way to combat provider overcharges.

Threats	Security Strategy	Probability of Occurrence Per Case	Potential Dollar Loss Range Per Case	Weighted Risk (WR) Loss Range*	New Rate As a Result of Strategy Implementation	New Weighted Risk (NWR) Cost	Risk Reduction Value
Misrepresentation of Recipient Eligibility		.10	$100-$200	$20,000-$40,000			
	Education				.08	$16,000-$32,000	$4,000-$ 8,000
	Audit				.07	$14,000-$28,000	$6,000-$12,000
	Investigation				.06	$12,000-$24,000	$8,000-$16,000
	Computers				.07	$14,000-$28,000	$6,000-$12,000
Provider Overcharge		.10	$100-$200	$20,000-$60,000			
	Education				.09	$18,000-$54,000	$2,000-$ 6,000
	Audit				.07	$14,000-$42,000	$6,000-$18,000
	Investigation				.08	$16,000-$48,000	$4,000-$12,000
	Computers				.06	$12,000-$36,000	$8,000-$24,000

*Weighted Risk Loss Range computed on basis of program administering 2,000 cases per year.

Exhibit 9–4. Risk analysis for security expenditure choices for government programs.

Since the implementation of almost any strategy could be expected to affect more than one offense, the lower and upper risk reduction values can be combined across offense types to provide an overall estimate of a particular strategy's effectiveness. Using education as an example from Exhibit 9–4, the upper and lower risk reduction values for misrepresentation can be added to those for provider overcharges as follows:

Misrepresentation	$4,000	$ 8,000
Overcharge	2,000	6,000
	$6,000	$14,000

Thus, a liberal estimate of the amount of money that could be saved through the implementation of an education strategy ranges from $6,000 to $14,000.

The cost of implementation is a major factor when considering which security strategy or strategies to pursue, if any. Exhibit 9–5 presents the range of risk reduction values from Exhibit 9–4, along with some hypothetical implementation costs. By subtracting the implementation costs from the range of risk reduction values, the decision-maker can compare the relative value of various security strategies.

The range of return column in Exhibit 9–5 shows that all strategies except education may fail to break even with the implementation cost. Investigation offers the least effective alternative. It costs the most to implement and has the next to lowest maximum potential return. Computers and audit appear equal in that each could produce an overall loss of $4,000, but computers could potentially return $4,000 dollars more than an audit. However, this figure is offset, to some extent, by the fact that computers would cost $2,000 more to implement. Education shows the smallest maximum potential return at $8,000, but costs only $6,000 to implement and has the least possibility of operating at a deficit.

While these values are rough at best, they do provide the manager with some guidance in adopting and choosing security strategies. The calculations show that, given limited funds, education would be the best solution for the government example. Funds earmarked for investigation could be better spent on other strategies.

Strategy	Summated Risk Reduction Values	Strategy Implementation Cost	Range of Return
Education	$ 6,000-$14,000	$ 6,000	0 to $8,000
Audit	$12,000-$30,000	$16,000	–$4,000 to $14,000
Investigation	$12,000-$28,000	$19,000	–$7,000 to $11,000
Computer	$14,000-$36,000	$18,000	–$4,000 to $18,000

Exhibit 9–5. Security strategy cost/benefit table for government program strategy.

RETAIL SETTING

To apply this risk analysis technique in retail security, the procedures described in the previous example can be followed with only minor variations. First, a vulnerability analysis would be conducted to identify the nature of the security threats and the types of individuals who pose them. As an example, Exhibit 9–6 shows a list of potential offenders and the types of crimes they might commit in a small retail convenience store. To simplify this illustration, customers that hide merchandise in clothing or parcels, or pass merchandise to an accomplice can be combined into one threat—shoplifting. Employee theft also includes several risks that the convenience store manager may need to address.

To compare these two threats, shoplifting and employee theft, the manager must estimate the probability that inventory losses can be attributed to these two crimes. For example, assume that five percent of a total 60,000 item inventory cannot be accounted for annually.[6] Assume further that the manager, based on personal research, estimates that sixty percent of the losses (or three percent of the total inventory) is caused by customer shoplifting and that forty percent of the losses (or two percent of the total inventory) is caused by employee theft. In this example, the proportion of total inventory lost is used as a measure of the probability that an offense will occur (see Exhibit 9–7).

Exhibit 9–7 indicates that the loss potential is smaller for the average case of customer shoplifting than for an incident of employee theft. These figures are based on the assumption that an employee is more trusted and more aware of the best times to steal.

Once these figures have been computed, the security manager can

	Potential Offenders		
Potential Threats	**Customers**	**Employees**	**Stockers**
Hiding Merchandise in Clothing or Parcels	•	•	•
Passing Merchandise to Accomplices	•	•	•
Underringing Cash Register		•	
Taking Money from Cash Register		•	
Falsifying Invoices			•
Switching Tickets to Obtain a Markdown	•	•	•
Collusion with Deliverymen			•
Giving Employee Discounts to Friends		•	•
Falsifying Sales Records		•	
Underweighing		•	•

Exhibit 9–6. Offenders and offenses for convenience store.

---

[6]Note that this figure is not equivalent to inventory "Shrinkage" in the accounting sense. We refer instead to an estimate of the number of missing items. Obviously, only a sound inventory control system can provide accurate estimates of this nature. While most convenience stores currently lack systems that would provide such data, it seems likely they will become more commonplace here as they are in larger retail stores.

Threats	Proportion of Total Inventory Stolen Annually	Potential Dollar Loss Range Per Item
Customer Shoplifting	.03	$ .50-$ 5.00
Employee Theft	.02	$1.00-$10.00

Exhibit 9-7.   Risk costs for convenience store.

proceed with the four steps for comparing security implementation costs and strategy effectiveness.

Step I: To compute the weighted risk (WR) loss ranges for this retail example, the proportion of items stolen is converted to the actual number of items. Previous estimates indicated that customers stole three percent of the total inventory (.03 × 60,000), or 1,800 items, and the potential loss per item ranges from $.50 to $5.00. Therefore, the weighted risk would be:

$$(\$.50 - \$5.00) \times 1,800 = \$900 - \$9,000.$$

For employee theft the estimates would be (.02 × 60,000) or 1,200 items, and the weighted risk would be:

$$(\$1.00 - 10.00) \times 1,200 = \$1,200 - \$12,000.$$

Step II: The manager must now consider the value of alternative security investments by calculating their effect on these weighted risk values. A new rate, the proportion of inventory stolen, is estimated for each potential security strategy. These rates can be viewed as the frequencies with which the offenses will continue to go undetected or undeterred after investing in a particular strategy. For example, the manager may conclude, based upon personal experience or the experience of others, that installing a closed circuit television (CCTV) system may reduce customer shoplifting from .03 to .025, or that CCTV would reduce customer shoplifting by 300 items (almost seventeen percent).

Step III: Using the estimated new rates of occurrence, new weighted risk (NWR) values are computed for each potential security strategy. To continue the example, installing a CCTV system to combat customer shoplifting would result in the following new weighted risk values:

$$(.025 \times 60,000) = 1,500 \text{ potential customer shoplifting}$$
$$\text{cases per year}$$

$$(\$.50 - \$5.00) \times 1,500 = \$750 - \$7,500 \text{ potential annual losses}$$

Step IV: Next, the new weighted risk (NWR) values are subtracted from the original weighted risk (WR) values to obtain "risk reduction values." These risk reduction values reflect the potential dollars to be saved as a result of implementing each possible security strategy. Proceeding with the CCTV/customer shoplifting example, the manager would compute:

$$\begin{array}{r} \$900 \\ -\ \underline{750} \\ \$250 \text{ Low Risk Reduction Value} \end{array}$$

$$\begin{array}{r} \$9,000 \\ -\ \underline{7,500} \\ \$2,500 \text{ High Risk Reduction Value} \end{array}$$

Thus, between $250 and $2,500 in customer shoplifting costs would be saved annually if CCTV were introduced.

Exhibit 9–8 presents a hypothetical risk analysis for a retail convenience store where seven different security measures are being considered. Exhibit 9–9 presents a summary of the risk reduction values, which combines the effects of each strategy on both customer shoplifting and employee theft, and indicates an approximate cost for implementing each strategy. By subtracting the implementation costs from the risk reduction values, the manager can calculate the potential range of return on each alternative strategy. In cases where return ranges are not immediately apparent, the manager can determine an average return and rank the strategies accordingly.

A manager with limited available resources may be required to choose the cheapest security option regardless of any potentially higher return for other options. On the other hand, options with a high loss potential, regardless of their gain potential, may be unsatisfactory to more conservative managers. Thus, the financial circumstances of the firm and the company's management philosophy will ultimately affect the final decision. Only in cases where the strategy implementation cost is low and the rank order of its effectiveness is high will the choice be as obvious as the decision to rearrange store layout is in Exhibit 9–9. While more refined methods of analysis are available, such analyses require more detailed specification of program and business costs.

IS RISK ANALYSIS WORTH THE INVESTMENT?

Managers concerned about investing limited security resources in the most rational manner possible must first decide whether conducting vulnerability and risk analyses are worth the resources they consume. While no simple answer to this question is available, certain principles should guide the decision. First, for a manager to make responsible policy choices, any information is better than *no* information. Risk analysis provides relevant information useful for decision-making. Second, the ability of any risk anal-

Threats	Security Strategy	Proportion of Total Inventory Stolen Annually	Potential Dollar Loss Range Per Item	Weighted Risk (WR) Loss Range	New Proportion As a Result of Strategy Implementation	New Weighted Risk (NWR) Cost	Risk Reduction Value
Customer Shoplifting		.03	$ .50-$ 5.00	$900-$9,000			
	Signs/Mirrors				.025	$750- $7,500	$150-$1,500
	CCTV				.025	750- 7,500	150- 1,500
	Part-time Security				.022	660- 6,600	240- 2,400
	Employee Training				.027	880- 8,100	90- 900
	Rearranging Store Layout				.024	720- 7,200	180- 1,800
Employee Theft		.02	$1.00-$10.00	$1,200-$12,000			
	Inventory Control System				.013	$ 780-$ 7,800	$420-$4,200
	CCTV				.017	1,020- 10,200	180- 1,800
	Preemployee Screening Procedures				.015	900- 9,000	300- 3,000
	Part-time Security				.012	720- 7,200	480- 4,800

Exhibit 9–8. Risk analysis for security expenditure choices for convenience store.

Strategy	Summated Risk Reduction Values	Strategy Implementation Cost	Range of Return
Signs/Mirrors	$150-$1,500	$ 200	-$ 50 to $1,300
Closed Circuit TV	330- 3,300	1,500	– 1,170 to $1,800
Part-time Security	720- 7,000	4,900	– 4,180 to $2,300
Employee Training	90- 900	350	– 260 to $ 550
Rearranging Store Layout	180- 1,800	300	– 120 to $1,500
Improving Inventory Control System	420- 4,200	2,000	– 1,580 to $2,200
Preemployment Screening	300- 3,000	1,200	– 900 to $1,800

Exhibit 9–9. Security strategy cost/benefit table for convenience store.

ysis exercise to predict outcomes accurately increases as the accuracy of the quantitative estimates increases. Indeed, the cost of obtaining accurate estimates is a key factor in assessing the total cost of conducting a risk analysis.

To review, three methods of obtaining such estimates were discussed previously. The first method uses existing data. The cost of obtaining accurate estimates in this instance may be as low as the value of resources required to retrieve the data and perform simple quantitative analysis. But managers are likely to discover that some, if not all, of the data required for these estimates is lacking. In this situation it would be necessary to employ one or both of the other estimation techniques suggested: consult with a panel of experts or, with management approval, conduct interviews or surveys with clients/customers and employees.

Any one of the three techniques described can be employed alone. Using only one approach clearly keeps costs to a minimum. However, where validity of the estimates is essential, the manager should consider using more than one technique, despite the added cost.

Ultimately, the decision to pursue risk analysis must be based on four factors: the resources available; the need for information relevant to decision-making; the cost of obtaining the needed information; and an estimate of the dollars currently being lost through inefficient use of existing security resources. In a field where hard data is often difficult to find, risk analysis offers concrete numbers that can be understood in management circles.

CHAPTER 10

Security Program Evaluation: The Facility Survey

Thomas B. Nagle
Director, Corporate Security
Levi Strauss & Co.

In reviewing cost-effectiveness and manpower utilization in security programs, one question that requires substantial thought is the decision to conduct annual facility inspections or surveys. With many companies now operating multiple facilities, some in excess of 250 separate operations engaged in manufacturing, distribution, research, service, or administration, the security manager is pressed to maximize departmental resources. Simply to remain abreast of the current security posture and to address the immediate needs of these various facilities strains many. Establishing a formal program of assessment adds yet another burden.

Nevertheless, a number of benefits are to be derived from annual inspections:

- Current evaluation of existing conditions in relation to established security standards.
- Identification of deficiencies and recommendations of remedial action based on firsthand observations by the security professional.
- Identification of trends and concerns requiring a company-wide response.
- First person interaction with field management and improved lines of communication.
- Assessment of the effectiveness of existing security programs and procedures.

All of these benefits are positive justifications for instituting a program of annual facility inspections, but in the real world of practical asset protection another reason is overwhelming. As a famous politician once said: "Until

Reprinted with permission of the American Society for Industrial Security, from *Security Management,* May 1981, pp. 93.

you squeeze the flesh, smell the smell, and hear the word yourself, you simply cannot know how the people think."

This one reason alone overrides the negative aspects of increased travel costs, added administrative burden for report preparation, reduced minimum effectiveness and response from line management, and all the many other priority requirements usually given to support a decision against conducting annual inspections.

Given this preamble, I believe the central question a security manager faces is not whether a program of annual inspections is necessary, but rather how to construct a program. The ideal is a program that not only supports the basic requirements for facility assessment, but one that minimizes or eliminates the negative aspects as well, *and* is cost-effective. The remainder of this article will address an approach to a facility inspection program developed by the Corporate Security Department of Levi Strauss & Co. (LS&Co.).

The world's largest garment manufacturer and distributor, Levi Strauss & Co. has facilities located on five continents in more than twenty-five different nations. In the United States alone, Levi Strauss operates more than fifty manufacturing facilities and six major distribution centers. In addition, the company has numerous regional sales offices, off-site storage facilities, a research and development center, and a corporate headquarters complex that houses approximately one thousand five hundred employees.

Three years ago, the Director of Corporate Security, the Security Manager, Western United States, and the Security Manager, Eastern United States began discussing the ineffectiveness of our facility inspection system. At that time, our procedures called for a facility survey to be conducted on the first visit. These surveys went far beyond our normal inspection criteria, identifying all information necessary to establish a facility security file. The file provided all the background information the security professional should need to make the many security-related recommendations regarding that particular facility.

Once an initial survey report had been prepared on a facility and reviewed, that particular facility was incorporated into an annual inspection schedule. The findings of these annual inspections were recorded in a narrative inspection report which concentrated on particular aspects of physical security that required improvement, and explained what was needed for such improvement.

Our examination of this facility inspection system revealed the following shortcomings:

- Although the security staff used a general format to conduct inspections, the narrative report, which was time consuming, allowed for inspection gaps.
- Field managers complained that their time constraints did not permit the thorough digestion of these inspection reports. Follow-up responses

clearly indicated that only the summaries of recommendations were being addressed.

- Due to emphasis on items requiring improvement, the reports tended to be negative in construction.
- No distinct basis existed for comparing facilities with one another or to established company standards.
- Report preparation was not cost-effective in terms of inspector preparation time and secretarial completion. Also, oftentimes, unnecessary delays in distribution occurred because the inspector was away from his office for two or three weeks at a time.
- The inspection report was a poor motivational and management tool.

To correct these deficiencies, the following system was designed and implemented:

The narrative report was eliminated entirely and replaced by a numerical grading system.

This grading system would relate to specific categories of physical protection common to most LS&Co. facilities worldwide.

The specific categories to be graded would be identified by specific standards established within the company's security manual.

Fourteen specific categories were identified for grading purposes:

1. Guards
2. Alarm Systems
3. Visitor Control
4. Perimeter Security
5. Key Control
6. Trailer Security
7. Security Coordinator Program
8. Sundries Control
9. Trash Disposal
10. Office & Administration
11. Housekeeping
12. Access Control
13. Emergency Procedures
14. Outside Storage

Our manuals were revised to ensure inclusion of complete definitions of criteria to meet the company's standards and criteria were identified in the manual as Physical Security Guidelines. For example, in the category of *Guards,* we decided what criteria should be used in determining the effectiveness of a facility's use of guards. We then amended the guideline in the security manual entitled *Guidelines for the Utilization of Guards at Manufacturing and Distribution Sites* to ensure that all the criteria used in grading that category were covered either in this guideline or in a series of guidelines.

For example, a separate guideline entitled *Guard Instructions and Orders* contained some of the criteria applicable to the overall category of guards.

A security manual dealing with physical protection should not be restricted to the categories identified for grading purposes. It must, however, through a combination of guidelines or topics, include all the criteria that will be used in the grading process. Awareness that what will be graded is covered in the security manual automatically increases security manual use. Getting people to use the security manual has been a nagging problem for the security professional, so the tactic solves two problems.

The most difficult task was developing the specific mechanics for category scoring and, consequently, facility scoring. This was accomplished by establishing certain ground rules:

- The basic purpose of the facility grade (identified as the facility mean score) was to reflect as accurately as possible how that particular facility measured up to the company's security standards.
- Each category applicable to a given facility would receive equal weight in establishing the facility mean score.
- The grading scores should allow sufficient flexibility per criterion or category to identify slight differences in facility performance.

Using these guidelines, we decided that each criterion in a given category would be graded as follows:

Below Standard = 0 − 4 points
Standard   = 5 − 8 points
Exceptional   = 9 − 10 points

A definition for each of these classes of grading was then developed.

A *Below Standard* rating applies to those conditions wherein a recommendation has been made previously but no evidence of implementation or response to the recommendation is apparent. Also, any security criteria in effect that obviously need attention or fail to meet the main thrust of a given guideline within the security manual would be rated *Below Standard*.

The *Standard* rating applies to circumstances conforming to the recommended means of security defined in the security manual for a given category.

A rating of *Exceptional* is to be used only in cases that the facility's managers have obviously made an extra effort to surpass the company's standards for a particular security requirement.

A criteria sheet for conducting inspections and computing category scores was developed next (see Exhibit 10–1). Using the criteria sheet, an inspector could calculate a mean score for each category to be graded at a facility. Criteria scores would be graded on a scale of zero to ten. We decided

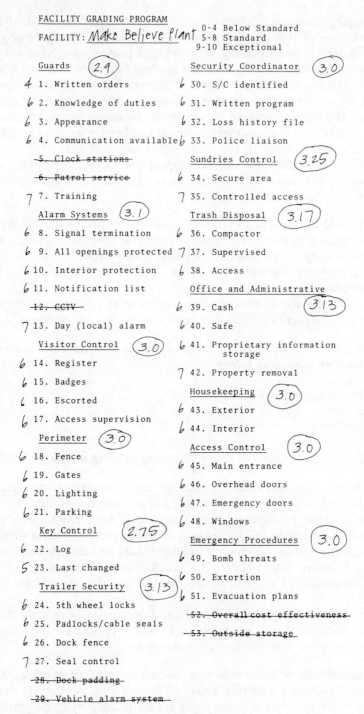

FACILITY GRADING PROGRAM

FACILITY: *Make Believe Plant*   0-4 Below Standard
                                  5-8 Standard
                                  9-10 Exceptional

Guards (2.9)

4 1. Written orders
6 2. Knowledge of duties
6 3. Appearance
6 4. Communication available
~~5. Clock stations~~
~~6. Patrol service~~
7 7. Training

Alarm Systems (3.1)

6 8. Signal termination
6 9. All openings protected
6 10. Interior protection
6 11. Notification list
~~12. CCTV~~
7 13. Day (local) alarm

Visitor Control (3.0)

6 14. Register
6 15. Badges
6 16. Escorted
6 17. Access supervision

Perimeter (3.0)

6 18. Fence
6 19. Gates
6 20. Lighting
6 21. Parking

Key Control (2.75)

6 22. Log
5 23. Last changed

Trailer Security (3.13)

6 24. 5th wheel locks
6 25. Padlocks/cable seals
6 26. Dock fence
7 27. Seal control
~~28. Dock padding~~
~~29. Vehicle alarm system~~

Security Coordinator (3.0)

6 30. S/C identified
6 31. Written program
6 32. Loss history file
6 33. Police liaison

Sundries Control (3.25)

6 34. Secure area
7 35. Controlled access

Trash Disposal (3.17)

6 36. Compactor
7 37. Supervised
6 38. Access

Office and Administrative

6 39. Cash (3.13)
6 40. Safe
6 41. Proprietary information
       storage
7 42. Property removal

Housekeeping (3.0)

6 43. Exterior
6 44. Interior

Access Control (3.0)

6 45. Main entrance
6 46. Overhead doors
6 47. Emergency doors
6 48. Windows

Emergency Procedures (3.0)

6 49. Bomb threats
6 50. Extortion
6 51. Evacuation plans
~~52. Overall cost effectiveness~~
~~53. Outside storage~~

Exhibit 10–1. Inspection criteria sheet.

category scores would be graded on a scale of one to five. A formula was derived to convert criteria scores to category scores.

$$\frac{\text{Criteria Score Total}}{\text{Number of Criteria}} \div 2 = \frac{\text{Category}}{\text{Score}}$$

These criteria sheets are generally not given to the facility manager. They are retained in the security office, as support in case any question arises regarding a grade given.

The next step in setting up our new facility inspection system was to devise an inspection report (see Exhibit 10–2). Using the criteria sheet, a category score for each applicable category is computed, the category scores are summed and the total is divided by the number of categories graded, to arrive at a mean score for the facility.

$$\frac{\text{Sum of Category Scores}}{\text{Number of Categories}} = \frac{\text{Facility Mean Score}}{}$$

In a meeting of the security staff, all inspectors were briefed on the criteria to be used. The need for complete objectivity and uniformity in the grading process was emphasized. The inspectors agreed that any category receiving a mean score of 2.9 or below would require a specific recommendation for improvement on the inspection report.

The final step before beginning the actual inspection program was to prepare a detailed explanation of the program for inclusion in the administrative section of LS&Co.'s security manual. Once that task was accomplished the program could begin.

As with any program, bugs did occur. Careful examination of the early inspection reports revealed that the inspector had to be extremely judicious in assigning a value of 8 to a rating of *Standard*. A final category grade heavily influenced by criteria scores of 8 would come out above standard rather than standard. For example, if the category of *Guards,* with seven

Category	Criteria	Score
Guards	Written Orders	7
	Knowledge of Duties	8
	Appearance	6
	Communications Available	5
	Clock Stations	9
	Patrol Service	N/A
	Training	7

CATEGORY SCORE: $(42 \div 6) \div 2 = 3.5$

Levi Strauss & Co.
INTER-OFFICE CORRESPONDENCE

TO: Sam Spade   DATE: January 10, 1981

DEPT. Plant Manager   FROM: John Doe   EXT. 333

SUBJECT: SECURITY INSPECTION –   DEPT. Corporate Security
Make Believe Plant

Date of Inspection   January 5, 1981

The following applicable areas related to the physical security of
your facility were reviewed and graded: (A new Security Manual
insert will be issued describing this program.)

1. Guards	2.9		8. Sundries Control	3.25
2. Alarm System	3.1		9. Trash Disposal	3.17
3. Visitor Control	3.0		10. Office & Administration	3.13
4. Perimeter (outside)	3.0		11. Housekeeping	3.0
5. Key Control	2.75		12. Access Control	3.0
6. Trailer Security	3.13		13. Emergency Procedures	3.0
7. Security Coordinator	3.0		14. Outside Storage	N/A

$$\frac{\text{TOTAL SCORE} \quad (39.43)}{\text{NO. OF ITEMS} \quad (13)} = \text{MEAN SCORE } 3.03$$

1 – Unsatisfactory
2 – Below Standard
3 – Standard
4 – Above Standard
5 – Exceptional

The following recommendations are being submitted to improve items
rated below standard or unsatisfactory:

1. Guards--Rick Smith, owner of the guard company, should
    be requested to furnish the guards with written orders
    for this plant.

2. Key Control--Since there has been a change in managers
    at this facility, the main entrance(s) locks should be
    changed in the immediate future.

cc: Security Coordinator, Group President, Risk Management

Exhibit 10–2. Facility security inspection report.

criteria, rated eight on five criteria, seven on one criterion, and nine on the
seventh criterion, the total criteria score would be 56. When adjusted to get
a category score, the facility would end up with a score of 4, which is above
the standard (a score of 3 on the 5-point scale). The facility would not,
however, actually have merited an *Exceptional* rating.

These small administrative problems were overcome by frequent communication among the various inspectors. This communication is critical if
several inspectors are to be used in an inspection program.

F A C I L I T Y   G R A D I N G   S U M M A R Y

A.   FACILITIES LISTED BY TOTAL MEAN SCORE:

	Pantswear	Mean Score
1.	Minneapolis	3.81
2.	Hibbing	3.61
3.	Stone City	3.58
4.	Sauk Center	3.38
5.	Willow Lake	3.24
6.	Grand Rapids	3.16
7.	Glyndon	3.15
8.	Detroit Lakes	3.13
9.	Pine River	3.13
10.	Wadena	3.12
11.	Brainerd	3.09
12.	Fargo	3.08
13.	Mooreshead	3.07
14.	White River	3.06
15.	Menahga	3.03
16.	Park Rapids	3.02
17.	International Falls	3.02
18.	Fairmont	3.02
19.	Austin	3.00
20.	Robbinsdale	2.95
21.	Watertown	2.92
22.	Little Falls	2.90
23.	Lake George	2.88
24.	Minnetonka	2.87
25.	Gedker	2.86
26.	Itasca	2.85

B.   DIVISIONS RANKED BY CATEGORY

Pantswear

Category	No. Possible	No. Below 3.0
1.	11	5
2.	26	4
3.	26	9
4.	26	7
5.	26	5
6.	26	4
7.	26	11
8.	24	10
9.	26	10
10.	26	3
11.	26	5
12.	26	10
13.	26	1
14.	7	1

This is an example of the report that would
be sent to the President of the Pantswear
Division.

Exhibit 10–3.   Annual facility grading report.

As soon as the program commenced, a number of positive things began to occur. Field managers were quick to realize that the numerical grades allowed comparison of facilities. They also recognized that senior line managers would capitalize on this comparison data. As a result, a spirit of competition began to develop with field managers becoming much more interested in the specific reasons for category and facility grades. Inspectors found they were able to complete inspections in about half the time previously required. Inspection reports could be completed immediately at the site and submitted to the facility manager, cutting down distribution time. The security department reduced its typing load from inspection reports by nearly eighty percent.

At the end of the inspection cycle, the security director had a tremendous amount of raw data that could be used to develop specific annual reports for review by executive management. Exhibit 10–3 is a sample of one such annual report.

These annual reports provide executives with several types of information:

- Specific facility scores for each facility within an executive's area of responsibility.
- A basis of comparison of the current posture of all facilities.
- Identification of specific categories needing general improvement throughout any part of the organization.

In addition, individual executives now had solid data to stimulate needed change within their organizations and they had a measurement against monies spent in an asset protection program. Levi Strauss's security staff is now completing the second cycle of gradings and will be able to provide, in annual reports, comparative scores for each facility graded against their performance last year, as well as against the percentage of change for a given group of facilities. We are also exploring the use of this data in terms of cost-effectiveness. Response to organizational action on previously identified category weaknesses can now be measured.

This approach to multiple facility inspections has generally been well received throughout the organization and fulfills the purposes for which inspections are established. Its benefits, in terms of motivation, cost savings, and overall effectiveness, again support the axiom that, "Oftentimes, we do not have to work harder—only smarter."

CHAPTER 11

Efficiency Evaluations
Stephen A. Krohne
Manager, Plant Security Operations
Iowa Beef Processors, Inc.

If executive management were to request an efficiency rating of your security program, how would you determine the rating? And what would be the best way of communicating that information?

Unfortunately, security managers and company executives don't always communicate effectively with each other. Company officials, whose expertise lies outside the field of security, are often unacquainted with the high technology hardware and jargon of the security industry. Therefore, for management to communicate effectively with security personnel, language comprehensible to both parties must be used.

The method of multi-plant security evaluation described in this article was developed to facilitate communication between security and upper management. It provides a format for rating security programs using concepts and language common to both security professionals and company executives.

Before undertaking an efficiency evaluation, determine departmental objectives. When using efficiency ratings, three objectives must be considered: (1) evaluate the strengths and vulnerabilities of plant facilities with respect to specific hazards; 2) evaluate all facilities with identical criteria and compare the results to determine average risks and common problem areas; and 3) make constructive, cost-effective recommendations to reduce risk.

Next, identify the risks that must be evaluated. Listed below are potential risks facing a hypothetical multi-plant facility.

1. Fire and explosion hazards
2. Risk of fire in plant, office, and service building
3. Safety hazards other than fire and explosions
4. Theft of company product
5. Theft of company property

Reprinted with permission of the American Society for Industrial Security, from *Security Management*, October 1981, pp. 39.

6. Theft of company documents and data
7. Theft of employee property
8. Vandalism to employee property
9. Assault on employees

CONTROL RATINGS	Control likely	Control uncertain	Control impossible
1. Fire and explosion hazards		✓	
2. Risk of fire in plant, office, and service building		✓	
3. Safety hazards other than fire and explosions		✓	
4. Theft of company product	✓		
5. Theft of company property	✓		
6. Theft of company documents and data	✓		
7. Theft of employee property		✓	
8. Vandalism to employee property		✓	
9. Assault on employees	✓		
10. Use or sale of drugs or alcohol on premises	✓		
11. Vehicle traffic	✓		
12. Pedestrian traffic	✓		
13. Disorderly behavior on premises	✓		
14. Vandalism or sabotage to company property		✓	

SUBTOTAL __30__

DETECTION RATINGS	Detection likely	Detection uncertain	Detection impossible
1. Fire and explosion hazards	✓		
2. Risk of fire in plant, office, and service building	✓		
3. Safety hazards other than fire and explosions	✓		
4. Theft of company product	✓		
5. Theft of company property	✓		
6. Theft of company documents and data	✓		
7. Theft of employee property		✓	
8. Vandalism to employee property		✓	
9. Assault on employees	✓		
10. Use or sale of drugs or alcohol on premises		✓	
11. Vehicle traffic	✓		
12. Pedestrian traffic	✓		
13. Disorderly behavior on premises	✓		
14. Vandalism or sabotage to company property		✓	

SUBTOTAL __24__

TOTAL __54__

SECURITY EFFICIENCY RATING __$^{70}/54$ or 77%__

Exhibit 11–1.   Control and detection ratings.

10. Use or sale of drugs or alcohol on premises
11. Vehicle traffic
12. Pedestrian traffic
13. Disorderly behavior on premises
14. Vandalism or sabotage to company property

After the risks have been identified, integrate departmental goals into the evaluation system. This hypothetical evaluation has two primary goals: 1) controlling risk and 2) detecting risk.

It is also important to gauge the effectiveness of control and detection. The system described here provides three levels for each category:

CONTROL/ DETEC- TION RATING	RISK	FACTORS AFFECTING RATING	RECOMMENDATIONS FOR REDUCING RISK
1 2	Fire or explosion hazards	engine fuel in storeroom B, poor ventilation in supply annex	Install fans for cross-ventilation, store fuels at rear of building C, away from machinery
1 2	Fire in plant, offices, and service buildings	overloading of electrical circuits in plant and service buildings	automatic shut-off feature for electrical overloads
1 2	Safety hazards other than fire and explosives	high voltage generators, and cutting edges ing equipment	restrict access to high voltage areas heavy-duty work for machi ators.
3 2	Theft of company products	metal detectors at exits, CCTV monitoring employee work and rest areas.	risk control adequate
3 2	Disorderly behavior on premises	strict access control, personnel counseling available	risk control adequate
1 1	Vandalism or sabotage to company property	fork lifts and vans in open storage lot, poor lighting on northeast perimeter	install chain link fence around storage lot, place 2 additional floodlights at north entry to warehouse

Exhibit 11–2.   Recommendations for reducing risk.

FACILITY   St. Stephens Forge & Ironworks

DATE OF RATING   February 5, 1981

RATING CONDUCTED BY A.C. Helmo, Mgr. Security

RATINGS EXAMINED BY: DATE

J. D. Watson, VP   2-9-81

Robert Chase, Eng.   2/11/81

H. B. GOULD, DIV. II   2/12/81

Marie C. Loomis   2/13/81

Ted Bartlett   2/16/81

E. C. Waters, Div III   2/17/81

Henry McAdams, Mgr.   2-19-81

Exhibit 11–3. Distribution list.

1.   risk control likely,
2.   risk control uncertain, and
3.   risk control impossible.

The same levels apply to detection:

1.   risk detection likely,
2.   risk detection uncertain, and
3.   risk detection impossible.

Numerical values are applied to each level of efficiency. Within the category of control, a numerical value of 3 points is allotted to the "control likely" measurement. A numerical value of 1 corresponds to the "control uncertain" measurement; and in an area where no control is possible, a rating of zero is recorded. Detection measurements are similarly accorded numerical values. Since detection is secondary to control, the numerical values in this category are adjusted accordingly. Thus the "detection likely" measurement carries a value of 2 points, the "detection uncertain" measurement receives 1 point, and the "detection impossible" measurement carries a rating of zero.

As illustrated in Exhibit 11–1, a control rating is recorded for 14 types of risk, with a maximum of 3 points possible for each category. A total of 42 points is possible in the control evaluation. In rating detection capabilities, the same 14 risks are assessed, with a maximum of two points possible for each, or a total of 28. Thus, a perfect score for a given facility, the combined total of both control and detection measurements, is 70 points. The sum of the numerical ratings of both cateogries is then divided by 70. The resulting percentage is the security efficiency rating.

The last step of the evaluation provides recommendations for upgrading security and reducing risk (see Exhibit 11–2). The evaluation's results must be distributed among appropriate company officials. Exhibit 11–3 is a typical distribution list, specifying the officials designated to examine the security ratings. The list should include plant managers, operations managers, and division vice presidents.

This efficiency rating system, while not intended to provide a detailed, technical analysis of any security program, offers a simple, easy to understand way of communicating basic security information to non-security professionals.

CHAPTER 12

Justifying Your Budget
Stanley Price, CPP
Director of Security
NY University Medical Center

In nearly every business and industry, cost containment and budget reductions have been a reality for almost a decade. Security departments throughout the country face increased pressure to cut costs, reduce personnel, and increase productivity. In addition, the security directors of some firms, and the health care industry in particular, must cope with reimbursement formulas that fall short of expenditures and fail to compensate for double-digit inflation.

Because of these fiscal problems, security executives must learn to justify their budgets by clearly demonstrating the cost-effectiveness of their expenditures. They must convince administrators that funds spent on security will save the company money in the long run.

To persuade administrators to approve budget and manpower requests, security executives must understand and apply sound management principles to their budget formulations. Planning, accounting, and programming are essential tools for designing an effective security program for any business or institution. All too often security people fail to use these tools properly.

In the past, security administrators have relied very little on basic accounting procedures to justify their budgets. For example, when asked how many guards would be needed to cover one post 24 hours per day, 7 days per week, they would simply multiply 24 hours by 7 days and divide by 40 hours (or one work week):

$$24 \times 7 = 168 \div 40 = 4.2$$

Using this system, 4.2 guards would be needed to cover one post adequately for one year. This would be a realistic figure if guards never took a day off. But who covers the post when an employee gets sick, goes on vacation, or is picked for jury duty?

Reprinted with permission of the American Society for Industrial Security, from *Security Management*, October 1981, pp. 39.

A more realistic methodology for planning and justifying a security budget was developed by security executives and administrators at the New York University (NYU) Medical Center. To reach an accurate estimate of manpower requirements, the NYU team first calculated the number of tours, or eight-hour shifts, each guard works in one year. In making this estimate, they used actual figures from Medical Center personnel records.

All of the figures included in the example that follows were taken from the center's 1980 security budget.

Fifty-two guards out of a force of 72 worked the entire year, taking the following time off during this period:

Type of Leave	Total Days	Average Days Per Guard
Vacation	663	12.75
Swing	96	1.85
Sick	755	14.52
Bereavement	6	.12
Suspension	34	.65
Jury Duty	18	.35
Personal	5	.10
AWOL	3	.04
Comp. Time	2	.04
Total	1582	30.42

Based on this information, each security officer averaged 30.42 days off in 1980. Taking the computations a step further, each security officer therefore worked 229.58 tours per year:

$$\begin{array}{r} (5 \text{ tours per week}) \\ \times\ \underline{(52 \text{ weeks per year})} \\ 260 \text{ tours} \\ -\ \underline{30.42 \text{ days off}} \\ 229.58 \text{ days worked per year} \end{array}$$

Next, it requires 21 tours per week to cover one post 24 hours per day, 7 days per week:

$$\begin{array}{r} (3 \text{ 8-hour tours per day}) \\ \times\ \underline{(7 \text{ days per week})} \\ 21 \text{ tours} \end{array}$$

To cover one post around the clock for one year therefore takes 1,092 tours:

$$\begin{array}{r} (21 \text{ tours per week}) \\ \times\ \underline{(52 \text{ weeks})} \\ 1,092 \text{ tours} \end{array}$$

With each security officer working 229.58 tours per year, 4.76 full-time employees (FTEs) are required to cover one post for 1,092 tours:

$$1,092 \div 229.58 = 4.76$$

Using this methodology, security planners can realistically gauge the number of employees needed by the security department, given the certainty of illness, authorized absences, and attrition within the guard force. The simplified hypothetical example that follows makes the budgeting formula more clear.

As a security executive, you are asked to justify the 16 FTEs you have requested to cover 3 posts, 24 hours per day, 7 days per week; and one post 8 hours per day, 5 days per week. By using the NYU budgeting system, you should arrive at the figure 15.41, which would be rounded to 16 guards. The step-by-step computations used to reach this figure follow.

To cover one post 24 hours per day, 7 days per week:

$$(24 \text{ hours}) \times (7 \text{ days}) = 168 \text{ hours per week}$$

To cover 3 posts 24 hours per day, 7 days per week:

$$(168 \text{ hours}) \times (3 \text{ posts}) = 504 \text{ hours per week}$$

To cover one post 8 hours per day for 5 days:

$$(8 \text{ hours}) \times (5 \text{ days}) = 40 \text{ hours per week}$$

To cover all of the above posts for one week:

$$(504 \text{ hours}) + (40 \text{ hours}) = 544 \text{ hours per week}$$

Now divide the number of hours per week by 8, for each 8-hour shift, to determine the number of tours required per week.

$$(544 \text{ hours per week}) \div 8 = 68 \text{ tours per week}$$

Next, determine the number of tours per year:

$$(68 \text{ tours per week}) \times (52 \text{ weeks per year}) = 3536 \text{ tours}$$

$$\frac{(3536 \text{ tours per year})}{\div \ (229.58 \text{ tours per guard per year})}$$
$$15.41, \text{ rounded to 16 guards}$$

For the final computation, which determines the number of guards

1 PROGRAM NAME ACTIVITY OR DESCRIPTION	2 LEVEL OF SERVICE	3 MANPOWER (FTEs)	4 SALARY EXPENSE	5 NON-SALARY EXPENSE	6 TOTAL PROGRAM COST
I.D. BADGES	5000 badges issued per year	.2	$ 2,882	$ 8,500	$ 11,382
PARKING LOT PATROL	7 days per wk., 24 hrs. per day	4.76	$ 79,987	$ 2,947	$ 82,934
MAIN LOBBY	7 days per wk., 6 AM to 10 PM	3.18	$ 53,437	$ 1,968	$ 55,405
EMERGENCY ROOM	7 days per wk., 24 hrs. per day	4.76	$ 79,987	$ 2,947	$ 82,934
SPECIFIC POST	Mon. to Fri. 10 AM to 6 PM	1.13	$ 18,989	$ 714	$ 19,703
PLAINCLOTHES PATROL	7 days per wk., 12 hrs. per day	2.38	$ 39,994	$ 1,504	$ 41,498
TOTALS		16.41	$275,276	$18,580	$293,856

Column 1: program or post, i.e., lobby guard, perimeter patrol, etc.
Column 2: level of service—the days or hours the post is covered.
Column 3: manpower—the number of full-time equivalents
    (FTEs) needed to cover the post.

Column 4: salaries—the salary cost of covering the post.
Column 5: non-salary expenses—uniforms, equipment, etc.
Column 6: total cost for program—column 4 plus column 5.

Exhibit 12–1. New York Medical Center programmed security budget.

needed to cover all posts throughout the year, simply divide the number of tours per year by the number of tours worked per guard per year, which was determined by the NYU system to be 229.58.

Once the required number of security guards has been determined, computing the total security guard budget should be relatively simple. The system used by NYU Medical Center officials is called a "programmed budget" (see Exhibit 12–1). This methodology breaks the security department budget into separate programs, and specifies the anticipated cost of each program. This budget programming procedure simplifies things for the security director when administration gives the order to cut costs. When budget cuts are ordered, the security director can show administrators exactly what programs are included in the department's budget, and then administrators can decide what they want to cut.

The NYU programmed budget system is a flexible tool that can be used to illustrate graphically how department resources are consumed. High cost items or programs are easy to identify, allowing them to be isolated and examined in detail.

In this short article, two tools security executives can use to help justify their budgets are described. There are no hard and fast rules for budget justification procedures. These tools can be modified or expanded to suit any department's needs.

CHAPTER 13

Loss, Offense, and Incident Reporting
Don Walker, CPP
Corporate Security Director
GENESCO, Inc.

In recent years the word "Security" has been used interchangeably with the terms "Loss Prevention," "Assets Protection" and "Risk Avoidance." These terms are a more accurate description of today's mission for the security professional. Today's security professional should be a vital part of the management team of an organization. He, like other management personnel, must make decisions based on the best facts available and must also be able to predict or forecast future trends and events.

A major task of the security professional is to identify precisely the risks and the probable effects of the risks on the assets of the organization being protected. With adequate risk analysis, the security professional increases his ability to effectively plan and allocate protective resources which will prevent or minimize losses.

The first step in any risk analysis or security planning is DEFINING THE PROBLEM (Exhibit 13–1). Although various considerations are involved in defining the problem, one vital element and the subject of this article is a review and analysis of the company's historical experience. In security, you must know what your losses are and how they occur before you can provide adequate, cost-effective protection against such losses. Despite this basic premise, some companies do not actually know the "who, what, when, where, how" of their losses or why the losses occur. Neither do they realize the total impact these incidents have on the net profits of the company.

Management may be aware of the details of some major burglaries, hijacking or robberies, and may have heard brief accounts of minor pilferage, "a little gambling" or some "pot smoking." Some of the losses may even have been reported to the organization's insurance department and some to

Reprinted with permission of the American Society for Industrial Security, from *Security Management*, September 1977, pp. 82.

Exhibit 13–1.   Security planning cycle.

the fixed assets accounting department, while others have gone completely unreported. The latter is more commonly the case. The "losses," actual and suspected, are often absorbed into the manufacturing or operating costs of the organization. This absorption encourages the inclusion of losses in the organization's production or operating standards; therefore, the losses become a budget factor and are never investigated.

One can easily see that if those incidents have not been properly reported and analyzed, management cannot measure their impact on the organization nor justify adequate expenditures for security. In addition, management cannot be aware of the related or indirect costs of losses, the number of incidents avoided or the value of the assets recovered. These weaknesses in awareness may cause the company management to view security as a necessary expense and not realize the profit potential of an effective security program.

Proper loss reporting and analysis will assist in defining the problem and will provide top management with the type of information needed to make sound business judgments. Therefore, every professional security department should have a manual or automated system of loss reporting as dictated by the size and complexity of the organization.

Accurate, well-documented information about losses and loss events can be some of the most useful information maintained by the company. The information is vital for: initiating investigations; continuing investigations of unresolved past incidents; establishing the amounts and types of losses being encountered by the organization; and assisting in the evaluation and revision of physical security features. Such data can aid in the evaluation of the effectiveness of the total security effort and in predicting future loss probability.

The purpose of this article is to describe the approach one multi-division company has used to develop an automated "Loss, Offense and Incident

Reporting" system for Defining The Problem, periodically reevaluating the protection effort and providing top management with a loss forecast.

STARTING FROM SCRATCH

Since the company had never approached security on a corporate basis, the first step was to determine what the loss history had been. All logical divisions and departments, such as Audit, Insurance, Transportation, Accounting, Finance, Personnel and Legal were contacted for their input. Previous audit reports, reports from private investigators and management letters from the company's independent accountants were reviewed. The next step was to visit a representative sample of the company's facilities.

The facility reviews involved the basic assessment of the existing security organization, programs, operating procedures, and basic internal controls; an analysis of known loss information at the facility and a cursory survey of the physical security. The results of the interviews, reviews and inspections revealed a weakness in security programs and a records situation similar to that previously described. That is, a lack of identification of losses was apparent, as was the lack of a system for reporting losses and a lack of accurate records.

The best records were found in the insurance department, but they included only those amounts over the amount of the deductible claim. The retailing operations revealed known dollar amounts for unexplained stock shortages, however, the losses in manufacturing were hidden in the cost of goods and manufacturing variances.

The information developed during this review was presented to top management in a slide presentation which depicted the physical condition of representative facilities and summaries of known losses. The presentation also highlighted the voids in information as well as a recommended plan to capture the information necessary to establish effective security programs. Management approved the plan which included the automated systems approach for the "Loss, Offense and Incident Reporting Systems."

SYSTEMS GOAL

The goal of the Loss, Offense and Incident Reporting System is to depict the known security problems of the corporation. The system maintains a historical record of all known and suspected security-related incidents that are reported from all company locations.

The analysis of the data obtained through proper reporting is the basis for effective planning and control of the corporation's security program. A Corporate Security Policy sets forth the purpose, scope and responsibility of the program. The policy requires that the supervisor be responsible for the asset report as follows.

"All losses, suspected losses, disappearances, thefts, criminal offenses, violations of company security policy and other incidents which result in a loss, damage or compromise of a company asset, must be reported within 48 hours of the incident or discovery of the incident, and where appropriate, investigated. Such reports must be in writing and submitted on the Corporate Loss, Offense and Incident Report (Exhibit 13–2).

In addition, incidents involving a management employee or a loss or suspected loss of more than $1,000 must be reported immediately to the Division or Corporate Security Department within 24 hours after discovery of the incident.

For the loss reporting system to perform at the optimum level, the definition of a reportable incident must necessarily be broad and include as many items as possible. The type of incidents to be reported in the system described herein are outlined in Exhibit 13–3.

SYSTEM OVERVIEW

The following is an overview as to how the Loss, Offense and Incident Reporting System described in this article actually operates.

At the site of any known or suspected loss, security policy violation or incident, a "Loss, Offense and Incident Report" form is prepared by the designated representative (the Supervisor responsible for the asset) at that location.

The "Loss, Offense and Incident Report" is a four-part form and is the basic data collection document. It must be submitted to the Division Security Director within 48 hours of the loss, suspected loss or incident. (The original and canary yellow copy of the form should be forwarded to the Division Security Director). Each division has the flexibility of determining how to use the division (pink) copy. For example: it may be used by the Controller, District Managers, Plant Manager, Director of Stores, Operations Manager, etc. The pink copy is sent to the Division Representative as specified by the Division Security Director. The four copy (goldenrod copy) is retained at the facility where the incident occurred.

The original and second (white & canary) copies are reviewed and appropriate codes are added by the Division Security Department. The canary copy is then submitted to Corporate Security. The original (white) is maintained by the Division Security Director. Changes to previous incidents are coded by the Division Security Director or where appropriate, by Corporate Security on an "Incident Reporting System—Incident Update" form (Exhibit 13–4).

Once a week all incident forms received are batched by Corporate Security and sent to Central Input Preparation, where the information is

1. Facility name and complete address. Include Zip Code.

2. Leave Blank. To be completed by the Operating Company Security Dept.

3. Data and time the loss or incident occurred, or estimate of when it occurred.

4. Amount of loss rounded to nearest dollar. Do not include cents. If the asset is recovered at the time of the incident, record it as a loss and enter the same amount as a recovery.

5. The rate at which the loss was computed:
   (1) Cost–Use for raw materials or work-in-process, or cash.
   (2) Wholesale–Use for finished goods in transit prior to reaching a retail store or warehouse.
   (3) Retail–Use for all merchandise in a retail store or in a retail inventory (warehouse or transit).
   (4) Book–Use for fixed assets.
   (5) Replacement–Use for supplies or other expense items, such as building damage.

6. Leave Blank. To be completed by the Operating Company Security Dept.

7. Describe event giving in as many details as available. If additional space is required, use regular line paper.

8. Describe what action has been taken, including:
   —Insurance Claims Filed
   —Promissory Notes taken from employee(s) involved
   —Employee(s) Separated
   —Police Involvement

9. Name and title of person submitting the report.

10. Signature of person submitting report.

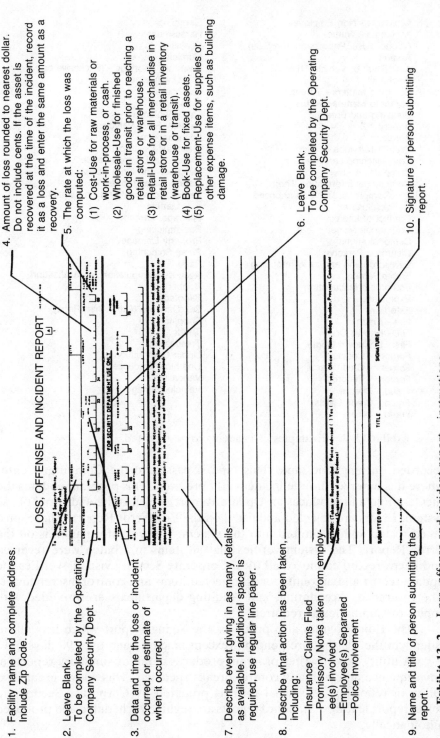

Exhibit 13–2.   Loss, offense and incident report—instructions.

Accidents - Non-Employee
Accidents - Traffic
Alcohol (Use, Possession and Sale)
Assault
Auto Theft or Vehicle Theft
Blackmail
Bombing Matters - Threats
Bombing Matters - Actual
Breaking and Entering
Bribery
Burglary
Civil Disturbance or Riot
Coin Machine Larceny
Computer Abuse
Confidential Information Theft,
    Compromise or Unauthorized
    Disclosure
Conflict of Interest
Counterfeit Money
Demonstrations
Disturbed Persons
Eavesdropping and/or Wiretapping
Embezzlement
Equipment Malfunction
Explosion
Extortion
Fire - Arson
Fire - Known Origin
Fire - Unknown Origin
Forgery - Checks
Forgery - Credit Cards
Forgery - Records
Fraud - Checks
Fraud - Credit Cards
Fraud - Other

Gambling
Harassment
Hijacking
Homicide
Inventory Shortage - (Excessive or
    Unexplained)
Kickbacks
Kidnapping
Labor Violence
Larceny From Vehicles
Loansharking
Malicious Destruction
Mysterious Disappearance
Narcotics and Drug Abuse
Natural Catastrophe
Patent, Copyright and Trademark
    Matters
Pilferage/ Larceny
Pocketpicking
Property Damage
Purse Snatching
Rape
Records Manipulation or Falsification
Robbery
Sabotage
Sex Offenses (Other than Rape)
Shoplifting
Thefts
Trespassing
Unfair Competition
Unethical Practices
Vandalism
Vehicle Damage

Exhibit 13–3.   Examples of incidents to be reported.

recorded on magnetic tape. This tape is passed to the Computer Center where it is entered into the incident edit program. This program updates the Incident File and produces an Update Report, which is the audit trail of the system. Errors are rejected and listed on the Edit Error Report. These must be corrected and re-entered into the system. Control information is on the Error Report. The system verifies that all items in a batch were received and keeps record counts of all files. Corporate Security visually verifies the update report and accounts for all rejected items and control discrepancies. The Insurance, Accounting, and Auditing departments are provided with copies or summaries as required.

The Edit Program also produces the Aging Report which lists all incidents in the file that are pending (except inactive) and over 90 days old.

A utility report writer program produces detail or summary reports in any sequence and with any control breaks specified. This allows great flexibility in reporting. A special form is prepared by Corporate Security to select report features. Standard reports are regularly scheduled and produced automatically.

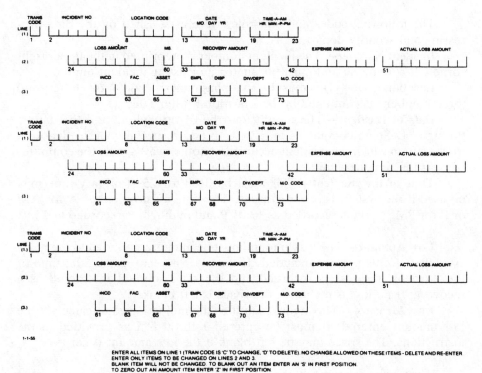

Exhibit 13–4. Incident reporting system—incident update form.

The Location Master File, which identifies over 2,000 locations, is maintained by entering transactions through Central Input Preparation into the file maintenance program. The Location Master File contains all information pertinent to each location and a list of security features available at that location.

Incidents are purged from the Incident File once a year. The purged incidents are saved on an archival tape for use in multi-year reports. The Location Master File is saved once a month to keep a history of the location's security features and results.

DATA COLLECTION

The "Loss, Offense, and Incident Reports" form (Exhibit 13–2) was designed by the security and data processing departments so that the pertinent information could be converted to a format that could be processed by machine. Most of the information is basic to any company and must be included for the system to be effective.

The following codes and edit rules were established by the data processing and security departments.

Incident Number—The incident number is preprinted in the upper right corner. It is numeric and must not match an existing incident number.

Location Code—This must be an alpha-numeric code of two letters and three numbers as contained in the Location Master File.

Date of Incident—The month must be 01 through 12 and the day 01 through 31. Some companies may wish to add a special code to denote a work shift on which the incident occurred. Another way is to let the computer convert the time to a shift.

Time of the Incident—This must be 0100 to 1259 (military time may be used if the system is so structured). The time must be either A for AM or P for PM. Noon is recorded as 12:01 P and midnight is recorded as 12:01 A.

Loss Amount—The loss amount must be numeric, rounded to the nearest dollar. Cents are not included. If the asset is recovered at the time of the incident, the loss is recorded and the same amount is entered as a recovery. If no loss is involved, the space is left blank.

Loss Measure—This figure identifies the method used to calculate the loss amount entered. It must be entered 1 through 5 as provided in the instructions. The space may be left blank if the loss amount is zero.

1. *Cost*—Use for raw materials through the manufacturing cycle. Cost of materials and labor, and/or cash.
2. *Wholesale Price*—Finished goods in storage or in transit prior to reaching a retail facility (store or warehouse).
3. *Retail Price*—Finished goods in a retail store or in transit from a retail warehouse to a store.
4. *Book Value*—Value of asset as shown on division records. Used for fixed assets, such as machinery and furniture, etc.
5. *Replacement Cost*—Cost to replace the asset. Use for supplies and other expense items, such as building damage.

Incident Code—The Incident code identifies the type of criminal act or violation of Security Policy. The definitions and descriptions must be designed for internal use and may, in some cases, differ from purely legal definitions. As an example, the following incident definitions have been established for Burglaries and Drug Abuse:

25. *Burglary and Breaking and Entering*
    The unlawful entry into or remaining in any building with the intent to commit a crime or the attempted unlawful entry into a facility with the intent to commit a crime.
78. *Narcotics and Drug Abuse*
    Any instances involving the use, sale, possession, growing, manufac-

turing or making of drugs or narcotics while on company business, on company property or in a company vehicle.

Facility Code—This code indicates the type of facility at which the incident occurred. For example:

10—Administrative Offices	40—Terminal or Warehouse
20—Plant	50—Transportation
30—Retail Store	60—Non-Company
32—Leased Department	70—Other
35—Sales Office and Showrooms	

Asset Code—This code designates the type of asset affected by the incident, i.e., what was stolen, damaged, hurt, or otherwise involved in the incident. For example:

10—Buildings (Plants, Warehouse, etc.)
11—Cash
12—Checks and Check Writing Equipment
13—Credit Cards
15—Computer Equipment
20—Employee—Person
21—Employee—Property
22—Equipment
23—Finished Goods Inventory
24—Fixed Assets—Other than Buildings
30—Information
40—Raw Materials
41—Retail Merchandise
44—Supplies
50—Vehicles
55—Work-in-Process Inventory
60—Other

As the system is refined, sub-codes will be established to identify specific assets, such as tools, machines, types of raw materials, etc. The sub-codes are particularly valuable for large installations.

Employee Codes—Here the type of employee responsible for the incident is noted. This code is to be completed only when an employee is involved in committing the incident, i.e., embezzlement, conflict of interest, etc. It is not used for a shoplifting, burglary or similar crime, unless an employee was part of a conspiracy. If an employee did not commit the act, leave the space blank. Such codes may be established by using The Equal Employment Opportunity Codes as follows:

A—Officials and Manager	G—Semi-Skilled Workers
B—Professional	H—Unskilled Workers
C—Technicians	I—Service Workers
D—Sales	J—Apprentices
E—Office and Clerical	K—Producting Trainees
F—Craftsmen (Skilled)	L—White Collar Trainees

Disposition code—Shows whether the incident is pending or closed and what the latest status is. The disposition code may be changed or updated by use of the Incident Update form (Exhibit 13–4).

01—Pending Investigation or Review
02—Pending Prosecution
03—Pending Civil Suit
04—Pending Management Action
05—Pending Promissory Note
06—Pending Insurance Claim
07—Pending Inactive
19—Pending Other
20—Closed Administratively
21—Closed Employee Termination
22—Closed Successful Prosecution
23—Closed Unsuccessful Prosecution
24—Closed Settlement for Company
25—Closed Settlement Against Company
26—Closed Insurance Settlement
39—Closed Other

The system's flexibility will allow for additional codes as required.

Division Department Code—This code is primarily for division use; however, it can be used by both the Division and Corporate levels to identify specific locations of loss, type of material lost, i.e., sweaters, fine jewelry, cosmetics, etc. This code may be used to break down reports by department, floor, or any other desired grouping established by the division. The division is responsible for establishing its own coding system. Blanks will be ignored by the system.

As a general guideline, when there is an external incident against an asset, the department number where the asset was located is recorded. If an employee is involved in committing the offense, the department number of the employee is used. The information collected in this section will differ depending on the type of organization using the information. For example, a major industrial plant may need five or six digits to code the exact location within the complex.

Modus Operandi (MO) Codes—Modus Operandi (MO) Codes are necessary for analyzing the means by which incidents have occurred. We must know the characteristic methods employed in repeated incidents to best determine how to prevent incident recurrence and future losses. Not all incidents will have or require an MO code. MO Codes should be established for the most frequent incidents as well as those incidents that require detailed analysis, e.g., burglary, robbery, etc.

The MO Code section may be completed by inserting the proper Alpha Character in the three position "MO Code" space. It is not necessary to complete the MO Description unless the codes do not adequately describe the incident, loss or offense. If it is necessary to complete the MO Description, use abbreviations that will be readily understood. For example: "A thief broke a window in a company-owned tractor and was attempting to remove the CB radio when he was apprehended by the police". The above incident would be coded as follows:

B	R	K	E		C	O		T	R	U	C	K		W	I	N	D	O	W		S	T	O	L	E		C	B

SAMPLE CASES

Set forth here are examples as to how an employee theft and a burglary are reported in the system as described above. The cases and all information pertaining to them are hypothetical and do not describe any actual person, location or actual occurrence.

Case A

At 5:10 PM on April 8, 1977, a sales clerk by the name of John J. John attempted to take five gold bracelets, valued at $20 each from the store where he was employed, Retail Retail Co. (Store Number 4) 882 8th Avenue, Anywhere, New York 10004. John attempted to conceal the bracelets in a package that appeared to be a purchase from another store. The Store Manager noticed that the package did not have a "package pass" stapled to the outside and stopped John as he was about to leave the store. John confessed that he had taken the bracelets for his friends, but that he had never stolen anything from the store before. The police were called and Office H. R. Rodes, Badge #4214, Manhattan South Precinct, responded. A complaint was filed by the Store Manager and a report was written by the Officer (Complaint No. A440996). The case is awaiting a hearing.

The case should be reported as indicated in Exhibit 13–5.

Case B

At about 3:10 AM, April 12, 1977, four men were apprehended by Metro Police in the parking lot of Suit Company, Warehouse Number 40, located

INCIDENT NO

To: Director of Security (White, Canary)
    Division Copy (Pink)
    File Copy (Goldenrod)

| A | 0331 |
| 1 | 2 |

DIVISION NAME	ADDRESS		CITY	STATE & ZIP
Retail Retail	882 8th Avenue		Anywhere	N.Y. 10000

LOCATION CODE	DATE	TIME A-AM	LOSS AMOUNT	MEASURE:
	MO. DAY YR.	HR. MIN. P-PM		1—COST

R R 0 0 4   0 4 0 8 7 7   0 5 1 0 P   1 0 0   3

8   13   19   23   24   60

1—COST
2—WHOLESALE
3—RETAIL
4—BOOK
5—REPLACEMENT

FOR SECURITY DEPARTMENT USE ONLY

INCIDENT TYPE	FACILITY CODE	ASSET CODE	EMPL TYPE	RECOVERY AMOUNT	DISPOSITION	DIVISION DEPARTMENT CODE
7 1	3 0	4 1	D	1 0 0	0 2	3 0 1
61	63	65	67	33	68	70

M.O. CODE   M.O. DESCRIPTION

B A D
73

NARRATIVE: (Detail in concise terms what occurred; when, where, how, by whom and why. Identify names and addresses of witnesses. Fully describe property taken by quantity, serial numbers, shape, size, color, model number, etc. Identify who was responsible for the asset, what security was in effect at time of theft? Modus Operandi — what means were used to accomplish the incident?)

John J. John, sales clerk was caught taking five gold bracelet out of the

store. The bracelets were concealed in a package which looked like a

purchase from another store. He was caught by the store manager because the

package did not have a "package pass" approved by the manager. The incident

occurred at 5:10 p.m. on April 8, 1977.

ACTION: (Taken or Recommended   Police Advised (X Yes ( ) No   If yes, Officer's Name, Badge Number, Precinct, Complaint Number and Disposition of any Evidence)

Patrolman H. R. Rodes, Badge 4214, Manhattan South Precinct responded and
complaint A440996 was issued.

SUBMITTED BY: R. B. Costello   TITLE: Security   SIGNATURE: _____
                                         Manager

Exhibit 13–5. Loss, Offense, and Incident Report.

at 333 Seventh Avenue North, Anywhere, Tennessee 37202, with 100 men's
3-piece suits, total wholesale value of about $10,000. The police had re-
sponded to a burglar alarm and upon arriving at the store they spotted the
men loading the suits into a white panel truck. An investigation by the police
and the Store Manager, B. B. Burney, who was also called by the alarm
company, revealed that the offenders had broken the glass out of a window

on the rear (northeast) corner of the building and unlatched the window lock. The windows on the rear of the store are not protected and exterior lighting has not been installed. A report was written by the police officers at the scene and is on file at police headquarters. (File #MPD 44663-77). The case is awaiting prosecution.

The case should be reported as shown in Exhibit 13–6.

INITIATING THE SYSTEM

The Division Security Director is responsible for assuring compliance with the reporting requirements of the Corporate Policy and for the coding in the section labeled "For Security Department Use Only." Therefore, a series of Corporate and Division level orientation meetings were held to define reportable losses, to familiarize people with the forms and to explain the system.

All reports are reviewed by Corporate Security prior to submission to Central Input Preparation. Central Input receives only the top portion of the form. The narrative and action portions are removed by the security department in order to maintain system confidentiality. Subject names and narrative details are not included as part of the data file.

DATA RETRIEVAL

The System has been designed to provide analysis and reporting on both a standard report schedule and upon special request. Such reports include the following.

1. By Incident Type/MO Code
2. By Incident Type/Day/Hour
3. By Division/Location/Department/Incident Type/Day/Hour
4. By Geographical Area/Location/Incident Type, Frequency, Value
5. By Employee Type/Incident Type, Frequency, Value
6. By Asset—Ranked by Loss Frequency (High Frequency Report)
7. By Asset—Ranked by Loss Amount (To show distribution of assets value)
8. By Facility Type/Incident
9. By Incident/Value (To provide a Value/Frequency ratio—which losses represent the highest costs.)
10. By whether or not the asset was recovered, if prosecution or legal action was instituted or if administrative action was taken.

INCIDENT NO

To: Director of Security (White, Canary)
    Division Copy (Pink)
    File Copy (Goldenrod)

| A | 0332 |
| 1 | 2 |

DIVISION NAME	ADDRESS	CITY	STATE & ZIP
Retail Retail	882 8th Avenue	Anywhere	N.Y. 10000

LOCATION CODE | DATE | TIME | LOSS AMOUNT | MEASURE: 1=COST

| R R 0 0 4 | 0 4 0 8 7 7 | 0 5 1 0 P | 1 0 0 | 3 |
| 8 | 13 | MO. DAY YR. 19 HR. MIN. 23 P.M. 24 | 80 |

MEASURE: 1=COST 2=WHOLESALE 3=RETAIL 4=BOOK 5=REPLACEMENT

FOR SECURITY DEPARTMENT USE ONLY

INCIDENT TYPE	FACILITY CODE	ASSET CODE	EMPL TYPE	RECOVERY AMOUNT	DISPOSITION	DIVISION DEPARTMENT CODE
7 1	3 0	4 1	D	1 0 0	0 2	3 0 1
61	63	65	67	33	68	70

M.O. CODE   M.O. DESCRIPTION

| B A D | |
| 73 | |

NARRATIVE: (Detail in concise terms what occurred; when, where, how, by whom and why. Identify names and addresses of witnesses. Fully describe property taken by quantity, serial numbers, shape, size, color, model number, etc. Identify who was responsible for the asset, what security was in effect at time of theft? Modus Operandi — what means were used to accomplish the incident?)

John J. John, sales clerk was caught taking five gold bracelet out of the store. The bracelets were concealed in a package which looked like a purchase from another store. He was caught by the store manager because the package did not have a "package pass" approved by the manager. The incident occurred at 5:10 p.m. on April 8, 1977.

ACTION: (Taken or Recommended   Police Advised (X Yes ( ) No   If yes, Officer's Name, Badge Number, Precinct, Complaint Number and Disposition of any Evidence)

A complete police report is on file - Metro PD Number MPD44663-77

SUBMITTED BY: B. B. Burney   TITLE: **Manager**   SIGNATURE:

Exhibit 13–6.   Loss, offense, and incident report.

An example of one of the reports is shown as Exhibit 13–7 and displays the information from the proceeding hypothetical cases A and B.

DEVELOPING THE SYSTEM

The first phase of the system, which took six months to develop, has been in effect in some divisions for approximately eight months and throughout

INCD. NO.	LOC. CODE	INCIDENT DATE	TIME A P	LOSS AMOUNT	M S	INCD. CODE	FAC. CODE	ASET CODE	EMPL CODE	RECOVERY AMOUNT	DISP	DIV. DEPT.	M O CODE	M.O. DESCRIPTION
330	RR004	04/07/77	03:00 A	300	2	25	30	41		0	01		AAA	Cut Bolt on front door
331	RR005	04/08/77	05:10 P	100	3	71	30	41	D	100	02		BAB	Pilfer by conceal in packg.
332	SC040	04/12/77	03:10 A	10000	2	25	40	23		10000	02		BBC	Smash glass rear window
333	SC040	04/12/77	05:10 P	755	3	71	40	41	I	755	02		HAH	Dock theft concealed scrap
334	SC040	04/14/77	03:30 P	350	3	94	40	41		350	22		AAA	Conceal under clothing
335	SC040	04/14/77	03:55 P	800	3	94	40	41		800	22		AFA	Conceal on person

Exhibit 13–7. Security system edit update report.

the entire corporation for four months. Although it is too early to properly evaluate the results, some preliminary information has provided the basis for further study. For example:

a. Some locations and departments have been identified as having higher losses than suspected.
b. Most incidents occur on Wednesday afternoons, followed by Thursdays and Tuesdays.
c. The highest average loss is on Wednesday, followed by Tuesdays and Thursdays.
d. Some prevention and detection efforts have not been as effective as they were previously thought to be.

A SECURITY MANAGEMENT SYSTEM

As outlined above, the Location Master File contains all information pertinent to each location and a list of security features available at that facility. The information includes the location code, name of the location, address, facility type, location size, number of employees, types of security at the location, annual cost of the types of protection, relative security risk of the area, relative security risk of the facility, date of last survey, date of next scheduled survey and control information.

The control information, by location, is made up of a total of losses, total recoveries, number of incidents (by classification), number of incidents pending (by classification), date the location was added to the file and the date of the last incident.

The Location Master File was designed for future expansion and will provide a wide variety of analytical reports as part of the security management information system. For example, by using a table of codes of the types of security at a location matched with reported incidents, analysis may be undertaken regarding incidents by security countermeasures. Likewise, cost-effective analysis may be prepared by comparing types of security, security costs, losses and recoveries. This reporting is most effective when it indicates the specific security resource that was responsible for the cost avoidance or asset recovery.

SUMMARY

Being able to predict or forecast future occurrences is a key element to the success of any "loss prevention"-oriented security program. If we depend on reaction to problems, we are too late.

A loss reporting system is, therefore, an essential element in defining the problem, adequately managing a security program and forecasting loss probability. An automated system, such as that described in this article, should be a fundamental part of the security program for any major department store, chain of small retail stores, major hospital, college, major industrial complex or other multi-location organization. The reporting system, whether manual or automated, must be designed to be flexible for expansion and modification as indicated by experience. The premise is consistent with the Security Planning Cycle (Exhibit 13–1) and is necessary in a dynamic organization.

PART III

The People Resources
of Security

Four categories of people can be security resources: the direct employees of the security operation such as guards and investigators, nonsecurity employees of the organization, outside contractors such as security consultants and contract guard services, and the general public, including the organization's clients. The primary resource, which occupies much of most security managers' time, is the first group.

While few managers of any sort have the staffing level they would like, security usually takes a back seat to so-called productive staff when personnel are added. Consequently, the resource of direct security employees is often limited. It is also a group commonly prone to high turnover and subject to the problems of low morale. Good management of security employees can do much to alleviate both weaknesses.

Since money is, like personnel, a limited resource, other motivators must be combined to boost morale and reduce turnover. Just as information is gathered in the security program for assessment of vulnerabilities, so should information about the state of security employees' morale be accumulated and analyzed by the security executive.

On the basis of this information and an evaluation of organizational needs, the security manager can determine development needs of security personnel. Sometimes, the structure of the security organization can be used to make employees feel involved. Other times, the security manager must counsel individual employees to aid them with their job performance. The security manager often must devise training programs to strengthen employee skills.

Leadership through the application of well-developed human relations skills is particularly necessary for the security executive who wishes to make the best use of the limited people resources of the security program.

CHAPTER 14

Give Your People the Opportunity to Fail

Charles A. Sennewald, CPP*
Director of Security
The Broadway Department Stores

Most enlightened managers today knowingly, or otherwise, subscribe to Dr. Frederick Herzberg's work motivation theory. This theory contends that employees, generally speaking, are not motivated by improved working conditions, improved supervision, social relationships, benefits or even money. The absence of these so-called "hygiene" factors can be de-motivating, but the presence, improvement or increase of the factors does not lead to sustained higher work performance. Interestingly enough, the "shot in the arm" effect on productivity created by a salary increase is short lived, and the varying income levels of people doing the same kind of work but compensated on a commission basis shows that the dollar is not the sole influence on productivity.

Behavioral scientists, such as Dr. Herzberg, and working managers alike can point to the positive performance results achieved by employees who find their work rewarding. What makes work rewarding? Responsibility, achievement, recognition, challenge and growth are rewarding and genuine motivators. A close look, therefore, at responsibility and at achievement in terms of what goes into or is necessary for both is of some interest.

In my opinion, giving an employee the opportunity to succeed is not so important as is providing him or her with a climate in which they have the opportunity to fail! Theoretically, we all have the opportunity to succeed: every school child is told that; parents point to the highest political offices as opportunities for achievement and success; new employees are told they have unlimited opportunities for success within the organization and recite glowing examples of same. Everyone knows what opportunities for success they have . . . but do they? A great number of employees also know that, more often than not, in real life . . . in the work environment, IT'S NOT

*Charles A Sennewald is presently President of Charles A. Sennewald & Associates.
Reprinted with permission of the American Society for Industrial Security, from *Security Management*, May 1979, pp. 20.

OK to make mistakes. . . . IT'S NOT OK TO FAIL AN ASSIGNMENT OR TASK. They know if they do err or fail, they'll get "chewed out" or psychologically battered. That being the case, and it is, how many employees are quietly de-motivated, marginally performing and unwilling to poke their heads up too high from the trenches?

A closer look at this "opportunity to fail" concept reveals that the decision-making process underpins genuine motivation. The employee should be the one who decides how, what, where, who or when in connection with an assigned task or area of specific responsibility—not the manager. Looking even closer yet we find that the decision-making process is the result and reflection of one's judgement and/or creativity. Management either respects and values the judgement and/or creativity of each employee, or they don't. How can an employee's true capabilities be known if the individual is over-supervised, over-ruled, unduly limited, reversed and corrected. Too many employees are valued and respected for reasons other than their judgement or creativity. Too many employees' judgemental depth and breadth have never been explored, tested, tapped or measured, because supervisors and managers won't allow it or have inhibited employees from exercising judgement.

The employee's performance evaluation should reflect the judgement and creativity which dictates the quality of that individual's decisions. Yet everyone knows the "boss" (anywhere in the management hierarchy) has a proven track record of good decisions, likes to make decisions, especially "important" ones, and does so, eroding away real responsibility. Though done with good intentions because the employee's decision could lead to a failure, and the "boss" doesn't want failure in his organizational pyramid such tactics on the part of the "boss" erode the employee's sense of re-sponsibility. Therefore the employee clearly sees it is NOT OK to make an error, there is limited or no opportunity to fail. The point comes down to this: if responsibility and achievement are true work motivators, and I believe they are, then managers should encourage employee motivation by providing the *opportunity to fail*. That is done by managing *people* rather than their *tasks*. In other words, by exercising good judgement in terms of who is assigned what task and with what parameters and then stepping aside. Certainly the manager should continue to monitor from a distance and should be available as an advisor. The key is to give the employee room to breathe and *to make an error* (unless, of course, the error could have disastrous consequences).

The *good* manager creates the climate wherein employees profit from their failures and errors, because mistakes are a proven and powerful teacher, e.g. "I learned the hard way to avoid that." Instead of managing to avoid mistakes, the *good* supervisor manages the mistake after the fact—in a positive, helpful and instructive way. This approach earns respect for and loyalty to the supervisor and is a meaningful growth experience for the employee. If the employee does not profit from mistakes and continues to fail at the same task, you now know his or her limitation and can assign more limited tasks in the future.

This opportunity to fail climate encourages and permits the exciting rewards of responsibility, achievement, recognition, challenge and growth. The bottom line for everyone—achievement—contributes to the success of all: the employee, the manager and the organization. That is what I call real work motivation. What do *you* think??

CHAPTER 15

Give Your People the Opportunity to Fail: A Reply

David L. Steeno
Assistant Professor
Western Illinois University

An article by Charles Sennewald about providing employees the "opportunity to fail" concluded with a query as to what the reader thought.[1] The question was too much of a challenge to simply pass over. It appeared to be an attempt to stir discussion of work motivation theory, organizational climate and leadership style. Fearing that others might not have the time to pick up the gauntlet thrown by Mr. Sennewald, the following observations are offered.

Anyone who has dealt with people in any type of organizational setting has probably noticed the variations in performance levels. Some people generate their own energy, performing at a high peak and requiring minimum direction, while others operate at marginal levels and require close supervision. Why? What accounts for the difference? Although managers seek the answers to these questions, few have the time or perhaps the inclination and resources to scientifically explain the variation in employee performance levels. The task of explaining differences in motivation has therefore most frequently fallen to the behavioral psychologist.

The reasons for differences in motivation among workers are varied and complex. Differences in individual characteristics, such as intelligence, ability and personality, plus organizational influences, such as the supervisory style, the reward-punishment system and the job itself, all contribute to an individual's motivation level.

Mr. Sennewald believes the key to employee motivation is to give the employee room to breathe and make an error. I disagree. The key to employee motivation is the recognition that there is no all-encompassing model of motivation, that various approaches to motivation exist, and that the

Reprinted with permission of the American Society for Industrial Security, from *Security Management*, September 1979, pp. 114.
[1]Charles A. Sennewald, "Give Your People the Opportunity to Fail," *Security Management*, Volume 23 Number 5 (May, 1979), pp. 20–21.

ability to diagnose motivational problems and adapt an approach to deal with the problem is one of the most important elements of the security manager's job.

Models of motivational behavior generally begin with a discussion of needs (physiological and psychological), which develop drives toward goals or incentives which are perceived as capable of satisfying a person's needs. Early motivation theories are sometimes called "prescriptive" models since they purport to tell a manager how to motivate. One such approach was F. W. Taylor's "scientific management," which concentrated on the study and design of work to maximize worker efficiency.[2] Taylor believed that efficiency could be increased by designing a system which used the single best method available. Industrial engineering is a development of Taylor's work. Taylor placed an undue emphasis on money as a motivator and neglected the human side of management.

Around 1940 management began to realize that it was wrong to view all workers as lazy individuals requiring constant supervision, motivated solely by money. Managers recognized certain "self-starters" who did not require much direction. The belief that worker motivation is influenced by the individual, the group and the job situation developed into a movement termed the human relations movement or more recently the "humanization of work."[3]

The genesis of the human relations movement is usually considered to be the study by Mayo, Roethlisberger and Dickson at the Western Electric Company's Hawthorne plant near Chicago.[4] The Hawthorne studies demonstrated that worker productivity is influenced by social relationships.

A major contributor to the human relations movement was Douglas McGregor who advanced two beliefs about human behavior that could be held by managers: Theory X and Theory Y.[5]

Theory X represented the traditional theory that the average person dislikes work, will avoid it if possible and must be coerced to work towards attaining the organization's objectives. According to Theory X, the average human prefers to be directed, wants no responsibility, has little ambition and, above everything else, seeks security.

Theory Y is based on a different set of assumptions. Theory Y assumes that employees do not inherently dislike work but will exercise self-direction and self-control in seeking to obtain goals. The theory suggests that the average individual seeks improved performance and increased responsibility under appropriate conditions.

---

[2]Frederick W. Taylor, *Scientific Management* (New York: Harper and Row, 1911).

[3]Robert L. Kahn, "The Work Module: A Proposal for Humanization of Work," *Work and the Quality of Life,* ed. James O'Toole (Cambridge, MA: The MIT Press, 1974), p. 200.

[4]Elton Mayo, *The Human Problems of an Industrial Civilization* (Cambridge, MA: Harvard University Press, 1933).

[5]Douglas McGregor, *The Human Side of Enterprise* (New York: McGraw-Hill Book Company, Inc., 1960).

The human relations approach has limitations too. The movement provides little information on the elements of human motivation and does not take into account that different individuals are motivated by different factors. Additionally, Theory X and Theory Y dealt with the "average" individual. As a practical matter, some individuals fit the Theory X model and the security manager who attempts to lead such people with Theory Y assumptions may fail in the attempt.

At least three major categories of contemporary motivation theory can be identified: 1) content; 2) process; and 3) reinforcement.[6]

The content theories focus on those factors which energize, arouse or start behavior. The content theories include Maslow's need hierarchy (primary needs satisfied before secondary needs—the highest being self-actualization), and Herzberg's work motivation or two-factor theory which is discussed later in this article.

The process theories are concerned not only with the factors that arouse behavior, but also with the process, direction or choice of behavioral patterns. The process theory includes Victor H. Vroom's expectancy theory which was discussed in the May 1979 issue of SECURITY MANAGEMENT.[7] Expectancy theory is also called cognitive expectancy theory, instrumentality theory and valence-instrumentality theory (VIE). The expectancy theorists maintain that the strength of a tendency to act in a particular manner is dependent on the strength of an expectancy that the act will be followed by a given outcome, and on the attractiveness of the outcome to the actor.

The third major category of contemporary motivation theory is the reinforcement concept based on learning theory and the work of B. F. Skinner. Reinforcement theory is also called "contingency" theory and, in its most elementary form, refers to the positive or negative consequences flowing from a particular behavior. It has some aspects of expectancy theory but attempts to avoid reference to internal psychological processes concentrating instead on changing behavior through a system of reward or punishment. Reinforcement theory involves operant conditioning and behavior modification concepts.

Managers use aspects of some or all of the contemporary motivation theories. No evidence can support the statement that "most enlightened managers today . . . subscribe to Dr. Frederick Herzberg's work motivation theory."[8] (The statement could be true, of course, if Mr. Sennewald defines an "enlightened" manager as one who subscribes to Herzberg's theory.)

The Herzberg work motivation theory has been criticized on the bases of the storytelling critical-incident method used, the procedural deficiencies

---

[6]John M. Ivancevich, Andrew D. Szilagyi, Jr., and Marc J. Wallace, Jr., *Organizational Behavior and Performance* (Santa Monica, CA: Goodyear Publishing Co., Inc., 1977), p. 103.
[7]John C. Cholewa, III, "Motivating the Other 99%," *Security Management,* Volume 23 Number 5 (May, 1979), p. 52.
[8]Sennewald, *op. cit.,* p. 20.

in the research, and the inconsistencies with previous empirical research concerning satisfaction and motivation. No correlation was demonstrated between job satisfaction and increased performance.[9]

Herzberg's original study was based on a review of published literature on job attitudes and a survey of 203 accountants and engineers in the Pittsburgh area who were initially asked to recall a time when they felt exceptionally good about their jobs. In a second interview these same subjects were asked to describe incidents where they felt negative about their jobs. Employees tended to describe different conditions as leading to their good and bad feelings. Herzberg concluded that many of the factors which managers thought contributed to motivation, such as pay and the nature of supervision, actually did not motivate.

The most controversial aspect of Herzberg's theory was, and still is, the idea that job satisfaction and dissatisfaction are not on the same continuum but are two distinct variables. In other words, while the presence of job content factors is satisfying and motivational, the absence of such factors does not result in dissatisfaction. And whereas the presence of job context factors is not motivational, their absence causes dissatisfaction. The opposite of job satisfaction is not job dissatisfaction, but no job satisfaction. The opposite of job dissatisfaction is not job satisfaction, but no job dissatisfaction. Job content factors (motivators intrinsic to the job) are achievement, recognition for achievement, advancement, responsibility, the work itself and growth. Job context factors (dissatisfiers or hygiene factors extrinsic to the job) are policy and administration, salary, supervision, relationship with supervisors, work conditions, relationship with peers, personal life, relationship with subordinates, status and job security.[10]

From Herzberg's sometimes confusing terminology it appears that pay, for example, is not a motivator. Such a conclusion flatly contradicts studies which have indicated that pay does motivate certain workers.[11] Advancement is a motivator. Yet advancement may be desired because of the resultant increase in pay and status (which Herzberg calls nonmotivators). The concepts become fuzzy and the distinctions become difficult to draw.

The value of Herzberg's theory is its recognition of the importance of job content factors.[12] One critic labels the theory an oversimplification.[13]

---

[9]Robert J. House and Lawrence A. Wigdor, "Herzberg's Dual-Factor Theory of Job Satisfaction and Motivation: A Review of the Evidence and A Criticism," in *Motivation and Work Behavior* by Richard M. Steers and Lyman W. Porter (New York: McGraw-Hill Book Company, Inc., 1975), pp. 104–114.

[10]Frederick Herzberg, "One More Time; How Do You Motivate Employees?," *Harvard Business Review*, (January-February, 1968), pp. 53–62.

[11]Edward E. Lawler, III, *Pay and Organizational Effectiveness: A Psychological View* (New York: McGraw-Hill Book Company, Inc., 1970).

[12]J. Clifton Williams, *Human Behavior in Organizations* (Cincinnati, OH: South-Western Publishing Co., 1978), p. 107.

[13]John P. Campbell et al., *Managerial Behavior, Performance, and Effectiveness* (New York: McGraw-Hill Book Company, Inc., 1970), p. 381.

Perhaps the difficulty with managers and behavioral psychologists trying to find *the* answer to motivation is similar to the problem faced by criminal justice administrators and criminologists in trying to find *the* answer to crime. In the end, managers may need to choose between trying to find a universal theory which can solve all problems, or a situational approch based upon the selection of a theory which seems to be the most relevant to the problem.

Why even discuss work motivation theories? Aren't some people just "natural" leaders? Isn't good management just "common sense"? In response to the latter, and with apologies to Benjamin Franklin, there is nothing as uncommon as common sense. As for the natural leader, he or she has most likely developed a sensitivity to the needs of others based upon experience.

Most of us, to a lesser or greater extent, operate on intuition or a "feeling" that a particular course of action will motivate an individual. If this "feeling" can be developed into an objective, conceptual framework it may further sharpen and refine the intuitive process and increase the security manager's effectiveness. Theorists such as Herzberg attempt to provide a conceptual model. Practitioners such as Chuck Sennewald use the model to assist them in the development of management programs to increase the productivity and professionalism of their security departments.

The thrust of Mr. Sennewald's article seemed to be that managers who provide a supportive climate with a non-directive, "stand aside" approach to leadership are going to obtain the highest production from their subordinates. Such an assertion does not necessarily follow from the Herzberg theory. For one who professes belief in Herzberg's theory of motivation, Mr. Sennewald spends an inordinate amount of space in his article discussing climate and leadership style—factors which Herzberg considers hygiene factors, not motivators.

Part of the difficulty I had with the discussion of Herzberg's theory and the "climate to fail" concept was the use of the term responsibility. Mr. Sennewald views responsibility as having the authority necessary to make the decisions required to complete the assigned task. Such a view of responsibility is more restrictive than Herzberg's use of the term. Herzberg considers responsibility to be an expansion of tasks—a job content, job enrichment idea. Giving an employee the authority and climate to make decisions is one way of enriching the job, but it is not the only way. Increased decision-making authority is not synonymous with increased responsibility.

If one accepts the proposition that responsibility and achievement do motivate, what then is the supervisor's role in motivating people? Does the supervisor strive to create a climate in which the employee can fail, as Mr. Sennewald suggests, or does the supervisor create a climate in which the employee can succeed? Is it merely a matter of semantics?

The work climate is important. Workers may have all the motivation in the world to perform, but if the supervisor is unable or unwilling to give them tasks to perform, they are stifled. Studies suggest that the most important influence on the climate of an organization is the manager's leadership style.[14]

Is it OK to fail? The answer depends on the context in which the question is asked. It is not OK to fail from the standpoint of conservation of human resources. "Failures" are not promoted. "Failures" do not contribute to productivity. "Failures" do not win promotions for their superiority or improve the department's reputation for efficiency. It is true that the bosses do not want failure in the organizational pyramid. Why should they? If achievement is the motivator, the boss wants the subordinate to succeed—to achieve, not fail. Failing is not going to motivate the employee to attempt more challenging tasks in the future. Would Vince Lombardi have striven to create a climate in which the Green Bay Packers felt comfortable losing?

When Mr. Sennewald asks if it is OK to fail, he is really asking, "When an employee does not achieve the results expected or desired, how should the supervisor react?" Will the experience be used as a learning device or will the supervisor "point the finger" at the employee and refuse to assign tasks to the person in the future under any circumstances? Does it make a difference what the supervisor does? If Herzberg is correct, will it matter if the employee gets "chewed out" or psychologically battered as long as the supervisor continues to present the employee with opportunities for achievement, responsibility, recognition, challenge and growth? After all, organizational climate is a job context factor. Mr. Sennewald aligns himself with the behavioral scientists and their focus on group sentiments, attitudes of individual employees and the organization's social and psychological climate. According to Herzberg, the work motivation theory is more properly aligned with the industrial engineer's emphasis on the content of the job.[15]

Keeping in mind that Herzberg's theory is *task* oriented and not *people* oriented, consider the following statements. A manager should "encourage employee motivation by providing the *opportunity to fail.* That is done by managing *people* rather than their *tasks.* In other words, by exercising good judgement in terms of who is assigned what task and with what parameters and then steppng aside."[16]

How far aside does the superior step? Completely? It would seem so as "Management either respects and values the judgement and/or creativity of each employee or they don't."[17] But a caveat: ". . . unless of course, the error could have disastrous [sic] consequences."[18]

So, we now know that we should give the employee room to breathe, but not too much room because disaster could result. Do we give some

---

[14]George H. Litwin and Robert A. Stringer, *Motivation and Organizational Climate* (Boston, MA: Division of Research, Graduate School of Business Administration, Harvard University, 1968).
[15]Herzberg, *op. cit.,* p. 58.
[16]Sennewald, *op. cit.,* p. 21.
[17]*Ibid.,* p. 20.
[18]*Ibid.,* p. 21.

employees more room than others? Who decides if an error could be disastrous? How is it decided? Is Mr. Sennewald *really* advising the "good" manager to manage the mistake after the fact rather than attempt to avoid mistakes? Is he saying, "Allow mistakes to occur because it is a wonderful learning experience for the subordinate"? Do we just keep making the same mistake over and over again or is there some value in a supervisor having experience so that he or she can pass the experience on to others? Is the supervisor's job to supervise (e.g., direct the activities of others toward the completion of a task), or is it to allow mistakes to be made so that employees will feel comfortable in taking risks in the future? Is Sennewald suggesting that a supervisor should not be arbitrary and capricious, making all the important decisions because he or she refuses to delegate real authority? If that is what he means, he never said it. He did tell us not to over-supervise (it must be OK to supervise—just do not supervise overly) and not to unduly limit, reverse and correct (it is OK to limit, reverse and correct—just do not do it unduly).

Suppose the employee does not profit from mistakes and continues to fail at the same task? Do we conclude that we "now know his or her limitation and can assign more limited tasks in the future?"[19] Do we even want to retain an employee who has such limited ability? How do we know that the "failure" was due to the employee? Perhas the employee was given too much room to breathe, became anxiety stricken, and suffers from hyperpnea. Maybe the employee would operate best under close supervision, with more structure and a clearer focus on the task. How do we know that a formal training program will not improve the employee's performance?

Maybe the employee was unsuccessful because of performance obstacles such as lack of time, conflicting demands on time, inadequate work facilities, restrictive policies, lack of authority, insufficient information about other activities that affect the job, or lack of cooperation from co-workers. Merely because one accepts the Herzberg idea that responsibility is a motivator, it does not follow that a manager must use only one leadership style which gives an employee room to breathe and make errors. The job of a supervisor is to guide, control and direct the behavior of others. Let us not abdicate our duty because we believe responsibility means allowing the employee to decide the who, what, where and when of an assigned task. The good supervisor exercises sufficient control to guide the employee to success.

Not every employee wants room to breathe. Some of us need more structure than others. Give the employee the climate he or she needs to succeed. Use those techniques of leadership which will best assist the employee in the attainment of the desired objective. Certainly one should not "psychologically batter" anyone, but there is nothing inherently wrong with "chewing out" an individual who has failed an assignment. Under the appropriate circumstances a "chewing out" can be very effective. The super-

---

[19]*Ibid.*

visor must keep in mind, however, that he or she must explore the reasons for the failure and continue to provide the opportunities to satisfy the worker's needs in the future.

An ability to understand why people behave as they do as well as an ability to motivate them to behave in a specific manner are two interrelated qualities important to the security manager. Managers do not need to understand the technical distinctions in motivation theory in order to make use of the research done in this field. Some knowledge of motivational theory is helpful for drawing generalizations and applying them to unique situations.

Where does all this leave the supervisor who is trying to motivate his or her subordinates to more positive work performance? It leaves the supervisor with the challenge to recognize that people have different needs, perceptions and abilities. The supervisor must consider the various theories of work motivation and leadership styles and select those approaches and techniques which are most appropriate to the particular work situation.

CHAPTER 16

Improving Job Satisfaction for Guard Personnel

Roger C. Clark
District Manager, Nuclear Security
Burns International Security Services, Inc.

High turnover among security personnel is one of the many problems facing the security manager today. Turnover can be expected in guard positions where pay is at the minimum wage or only slightly above, benefits are minimal or non-existent, training is generally on-the-job, and guards see little chance for promotion. In these cases, the job of a security guard appears to be, and frequently is, boring.

It is hardly surprising that turnover rates in situations combining all of these factors can be very high. But why does turnover continue to be high in security positions where the pay is good in comparison to other industries, where benefits are good and getting better, and where guard training is extensive?

In searching for an answer, I interviewed a large number of guard personnel from both proprietary and contract forces. Two attempts to elicit information through questionnaires proved unsatisfactory. A very low return on the first questionnaire seemed to indicate the guards did not wish to be bothered with answering the questions. Many of the guards who did return the questionnaires indicated their answers were less than candid (even though a cover letter stated the information was confidential and for research purposes only). In some cases, the questionnaires were distributed by supervisory personnel who told the guard to fill them out and even suggested answers to certain questions.

Finally, I decided to replace the questionnaires with face-to-face interviews. While these interviews restricted the number of guards who could participate, they provided a more in-depth discussion of the problems facing guards in their work.

Ninety-three individuals at eight locations participated in the interviews.

Reprinted with permission of the American Society for Industrial Security, from *Security Management,* May 1982, pp. 55.

Of that number, forty-one were proprietary guards and fifty-two were employed by contract agencies. Only four of those questioned were in supervisory positions, although the length of service varied from three months to nearly ten years. The interviews averaged ten minutes per individual. Little statistical significance was noted in the conclusions based on age, years of service, type of security function, racial or ethnic origin, education, or sex of the participants.

The answers revealed several inherent problems with the job of a security guard that contribute to job dissatisfaction and ultimately to high turnover. The problems cited most frequently during the interviews were (in order of reference):

1.   Inadequate pay and benefits.
2.   Boredom on the job.
3.   A feeling that other employees regarded guards as inferior.
4.   No room for personal growth.
5.   Fear of making mistakes that would lead to discharge, damage to property, and lawsuits directed against the guards and their employers.
6.   Personal problems, mainly drinking and family disputes over duty hours and compensation.
7.   Inadequate or poor supervision.

A security manager can address these problems and thereby increase job satisfaction and reduce turnover. The following suggestions for improving job satisfaction in each of the categories identified by the guards are offered as springboards to the development of programs tailored to individual needs.

INADEQUATE PAY AND BENEFITS

Inadequate pay and benefits for entry level guards generally exist throughout the security industry. In a competitive atmosphere where contracts for general guard services are awarded all too frequently on the basis of low dollar quotes, guard pay will remain low.

To enable guards to achieve better salaries and benefits, companies using contract security services must be willing to pay a few dollars more per hour for a professional security service. Security managers can ask contract agencies for a breakdown of how per-hour income is spent.

Contract security companies, on the other hand, must be willing to invest a large percent of their income for guard salaries and benefits—and most reputable companies do. Many of the contract guards who participated in the interviews believed that everything the company took in over and above their salaries was profit. Taking time to show how a guard-hour dollar is spent could help make guards more aware of what their employer is doing for them.

Security managers should also make financial counseling available to guards through the human resources department of the organization and through pamphlets and letters included periodically in pay envelopes. Lacking any training or experience with budgets or financial planning, many of the guards interviewed were deeply in debt. Only one out of the ninety-three had any regular savings program.

BOREDOM ON THE JOB

The second most frequent source of job dissatisfaction the guards named was boredom, caused primarily by repetition of duties. Admittedly, finding a relief from boredom for the guard who sits at a reception desk or who routinely makes key rounds is not easy.

Still, many avenues are available to the security manager who wants to reduce employee boredom, such as rotating guard duty stations. Tests can be set up along a guard route, asking the guards to identify mock security breaches or paraphernalia. Care must be taken to make these training materials readily identifiable so the guard does not discover an explosive device, for instance, and treat it as a test item and not a real threat. The location of the items should also be reasonable and not impossible to find.

When the guard identifies the problem or locates the material, he or she should be instructed to bring it back to the guard station. A point or bonus system can be incorporated into this training, so the guards are rewarded for good observation.

A supervisor who occasionally accompanies the guard on rounds can ask pertinent questions about the duty post. This technique shows that management is concerned about the guard's duties and considers the guard the expert on that assignment.

Periodic letters or memos asking guards for suggestions about ways to improve security at their assignments also helps keep the guards aware of their duties. But using this approach requires the security manager to follow up on the comments. Reasonable suggestions should be acted upon as soon as possible, and implemented whenever feasible. The reasons unworkable suggestions must be rejected should be reviewed with the guard. In either case, a guard's suggestion should never simply be dismissed. It should be used as a training vehicle to channel the guard's approach to security problems into acceptable limitations.

GUARD STATUS

During the interviews every guard said he or she felt as though other persons look down on them and hold them in low regard, although this problem was less prevalent among proprietary guards than it was among contract guards.

Interestingly enough, however, all of the guards felt they had a good relationship with many of their co-workers, and that their relationships with people outside of work were not adversely affected by their security employment. In fact, they said, neighbors and friends sought them out to arbitrate disagreements and to offer advice on many subjects.

Since the interviews did not include people outside security, the question of whether others actually held the guards in low regard or whether this concern was simply a perception was not explored. Generally, though, people in low-paying positions are not granted much status by the public at large. But, from information developed during the interviews, the guards did not seem to hold themselves or other guards in high esteem, and they may have projected this feeling into the attitudes of others.

Disregarding low wages, guards most frequently felt they were not highly regarded for three reasons: their appearance; a lack of knowledge by others about their duties and responsibilities; and general contempt by management, evidenced by making exceptions to rules the guards are employed to enforce and frequently complaining that the guards have not exercised good judgment when the guards felt they had, considering the circumstances.

A security manager cannot do much to change the attitudes of a public that regards income as a major critieria for judging the value of an individual. But the manager can help guards gain greater self-esteem. A faded, ill-fitting, threadbare uniform neither inspires confidence in people who deal with a guard, nor aids in developing a sense of pride and purpose among the guards themselves. Every manager should see that all guards are well-dressed and that uniforms or other duty attire are in good condition and fitted properly. Supervisors should inspect uniformed personnel daily, checking for worn material and badly tailored clothing. Guards should be required to report for duty with clean, pressed uniforms and polished shoes. Grooming and personal hygiene should meet high standards. Guards who don't shape up should be discharged to maintain morale among those guards who care about themselves and their appearance.

At least once a year, and more frequently if possible, company employees should be instructed, through films or handouts, on the many functions guards perform and how the guard is an integral part of the overall company profit picture. The guard should be pictured as a source of help to the employee, not a punitive threat.

As in any management situation, the guard should never be disciplined or made to appear foolish in the presence of others. The manager should not make judgments about a guard's decisions until all the facts surrounding the incident have been investigated. When, given all the facts, a guard has exercised poor judgment, or when a guard's decision must be overruled, the reasons for this must be clearly explained to the individual. Use the situation to help guards grow, while emphasizing they will still be supported in the future.

NO ROOM FOR PERSONAL GROWTH

Eighty-five percent of the guards interviewed (over ninety-six percent of the contract guards) felt they were locked into their current positions with little or no chance for advancement.

Career development programs offering specialized training not only prepare guards for future promotions, but also add career interest and create a more valuable and flexible staff. Correspondence courses can be developed in-house or purchased from outside companies. Tuition assistance or reimbursement for attending job-related classes at local colleges and universities should be considered.

Initiating guard levels is another approach managers can use to assist personnel in career planning. Progression to higher steps should be awarded when the guard completes a set number of training hours and receives a good evaluation, or when other specific criteria, spelled out in advance, are met. Some visual representation of these various levels should be added to the guard's uniform, such as a color-coded band slipped over one epaulet.

All guards should be made aware when an individual achieves a level change, not only to enhance the status of the individual but also to recognize the accomplishment as a future goal for others. Someone from management, not just the guard's direct supervisor, should present the new grade level indicator. The presentation should be made at a shift change so the greatest number of guards can participate.

FEAR OF MAKING MISTAKES

The attitude, "If I do nothing then I can't do anything wrong," was expressed by several entry-level guards during the face-to-face interviews. The reason for this attitude quickly became apparent—lack of training. The guards were afraid to take any action because they had not received any training beyond a few minutes of on-the-job explanations by other guards who had, in most cases, been trained the same way.

Guard training before assignment to a new post is critical to job performance. Guards must not only know what they are supposed to do and how they should do it, but they should also know why a procedure must be done and the legal rights and restrictions associated with the assignment. Guards must know who to contact in unusual situations or emergencies, and they must be confident that the contact person will be able to supply the necessary answers.

· Every guard post should have written post orders, and every guard should have a manual that spells out company rules and regulations, grievance procedures, and limitations on guard conduct.

Simply supplying guards with minimal preassignment training, and assuming they will keep abreast of changes on their own, is not sufficient.

Conditions change, needs change, and legal decisions affecting security change. Training must be ongoing, enabling the guard to control and adapt to pertinent changes.

Guard personnel must also be constantly reminded that management is there to support the guards and protect their interests. Trained guards, comfortable in knowing they are supported by management, will have the self-confidence necessary to perform to a high standard.

PERSONAL PROBLEMS

Proper preemployment testing and evaluation procedures, along with adequate background checks, can help prevent persons who suffer from severe personal and/or family problems from being hired as security guards. But no amount of testing is foolproof, and some people with preexisting problems will get through the screening process.

In addition, the duties, hours, pay, and general conditions of most security assignments contribute to built-in job stress. Alcoholism, drug abuse, wife or child beating, divorce, and suicide are extreme responses to this stress. Continuing domestic arguments are common symptoms.

Security managers cannot afford to overlook the problems of job stress and its effect on a guard's life and job performance. Corporate human resources department managers who share a concern for the welfare and performance of employees should be consulted when addressing an employee's personal problems. Printed materials can be made available to guards explaining the professional counseling services available to them and their families through the company.

This attention to a guard's personal health underscores management's concern for each employee's well-being. Guard supervisors must be trained to recognize the signs of job stress and to discuss potential concerns with employees. The wrong approach can trigger additional problems or cause employees to withdraw, passing up the assistance they may need.

INADEQUATE OR POOR SUPERVISION

As a security manager, do you know the background, qualifications, and training of each supervisor at each guard site? Are your supervisors continually evaluated? Do you personally review daily reports on discipline and inspections? Do you conduct periodic meetings and specialized training sessions for supervisors?

Answering "no" to any of the preceding questions sets the stage for problems at the supervisory level. Every guard interviewed said problems with supervisors directly affect job satisfaction. Stories ranged from the totally incompetent superior to personality conflicts of consequence only to the guard. However, even these personality conflicts must be taken seriously by the security manager. The morale of the entire force can be affected if employees start choosing sides in the dispute.

Except for one supervisor who had received management training while a law enforcement officer, none of the supervisors at the eight locations involved in this study had received any formal training in supervision. Three of the four interviewed had been hired when a contract agency was recruiting for personnel to fill a new assignment.

A good guard is not necessarily a good supervisor. Lacking formal training in supervision, employees will adopt a supervisory style of their own that may be detrimental to their position of authority. They may hold themselves aloof from other guards, or burn up the telephone wires calling someone else about every little problem.

Ideally, guards who want to be promoted or who show supervisory potential should be required to obtain training in supervision before a promotion is offered. In most cases, however, prior training is not possible or practical, and this education must come after the promotion takes effect. To add to their capabilities, new supervisors can enroll in management classes at local colleges or universities. A small but good library of management books can be set up in the security office. The company's training department can review or recommend appropriate training films and tapes.

In addition, every person placed in a supervisory position should serve a probationary period, including at least three reviews, before the promotion is made permanent. If it becomes apparent that an individual is not going to make a good supervisor, he or she should be removed from consideration and transferred to some other site, if possible.

After completing the interviews with the various guards, I have concluded that the problem of guard turnover is major but not insurmountable. I recommend that other security managers conduct a survey of their own to determine the problems contributing to turnover at their facilities and to develop approrpiate solutions. The survey process may be time consuming, but I found the benefits well worth the effort.

CHAPTER 17

A "Team Concept" of Management
Ronald R. Minion, CPP
President
Base-Fort Patrol Ltd.

American and Canadian workers are not producing with the same degree of motivation as workers in many other countries. This statement is validated by our quarterly trading deficits. Canada, for example, may well enjoy a temporary trade surplus when the dollar is seriously devalued, but when all of the international service, supply and borrowing considerations are weighed, the annual national indebtedness is staggering. An unhealthy industrial community must accept its share of responsibility for these serious economic woes.

The first step in getting to the core of the problem is to measure the degree to which employees are motivated in the organization. There are two proven methods that can be employed to help managers acquire the necesssry information.

- Interviews: Persons in the organization who are capable of gaining the confidence of the employees must carefully obtain information that will provide management with a clear picture of the state of industrial relations in the organization.
- Questionnaires: Employees are given a questionnaire and asked to provide frank and candid comments about their workplace and the people in it. They must be made to understand that no form of reprisal will follow if derogatory comments are made concerning management.

The services of a management consultant could be used to deal with the problem. However, managers will profit by undertaking the exercise without outside assistance. By getting involved in the initial investigation, analysing the problems, and developing workable solutions, managers have

Reprinted with permission of the American Society for Industrial Security, from *Security Management*, September 1979, pp. 96.

a much better insight into what is really going on in the organization. Then too, managers will be more involved in policing the new policies to ensure that they meet with ultimate success.

It has been said that security guards are the least motivated individuals of any industrial group. They are most certainly poorly paid, poorly supervised and poorly trained, yet are expected to perform an important function in society. The manner in which a security guard agency is structured makes it very difficult to identify effective individuals, as they are usually working in branch offices or remote locations. When they are effective, they prevent crime, fires and accidents, but positive achievement is not always evident.

The management of Base-Fort Patrol Ltd., a security guard company headquartered in Alberta, Canada, decided to attempt to improve morale, motivate employees and alter the faltering rapport between management and guards. The first step in the project was to send a questionnaire to all employees in approximately eighteen branches throughout the company. The company was broken into two main regions: North Regional Headquarters (located in Edmonton), and South Regional Headquarters (located at Calgary).

The company had been in business for approximately thirteen years, and had grown from a single employee (the president-owner) to over seven hundred employees. As the organization grew, so did the accompanying management problems. The most serious problem was employee morale which, at the time of the questionnaire, was at an all-time low. This fact was substantiated by a 400% rate of attrition and general employee discontent.

The questionnaire was designed to provide accurate information regarding employee morale. Each of the seven hundred employees completed the questionnaire. Many of them signed their names but a majority preferred to remain anonymous. Points covered in the questionnaire included:

- Employee attitudes towards management.
- Comments concerning security supervisors.
- General comments concerning shift work, wearing uniforms, short hair cuts, training, supervision and working on holidays.
- Identifying conditions leading to a high rate of staff turnover.
- Positive and negative comments concerning the job.
- General comments.

The response clearly confirmed employee alienation towards the existing style of management. A total of one hundred thirty-five interesting and valid points were extracted from the completed questionnaires. Of this total, only five were of a complimentary nature, while the remainder were complaints or general ill feelings about the organization. A few of the most prominent concerns follow (taken verbatim from the replies received on the questionnaire):

- There is little "esprit de corps" in the organization.

- Supervisors don't encourage employees by praising them.
- There should be better character checks made before they hire some of these "turkeys".
- Members should have more responsibility, and supervisors less authority.
- There should be more physical training and fewer fat guards.
- The company should treat everyone equal and they don't.
- At meetings, supervisors keep reminding us how dispensable we are.
- The one-way direction of information in this company has developed a "master-slave" atmosphere.
- Supervisors should request rather than order.
- Inspections are like this, Hi! How's it going—good night!
- There is a lack of consistent methods of discipline.
- Employees always get the "run around" from head office and supervisors.
- There is never any thanks for the job you do.
- The company is too military.
- Patrolmen and women don't have any say in what's happening.
- There are many promises by executives that are not fulfilled.
- I thought you were supposed to get promoted after one year . . . what happened to me?
- Promotions always seem to go to favorites.
- Good work should deserve some form of reward, a crest or trophy.
- There is no personal security working for this company, that is why so many people quit.
- There are far too many regulations to suit me.
- You don't get any recognition for working all night in the cold.
- There is little information reaching outlying contracts—we feel isolated.
- I have the feeling I'm not doing anything constructive.
- Minor problems are never corrected, and they lead to bigger ones.
- Questionnaires like this should come to us regularly.

Naturally, it was rather disturbing for management to learn that the employees of Base-Fort had so many points of discontent. It must be remembered, however, that although a number of the items raised in the questionnaire were suggested a number of times, others were mentioned only rarely, like the employee who questioned the promotion methods . . . "what happened to me?" The questionnaire did have positive results in that it made management realize that if they were to improve morale, motivate the employees, and reduce attrition and absenteeism, something very meaningful had to be done. As Edward Lawler stated, it may be necessary to change the organization to fit the plan, rather than fitting the plan to the organization.

One of the most serious problems isolated by the investigation into employee morale was the fact that good employees were leaving the company because they were frustrated. Always working with new employees had an adverse effect on the quality of the service. When clients began to complain about constantly seeing new faces on their premises, it gave ample warning that staff changes had to be greatly reduced.

After discovering the condition of employee relations in the organization, several management meetings were held. It was decided that the employees expected some positive results. The remark by one employee, "I don't really expect anything to come of these questionnaires" was not an uncommon opinion. Most employees felt that some form of "lip service" would be applied and nothing would really change. In view of this attitude and the critical nature of the problem, management decided to make wholesale changes in the organization. In other words, change the organization to suit the plan. The plan was drafted in the form of a message to new employees since a large percentage were new. Existing employees were supplied with a copy of the rough draft (see Exhibit 17–1).

```
WELCOME to BASE-FORT PATROL LTD.  I am glad you have chosen a career with
our firm.  I am proud of the achievements of our organization and place credit
for our fantastic growth on the shoulders of our people.  Men & Women of
BASE-FORT have worked hard to earn a good reputation for our Company.  As
a new employee you will most certainly have the opportunity to help maintain
this growth by applying your personal skills.

We are truly a PEOPLE COMPANY, placing real values on the manner in which
our employees are treated.  Each and every BASE-FORT person is shown respect
and given recognition for their contributions that are so vital to our suc-
cess.  As you will see in the paragraphs that follow, our company cares very
much about our valued employees.  It would be difficult for you to find an
organization that offers more ways of rewarding each individual for their
own achievement.  To earn the respect you will receive from your supervisors,
it is very important that you perform your duties in a responsible manner.
We care very much about:

                    YOUR - knowledge of work
                    YOUR - dress and deportment
                    YOUR - punctuality
                    YOUR - public relations

At BASE-FORT we believe in the TEAM CONCEPT of management.  What is this
kind of management?  Well, in simple terms it means that you will belong to
a "team" that will form part of the BASE-FORT system.  Your team will deter-
mine the method by which you tackle the day-to-day problems of providing
security service.  The more you put into the team, the more you may expect
to get from it.  We believe in the TEAM CAPTAIN - the TEAM LEADERS & the
TEAM MEMBERS, and we allow you to manage your own company affairs.

MORE ABOUT THE TEAM  (How is it evaluated?)

(1)  PERFORMANCE - A senior member of BASE-FORT is responsible to conduct
     inspections of each team.  The team will be rated in the following areas:
     (a)  DEPORTMENT - The  way you wear your uniform.
     (b)  KNOWLEDGE OF WORK - How well you know your duties.
     (c)  QUALITY OF REPORTS - How well you prepare reports.
     (d)  ATTITUDE AND INTEREST - The measure of enthusiasm exhibited to-
                                  wards duties and responsibilities.
     (e)  EQUIPMENT AND VEHICLE MAINTENANCE - The manner in which E & V are
                                  operated and cared for.
     (f)  "GUARDIAN" - Contributions to the monthly newsletter, "THE GUARDIAN".
```

Exhibit 17–1.   Message to all employees from the President.

(g) OVERTIME - How well overtime is managed.
(h) CLIENT SATISFACTION - Clients are interviewed to determine how
     well team members are performing their duties.
(i) TEAM WORK - How well do employees perform as a unit?
(j) COMMUNICATIONS - How effective is the method of "information flow"
     within the team?
(k) DECISIONS - Do all team members have the opportunity to participate
     in decision making?
(1) GOALS - Are employees aware of and working towards company goals,
     of the team and the organization?
(m) LEADERSHIP - Do team leaders provide inspiration for team members?
(n) MOTIVATION - That's what the team is all about.

(2) PROFITABILITY - As part of the overall plan, each team is given total
     responsibility for managing personnel and contract administration. How
     well employees are scheduled and contracts managed plays a key role in
     team profits. Quarterly, a computer margin report is provided to the
     team to help analyze operations for that period.

PERFORMANCE AND PROFITABILITY

Items a - n are assessed by a senior member of BASE-FORT and a written
report is made available to the team and discussed with the team leaders.
This report coupled with financial data makes it possible to rate the performance of each team. Contents of the performance and financial reports
form the basis for gauging how well each team and the company is progressing.

THE REWARD FOR ACHIEVEMENT

Each quarter; i.e. April 1st, July 1st, October 1st and January 1st, each
team will be rated on the strength of their performance and profits. There
are about 10 teams in each region, (North & South). A committee of three is
elected by members of the team. The team leader and the committee is responsible for recommending the quarterly profit sharing bonus to each team
member. The amount of profits to be disbursed will be based on the collective efforts of the team during the three month period. The best team from
each region will be individually listed in the "Guardian".

THE REWARD FOR GROWTH

Each quarter a team may warrant additional revenue through a "growth profit
sharing plan." For each "full time security officer" that is added to the team
through new security contract work, the "team" shall receive $100.00 per each
new security officer. For example, if ten more team members are added to
the total strength of the team, then that team would receive $1000.00 to be
distributed evenly among each member.

ADDITIONAL INCENTIVES

A special merit award in the form of a "gold pendant" will be made available
under the following conditions. The pendant is given to the employee per-
manently for exclusive personal use.

(a) Upon completion of five years of continuous service.
(b) Upon completion of the 1st class testing methods, attaining a
     pass mark.
(c) For special achievement above normal duty requirements.
(d) For providing a suggestion to administration that results in:
     - Increased efficiency
     - Increased economy

Our logo, "Knowledge to Protect", along with the book and sword insignia
is in the final stages of becoming a "registered trade mark". A silver badge
identical to the gold pendant will be made available to all members under
these conditions:

(a) COMPLETION of the basic PRE-JOB Training Course, and
(b) COMPLETION of the basic ON-THE-JOB Training Course.

The silver pendant shall be worn on the uniform and remains the property of
Base-Fort Patrol.

Exhibit 17–1 *(continued)*

REGULAR EMPLOYEE BENEFITS

Accident, Sickness and Health Guard Protection - London Life Insurance
Retirement Pension Plan - London Life Insurance
Free Uniforms - After one year, employees are supplied total uniforms at no
              cost.
Share Purchase Plan - After five continuous years of service an employee is
                     entitled to purchase shares in the company at a reduced
                     rate.

OUR SALES FORCE

We BELIEVE that each member of the team represents part of the BASE-FORT
PATROL LTD. sales force. We think our people can sell our product best of
all, so we don't employ any sales personnel. By professionally attending to
your duties, and exhibiting enthusiasm you play a key role in selling the
company. "Keep your ear to the ground" and always be aware of any potential
new security contracts. Remember, every person you encounter while in uniform just might be a potential new client. This means money in your pocket.

BASE-FORT PHILOSOPHY

* OUR EMPLOYEES are intelligent and have a right to know what is happening with BFP.
* OUR EMPLOYEES are capable of making decisions regarding matters that affect them.
* OUR EMPLOYEES deserve an opportunity to enjoy personal growth within the company.
* OUR EMPLOYEES deserve to feel secure, free from loss of employment.
* OUR EMPLOYEES deserve to utilize their personal skills in their work environment.
* OUR EMPLOYEES deserve the opportunity to participate to the fullest extent.

OUR GOALS (individual - team - company)

They are all the same, to become the biggest and the best in the country. To
do this it must be a total team effort. Management, Supervisors and Team
Members must work in trust and be confident in the future. We must maximize
the skills of every Base-Fort person so that our pooled human resources will
make us strong.

Good Luck !

Exhibit 17–1 *(continued)*

Employees, supervisors, managers and some clients were presented with the draft, and asked for input. The response was very positive. While people estimated the plan would certainly cost the company a good deal of money, the expected results would make the plan a good investment.

The plan was based on the "team concept" of management. To evaluate the various teams, two types of administration forms had to be devised. The first is the "performance evaluation," which is used to measure the standard of security service throughout the organization (see Exhibit 17–2).

The second is the "profitability evaluation" (see Exhibit 17–3). This form is used to measure the financial achievements of each team. Each quarter, management would carefully analyze each team based on the content of the two reports. Quarterly reports would be the "feedback" to team leaders for eventual examination by all team members. The teams were rated first, second, third, and so on. The managers responsible for evaluation had to be prepared to discuss results with team leaders. These team leaders, three from each team, were elected by the team members. The teams were then structured in this way:

Application:
This quarterly team evaluation form is submitted, with the quarterly margin report,
form BFP Pers. 13 and provides information that forms the basis for rating the
effectiveness of each team.

Date: _____   Team Number: _____

                                  Team Leader: _____

	EXCELLENT	VERY GOOD	FAIR	POOR
Deportment	_____	_____	_____	_____
Knowledge of Work	_____	_____	_____	_____
Quality of Reports	_____	_____	_____	_____
Attitude and Interest	_____	_____	_____	_____
Equipment & Vehicle Maintenance	_____	_____	_____	_____
GUARDIAN Submissions	_____	_____	_____	_____
Overtime Control	_____	_____	_____	_____
Client Satisfaction	_____	_____	_____	_____
Team Work	_____	_____	_____	_____
Communications	_____	_____	_____	_____
Decision Making	_____	_____	_____	_____
Participation Towards Goal Attainment	_____	_____	_____	_____
Leadership	_____	_____	_____	_____
Level of Motivation	_____	_____	_____	_____
Subtotals:	_____	_____	_____	_____

Total: _____

Point Scale

Excellent: 4   Very Good: 3   Fair: 2   Poor: 0

Evaluation

48 - 56 Excellent;   40 - 48 Very Good;   30 - 40 Fair

Conclusion

The contents of this report must be discussed with the Team Captain and the three
elected team Leaders. The information is to be relayed to all Team Members, who
are to have the opportunity to examine the report and discuss its contents at Team
Meetings. This evaluation and the quarterly Team Margin Report, (Profitability),
BFP Pers. 13, will form the basis of determining the amount of profit to be disbursed
to Team Members each quarter.

Exhibit 17–2. Team evaluation report.

Team number _____ LOCATION _____ Date _____
Financial Return for the Quarter of _____ to _____

	PREVIOUS QUARTER	PRESENT QUARTER	COMPARISON
TOTAL SALES			

Regular Hours			
Overtime Hours (non-chargeable)			
Overtime Hours (chargeable)			
Statutory Holiday Hours (chargeable)			
Total Guard Hours			
Total Guard Wages			
Percentage (wages to sales)			

PAYROLL BURDEN

(Canada Pension, Unemployment Insurance, Vacation Pay, Worker's Compensation, etcetera)
Total
Percentage (Burden to sales)

CONTROLLABLE COSTS

(Specific costs assigned to team such as auto, rent, travel, equipment abuse, supplies,
  inspections, team training) - See attached print-out

Controllable costs
Percentage C.C. to sales

NON-CONTROLLABLE COSTS

(Costs not controlled by team but incurred by entire company such as legal-audit, insurance,
  bonding, rent, utilities, supplies, depreciation, interest, etcetera)-See attached print-out

Non-controllable costs
Percentage N.C.C. to sales

MANAGEMENT-ADMINISTRATIVE SALARIES

Headquarters
South Region
North Region

Total

Percentage M-A.S. to sales

QUARTERLY RECAP PERCENTAGES TO SALES

P.R. Burden _____ Controllable Costs _____ N.C.C. _____ M-A S _____ Total _____

Net Profit before taxes _____ Bonus in dollars to team_____

ACKNOWLEDGED·

_____   _____
        Team Leader   Team Captain

Exhibit 17–3.   Team evaluation—profitability.

TEAM CAPTAIN
(picked by management)

TEAM LEADERS
(three elected by employees)

TEAM MEMBERS
(assigned to team by management)

The amounts paid to the team members, the team leaders and the team captain do not vary. There is, however, a difference in the amount paid to each team. A team rated #1 would receive slightly more than a team rated #2, and of course, the last place team members would receive the smallest individual remuneration. A team that placed consistently low was examined closely by management, with a view to improving productivity and profitability.

To implement the new program, each employee received a communication directly from the president outlining the plan, which had been approved by all levels of management after discussion with employees. The plan was drafted to reflect the new company attitude toward employees and to explain fully the manner in which each employee would benefit from the new policies.

The results of implementation of the "team concept" were all positive. Terminations and absenteeism dramatically declined. Security guards became more interested in their duties and worked very hard to earn a favorable report and good team rating. They worked together in solving team operational problems and became concerned about controllable costs. Profit margins in each team zone increased and so did employee efficiency. Further training was necessary for some supervisors who saw the "team concept" as a threat to their authority. They found it difficult to share the decision-making process. Once they realized that the real test in supervising was to channel the input from their subordinates, they became accustomed to the new style of management. The company as a whole profited from the involvement of ALL of its employees in the decision-making process.

Many theorists could gain a wealth of knowledge by closely examining the numerous business pressures that often make it difficult to look objectively at human behavior while still maintaining a "handle" on all of the other management functions that need constant attention. Theories, tests, experiments, text books, and group studies can't provide all of the solutions, but neither can a steady diet of the work environment without looking for challenges from outside of the organization. The ability to manage people effectively comes from a combination of experience, education and a broad understanding of human behavior.

Fellowship and social content in an organization is one of the most significant employee needs. The greatest power stems from a group working towards common objectives. If an organization is able to develop unity and group cohesiveness, a kind of "peer pressure" will be imposed on those employees who tend to lessen the group's effectiveness. If the group "norm" calls for twelve units per hour and a particular

---

Box 17–1. Leadership and group performance.

Continuum Of Leadership Behavior

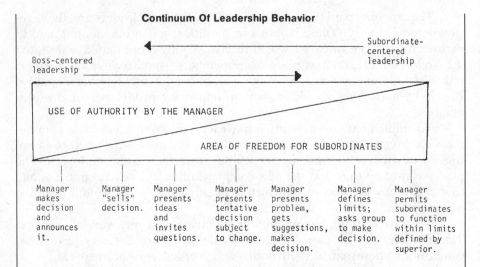

employee produces fifteen, this employee will be made to understand (by the group) that he or she should work within the median of the group. On the other hand, if an employee produces below group expectation, the same kind of direct or indirect pressures will be applied to force conformity. A motivated group requires very little supervision because they have the best interests of the organization in mind. An employee's need to belong and fear of group rejection is the most powerful kind of supervision.

American and Canadian managers require more knowledge about group performance. The Japanese seem to have mastered the ability to structure their industrial communities in a group or team setting. One Japanese executive said:

"Americans tend to think of themselves as individuals, distinct from the group, and are quick to take the defensive in order to protect themselves. Japanese have a primary responsibility to their group or company rather than themselves."

If a true team concept is to be developed there has to be a genuine concern for other members of the team and the team performance as a whole. Of all of the motivating factors discussed, it would seem that *recognition* is perhaps the most significant factor. The management that can recognize effective team performance as well as give credit to individual team or group members will undoubtedly find the solution to many of the employee relation problems in an organization.

Robert Tannerbaum and Warren H. Schmidt have developed some very appropriate observations concerning a manager's style of leadership in relation to group performance. Their diagram, taken from the

Box 17–1 *(continued)*

Harvard Business Review (March-April 1978), illustrates what is termed "Boss Centered Leadership" as opposed to "Subordinate Centered Leadership." (See Continuum of Leadership Behavior)

Assume that a company planned to establish a "team concept" and one of the problems that required a solution was "should the team leaders (other than the team boss, manager or supervisor) be elected or appointed by management."

Suppose the seven decision making techniques were applied to this question.

1. *Manager Makes The Decision And Announces It*

In terms of a "team concept" the team would be told that the leaders would be appointed or elected and team members or subordinates would have no say in the matter.

2. *Manager Sells His Idea*

This manager may wish to appoint the team leaders and strive to communicate with his subordinates to convince them that his is the best plan. He may or may not succeed and could ultimately face the prospect of having individuals or groups on the team resisting his plan to appoint the leaders.

3. *Manager Presents Ideas And Invites Questions*

This manager presents the plan as he feels it would be most successful. He invites input from subordinates and they explore the strong and weak points of the plan. If the manager's original idea is altered or varied to some extent, team members (employees) would feel that they had some effect on the net results of the original idea presented by the boss.

4. *Manager Presents a Tentative Decision Subject To Change*

The final decision remains the responsibility of the manager but subordinates have the opportunity to diagnose the plan and propose changes. Although the final decision is made by the boss, this kind of management makes employees feel that they have a rather wide latitude in influencing the final plan.

5. *The Manager Presents The Problem, Gets Suggestions And Then Makes His Decision*

In the previous four styles of management the plan is presented by the manager. In this case, the boss presents only the problem. This style of leadership involves the maximum use of the skills of the group (team). They have the opportunity to explore any range of solutions that affect the decision that is ultimately made by the boss.

Box 17–1 *(continued)*

6. *The Manager Defines The Limits and Requests The Group To Make the Decision*

The problem is first explained by the boss and then the team or group begins to work on the solution. A participative kind of manager may even wish to belong to the group during the period that they investigate solutions. Not only does the boss benefit from the human resources of the entire group, but he will find that there will be little if any resistance to the decision that is reached. The authoritarian boss described in item one would most surely be faced with resistance to his mandatory decision, but when the group is allowed to make the decision they are bound by their own findings.

7. *The Manager Permits The Group To Make The Decision Within Prescribed Limits*

This is an extreme form, a laissez-faire (free rein) style of leadership. Research groups, for example, would discuss the problem and then be allowed to work freely at finding a solution. In the case of a group deciding on a method of choosing their leaders, it is likely that very little influence would result from management and the team could become too distant from company influence. This style does, however, give employees an opportunity to creatively explore imaginative ideas without management influence.

Certainly there are risks involved in allowing employees to participate to a fuller degree in organizational decision making. What does a manager have to lose if he or she adapts this kind of managerial stance? When we examine our record concerning performance, employee morale, and corporate competitiveness, in most cases, there is very little to lose by altering our methods of management. Perhaps a team approach is the answer.

Box 17–1 *(continued)*

CHAPTER 18

The Security Director as Leader

John Fay, CPP
Assistant Director of Security
Charter Oil Company

Countless studies have been made of leadership and how it is exercised. But from this effort, no evidence has appeared to support the existence of a single set of qualities that guarantee a person will be a good leader. If anything can be said with certainty, it is that the qualities of successful leaders are not universal.

Most people think of leaders in descriptive terms, such as courageous, intelligent, stable, moral, and understanding. While one supervisor may possess courage and intelligence, another's strong suit may be stability and understanding.

The personal qualities a security professional brings to an organization should match the needs of that company for him or her to be most effective. The requirements of every situation will be met more readily by one combination of qualities than another. For example, the kind of leadership needed in a young and growing security organization differs from that suitable for an established, conservative organization.

Leadership styles vary from approaches that use little control to those that exercise absolute control. The choice of an approach is conditioned by the demands of the situation and the personality of the supervisor. A tight time schedule, a skimpy budget, or an outcome that poses critical consequences can dictate what type of management is needed. A supervisor may bring certain personal abilities to a situation that will help or hinder success. Decisiveness and prompt action may be appropriate to one situation, while another may call for caution and restraint. The self-discipline of subordinates, their degree of understanding, their acceptance of the work objectives, their individual and collective motivations, and the broader goals of the organi-

Reprinted with permission of the American Society for Industrial Security, from *Security Management,* July 1981, pp. 104.

zation will also influence the leadership style a supervisor chooses for a situation.

Three styles of leadership predominate—authoritarian, participative, and integrated. Most supervisors, security and otherwise, tend to combine characteristics of all three leadership styles.

The *authoritarian* leader directs people to do things without first soliciting their input. Directions given by the authoritarian leader do not reflect a give and take between supervisor and subordinates. The authoritarian leader usually holds exclusive decision-making power within his sphere of operations. An advantage of the authoritarian style is the speed with which decisions can be made.

An authoritarian leader is not necessarily dictatorial. Even a strict, paramilitary security organization is likely to provide a working environment that offers cultural, social, and legal strictures that prevent abuses of supervision.

The *participative* or democratic style of leadership attempts to merge employee opinions with organizational requirements. Its essential feature is its orientation toward those who are led. Subordinates participate in the arbitration of differences between their desires and the demands of the organization. Although employees may find their participation satisfying, they are sometimes frustrated by the length of time needed to reach collective decisions. Internal conflict may occur when differing viewpoints cannot be reconciled.

Integrated leadership lies somewhere between the authoritarian and participative styles. It is perhaps the most difficult to achieve. The supervisor stays in touch with the overall thinking of his subordinates, making them feel their own wishes are part of the motivating force, even when they are in fact being led. The supervisor creates or modifies work activities to correspond with employee desires, but always maintains the established organizational goals uncompromised.

When successful, the integrated approach provides strong support for the supervisor, particularly when productivity goals are easily met or exceeded. A problem with the integrated approach lies in the time required to build a team mentality and mold individuals into a functioning group.

The skills needed for *action* involve carrying out the options or alternatives selected to approach a situation. It is one thing to select an action, but quite another to execute it. Action skills are very likely the most important skills possessed by a security supervisor. The accuracy of a diagnosis becomes moot when a supervisor lacks the capacity to act. Assume, for example, that all or most security officers under a supervisor continually submit error-ridden incident reports. Diagnosis calls for simplication of the incident report, training employees to fill out the new form properly, and follow-up discussions when incorrect reports are submitted. The supervisor may recognize and accept the reality of what has to be done, but may not be capable of accomplishing it.

Action is conditioned by a leader's personality, background, confidence, and grasp of reality. Lack of experience, education, or initiative can severely restrict a supervisor's capacity to lead, as can rigidity, prejudice, and similar impediments.

Action is also influenced by forces outside the supervisor, such as the constants of politics, money, or time. A competent security supervisor understands the security department and the forces by which it is moved. Although sometimes powerless, he is usually able to exercise a certain degree of control over the limited sphere in which he operates.

The word leadership can suggest a special personal quality that captures the allegiance of followers. To be sure, leadership does have an aspect of charisma, but to give special significance to the inspirational influences of leadership detracts from the fundamental skills that produce a desired human performance.

The ultimate test of leadership is found in the quality of performance rendered by people, whether as individuals or as parts of an organization. Each leadership decision and each leadership act must take into account the attainment of desired results.

Capable leadership is not simply a matter of intuition, luck, or raw native ability. Leadership abilities are not inherited; they are acquired. Most people can learn the fundamentals of leadership. The skills and attitudes can be developed by persons who may differ widely in their natural traits and abilities. From this view, leadership is seen as an organizational function, rather than as a personal quality. The message for security managers is to think of leadership as a function or process that can be enhanced through the development and application of basic human relations skills.

All three leadership approaches can be applied singly or in combination. The nature of the approach is influenced by the leadership skills of the supervisor, the attitudes of the people to be supervised, and the demands of the work. Another consideration important to supervisors is not whether they influence their subordinates, but the nature of their influence.

How a leader exerts his or her influence over subordinates will determine the results achieved. An organization tends to be built from the top down. Leadership starts with the thinking and behavior of the supervisor and is translated into a variety of actions by the employee group. If the ideas of the supervisor are imperfect, the thinking and actions of the employee group are likely to be imperfect.

It would be a wonderful thing to have a clear set of rules for a security supervisor to follow whenever he or she is faced with a leadership problem, but this is not likely to happen. The constantly shifting nature of supervision and the infinite combination of methods to deal with problems rule out the chance that a single set of problem-solving rules will ever be found.

A useful conclusion can be drawn from the observation that no sure-fire method for handling all leadership problems seems to exist. To exercise effective leadership, the supervisor must discard any notion that every situation can be solved by a predetermined method. To succeed, the supervisor must be flexible. He or she must be willing and able to modify his or her approach in relation to changing circumstances. Flexibility requires accurate appraisal of a situation and decisive implementation of actions based on a sound prediction of consequences. To achieve these goals, the supervisor must have both diagnostic skills and action skills.

Diagnostic skills include observing, listening, analyzing, and predicting. Worthwhile diagnosis relies on an ability to differentiate between relevant and irrelevant elements in the situation being analyzed. Separating the important from the unimportant is preliminary but critical.

Noting and treating the symptoms of a problem are not enough to solve it; the key is to determine its underlying causes. A supervisor is sometimes prevented from finding the root of a problem because of his or her own predetermined beliefs. Supervisors are more likely to make a correct diagnosis if they start with a firm resolve to understand the true problem. To achieve this objectivity, the supervisor must be free of any unsubstantiated assumptions about people, groups, events, and other ingredients related to the problem. Things should be seen as they are, rather than as the supervisor thinks they should be or prefers them to be.

Being realistic helps the supervisor accept people as they are. This does not mean he or she must tolerate irresponsible actions, inadequate performance, or laziness on the part of his subordinates. But it should be recognized that people are not always perfect and that an assessment of any situation involving people must take that fact into consideration. A supervisor also needs to recognize his or her own limitations. Sometimes a problem is created by a supervisor's personal shortcomings, and a measure of self-understanding can help him identify where he has erred and to take corrective action.

To the extent that time and circumstances permit, a supervisor will find it useful to analyze specific leadership situations calmly and methodically. Supervisors should look at a situation in terms of human attitudes and behaviors, understanding that separate facts cannot be interpreted correctly except as components of a larger picture. When all the attainable facts are examined, their real significance becomes more evident.

Once the supervisor has made a realistic appraisal of a situation requiring leadership intervention, he is ready to develop a plan of action. Because each situation is unique, considerable skill is required in selecting and carrying out those options for action that are most appropriate.

CHAPTER 19

The Security Director as Trainer

Clay E. Higgins, CPP
Stone and Webster Engineering Company

The Task Force on Private Security reported in June 1976 on a vicious circle operating in the private security industry. Low salaries, marginal personnel, few promotional opportunities, high turnover, and little training all lead to ineffective performance by security personnel. Of these problems, the lack of training is the pivot point that can lead out of the circle.

The deplorable condition of personnel training in the security profession is found from top management down to the uniformed guard. Some major studies have recognized the problem, including one in 1972 by the Rand Corporation and later those by the National Advisory Committee on Criminal Justice Standards and Goals, and the Private Security Advisory Council of the Law Enforcement Assistance Administration (LEAA).

The poor rate of training and a common poor opinion of the quality of security personnel are in striking contrast with the rapidly rising crime rate and the growing sophistication of society in general. Security departments are expected to deal with increasingly sophisticated criminals, yet, because of the poor image of guards, security management is unable to offer salaries that would attract individuals with more training.

The security director is frequently caught in this paradox, with a big job to do and a staff poorly trained to accomplish it. To improve the staff's performance, the director is often forced to serve also as training manager.

The security director must decide how to handle this dual function to best advantage. His continuous duty must be to combat crime, establish loss prevention programs, and fight conditions conducive to crime and loss. But to have his training program successful, it must be attractive, meaningful, and relevant. It must meet the operational needs of the department and the realistic needs of the individual employees.

This article outlines the factors to be considered in planning and im-

Reprinted with permission of the American Society for Industrial Security, from *Security Management,* May 1980, pp. 77.

plementing a good security personnel training program. The first section provides guidelines for developing training strategies and making training as pertinent as possible. The next section deals with planning for training and how to construct annual, quarterly, and monthly training plans. The third part describes methods of instruction and suggests which are best for various circumstances and training situations.

HOW TO DETERMINE TRAINING NEEDS

Many subjects for training are obvious, but some must be determined by careful analysis of the organization and its employees.

Recurring training covers known material that employees may need to brush up on from time to time. Often, those individuals who resist these refresher courses most are those who most need the review.

Security officers need to be familiar with the legal restraints imposed on them, as well as the responsibilities they have under the law. Refresher classes on general law, criminal law, and the organization's rules and regulations should be given on a regular basis. In-house problems may require classes on crime prevention, loss controls, drug and alcohol abuse, emergency and disaster operations, public relations, etc. After the initial training period, these subjects should be repeated as necessary to maintain effective performance.

Individual training should be tailored to each employee to enable the person to perform the specified duties and tasks of the assigned job description. During the first three to six months of employment, individual security officers should be monitored and rated on a performance scale. Long-term employees also need constant performance ratings to ensure a high standard. This rating of a security officer's ability to perform the critical tasks of his job helps assess competence and the need for training.

All new security personnel should receive a minimum of eight hours training before assignment and forty hours of training during their first ninety days of employment. The type of training will depend on the background of each person hired.

When a weakness shows up as a common problem, department-wide training may be called for. In this case, employees should be divided into manageable units for instruction. The entire group cannot be taught at once as the security operation cannot be halted, and, in any case, teaching is usually more effective in smaller groups. It is important, however, that each unit receive the same instruction and the same number of class hours.

Suggestions and ideas for training will come from many internal sources, and these should be considered. However, the security director is in the best position to observe the security staff, and he should ultimately determine the training that will make them most effective.

The analysis of training needs can be reduced to five steps:

- Identify all duties required of and all laws and regulations pertaining to the security staff.
- Determine the capabilities required of the individual employees and of the staff as a whole to accomplish job responsibilities successfully.
- Establish training tasks that will enable employees to reach training goals.
- Determine alternative methods of training.
- Select and follow a course of action for achieving training goals.

The completed training analysis should include a list of all recurring training obligations, individual training desired, and unit training proposed. These lists will be the foundation of the annual training plan.

This process of analyzing training needs and methods should be continuous. Whenever classes have been held, the performance of employees should be evaluated and the training methods reviewed. Recommendations stemming from this scrutiny should be incorporated so the training program is continually updated.

HOW TO PLAN TRAINING

When the initial analysis of training needs is complete, the security director should prepare a training plan. This should account for the training of all personnel assigned to the security department, regardless of job category. A comprehensive unit training plan should contain annual, quarterly, and monthly training plans.

The *annual* plan should be of first concern to the security director in planning the unit's training program. It should be informal, flexible, and above all, workable.

No single month or quarter should be overcrowded in the preparation of the annual plan. To fill the calendar, start with recurring required training and those subjects that have been identified through analysis. Next add training that will require money to hire teachers or rent equipment. These topics should be listed first because budgeting and administrative requirements may be involved in executing them. Any other topics should complete the calendar.

The purpose of and need for all training should be clearly stated in the annual plan. Failure to identify training purposes may result in a lack of essential training and/or training that is not beneficial. In these instances, time and money are wasted with little or no return.

The preparation of the *quarterly* plan allows the security director to tie down any loose ends. The method of instruction should be incorporated in this document, and consideration should be given to the target audience and the availability of instructors, guest speakers, funds, equipment, references, and training facilities. Planning for subjects such as weapons qualifications, self defense tactics, arrest techniques, search and seizure, etc. must go into the quarterly plan to ensure availability of training areas, instructors, and training aids.

The quarterly plan should also be used to record the availability of training support. Following is a list of possible sources of support for an in-house security training program:

- Correspondence courses.
- Training programs at police academies or other law enforcement-related agencies, or programs run by the state government.
- Security training by private agencies.
- Programs at local colleges and universities.
- Educational departments in the organization itself.

The *monthly* training program is the final document in the planning phase. At this stage, the security director should consider the proper setting for the classes, the development of the right attitude in both the trainer and the security officers, and the format of scheduled classes.

After training needs have been determined and identified in the training plan, the next concern must be how to carry out the training.

HOW TO CONDUCT TRAINING

The ideal way to conduct training is to have an hour or two at a time set aside for "hands-on," practical training combined with lectures. This allows the guards or other employees to concentrate on the material at hand and to practice new techniques before they use them on the job.

The retention rate from training that includes practical experience is close to one hundred percent of the information. The retention rate for material taught solely through verbal presentation, television, or film, on the other hand, is more like seventy to eighty percent, but can be much less depending on the quality of the presentation.

Every effort should be made to have periodic training sessions that last long enough for all students to participate in the "hands-on" practice. In the security organization, it is difficult to get the time to implement this type of program. Company management is often unwilling to pay overtime for guards to receive training when they are off duty, and posts cannot be left vacant to train these employees during the hours they are on duty.

Because of these problems, the security and law enforcement professions have fallen into the habit of "roll-call" training. The half hour when one shift is gathered together for roll call before relieving the prior group is the most frequent training period. Only ten to fifteen minutes are left for presentation of materials.

This very limited time for training requires careful planning of the material and the method of presentation. Information selected for presentation must be sound and applicable.

Various methods of presentation can be used, and the one best suited to the subject matter should be selected. Standard methods of instruction recommended for training are lecture, conference, seminar, demonstration, practical exercise, on-the-job training, and exposure to local expertise. These terms are defined below:

- A *lecture* is a presentation by a single speaker to a group.
- A *conference* is a group discussion in which participants' opinions are shared. It is student centered and instructor controlled.
- A *seminar* is also a group discussion that is student centered and instructor controlled, but this talk is based on the research of the participants.
- *Practical exercise* is a simulated application of a true environment in which the students will have to perform.
- *On-the-job training* works best with one trainee and one experienced security officer. In this situation, the trainee can learn the job requirements through examination of situations that arise during a routine shift.
- Sources of *local expertise* are available from regional, national, and international associations with members all over the country, e.g., the International Association for Hospital Security, the National Fire Protection Association, Insurance Companies, Inc., and the American Society for Industrial Security. Excellent guest speakers may be obtained from your associates on a reciprocal basis.

The success of individualized training depends on the availability of instruction material and the motivation of the trainee. Suggested methods are correspondence courses, college courses, learning centers, and independent study.

The learning center has the best potential of all individualized learning situations, though it is the most overlooked of these methods. Learning centers provide a private area for individuals to study at a time they select. The center can be set up in a quiet room by the security director and stocked with security and law enforcement books and related materials, such as audio and video cassettes, filmstrips, programmed texts, slides, tape lessons, reference books, and workbooks with accompanying texts. The trainee then informs the security director when he feels he is ready for testing.

A vital source for the security director can be the in-service education or training department of the organization for which he works. Equipment, including projectors, tape recorders and cassettes, and other training aids, can be borrowed from these departments for use in the security training program.

CONCLUSION

Reports must be filed for all training conducted by the security department. A department file and an individual report for each employee should be made.

The department file should describe the type of training conducted; names of the unit personnel attending; name of the instructor, trainer, guest, or facilitator; and problems or information of significant interest concerning the training.

Finally, training must be evaluated. This is the quality control procedure that provides feedback on the total training effort. The security director must monitor both the trainer and the trainee to ensure that training standards have been satisfactorily met.

The security director is directly responsible for improving the effectiveness of security personnel. He can influence the total security of his organization by establishing a viable training program. To do this, the security director must be able to assess training needs; construct a total training plan with annual, quarterly, and monthly plans; and conduct the training necessary to meet the objectives of the needs assessment.

The security director is in the best position to influence the quality and effectiveness of his security program through training. If his security program is deficient, he has only himself to blame.

CHAPTER 20

The Security Manager as Counselor
John Fay, CPP
Assistant Director of Security
Charter Oil Company

When an employee's personal problems get in the way of acceptable job performance, intervention by others may be necessary. By offering subordinates assistance in solving such problems, supervisory personnel can help them reach solutions and return to their jobs with renewed attention and confidence.

Within a typical security organization, no one is better positioned than a supervisor to provide employee counseling. The supervisor can most accurately gauge an employee's attitude, interests, potential, and performance, and can base his guidance on knowledge of the employee as a person.

The role of counselor places considerable responsibility on the security supervisor. To help subordinates make intelligent decisions regarding work, long-range job aspirations, relations with fellow workers, and family or social activities outside the job environment, the supervisor must possess basic human relations skills. He or she must be adept at discerning an employee's problem and at providing opportunities for the employee to reach a solution. The security supervisor needs patience, good judgment, and the ability to communicate effectively. But above all, he must have a sincere desire to help a subordinate in trouble.

The first opportunity for counseling takes place when an employee is hired. Indeed, a well planned and well executed counseling session during initial orientation will often prevent small start-up problems from mushrooming into larger problems at a later time.

The new employee needs to become geographically oriented to his or her work environment, to meet new people, and to learn the rules of the organization and the procedures of the job. Initially, he is likely to be unsure of his ability to meet job requirements. During the hiring process, the security

Reprinted with permission of the American Society for Industrial Security, from *Security Management,* August 1981, pp. 147.

supervisor should acquaint a new employee with work standards, fitness reports, disciplinary procedures, and criteria for advancement. The supervisor can also help promote a sense of belonging by arranging an informal meeting between co-workers.

Appropriate settings for counseling are many and varied. Whenever the security supervisor is brought into contact with a subordinate for the purpose of helping him work out a personal problem, an opportunity for counseling is present. Counseling can occur at an employee's work station at the moment a personal problem surfaces; in the supervisor's office on a formal, pre-arranged basis; or in an informal setting such as a restaurant, coffee shop, or the employee's home.

There are three basic counseling approaches: directive, non-directive, and co-analysis. The choice of approach depends upon the supervisor's knowledge of the employee, and on a preliminary assessment of the employee's problem.

The *directive* approach is supervisor-centered. The supervisor takes the initiative in the dialogue with the employee. Information moves from the supervisor to the subordinate, with the supervisor choosing the topics of discussion. This approach is meant to help an employee understand what is expected of him and to help him eliminate deficiencies that hinder effective work performance. The directive approach can only succeed when the subordinate makes a genuine effort to face and solve his problems. If the supervisor believes a subordinate lacks the ability to recognize his limitations, the directive counseling approach is inappropriate.

The *non-directive* approach to counseling is employee-centered. The employee is encouraged to talk, to "get his troubles off his chest," to identify his difficulties, and to discover a solution to his problems by talking them out. The supervisor encourages the employee to take the initiative in proposing and implementing solutions to his problems. The non-directive approach can be very helpful in breaking down emotional resistance and in releasing the employee's desire for improvement.

The *co-analysis* approach lies somewhere between the directive and non-directive methods. It has the advantages of both the directive and non-directive methods, but offers the supervisor greater flexibility. Co-analysis is intended to produce an accurate diagnosis of problems through interaction between the supervisor and subordinate. Working together as a team, they identify the problem and work out a program to correct it. This approach will succeed only if the subordinate is willing to accept the supervisor as a partner and sincerely wants to help himself. Empathy is an important element of the co-analysis approach. A supervisor who can grasp how a subordinate sees himself in relation to his job and to other persons is in a better position to offer guidance.

Any of these approaches to counseling must be preceded by careful preparation. The supervisor should gather and study available data on the employee, giving careful consideration to the employee's abilities, aptitudes, and apparent career desires. Some of this data should be committed to memory, to minimize the distraction caused by leafing through notes, records, or files. The presence of official documents and note-taking during a counseling session can inhibit a free flow of information from the subordinate.

The physical setting for the counseling interview should be relatively free from interruption and out of public view—an employee being counseled does not want to be conspicuous. Privacy helps overcome a natural unwillingness to "open up" and communicate freely.

The physical features of the interview room should make the subordinate feel comfortable and at ease. Strong, bright lights can promote a harsh atmosphere; faint lights can produce a sinister atmosphere. A room that is too hot or too cold can be psychologically oppressive. Chairs placed too far apart can give the subordinate a feeling of isolation, while chairs placed too close together can make him feel trapped. If the subordinate has a timid personality it might be useful to provide a chair that is larger or higher than that of the supervisor, to give him a feeling of security and importance. But if the counseling session involves a disciplinary matter, it might be better to seat the employee in a chair smaller or lower than that of the supervisor. And, since the counseling session requires the subordinate's undivided attention, his chair should face away from a window or outside area.

The beginning phase of a counseling session is critical; it establishes the tenor of the interview and influences the employee's confidence in the superviosr. Time spent showing interest in the employee at the outset may yield benefits later in the session. A few moments spent in establishing rapport saves interviewing time in the long run.

An effective method of establishing rapport is for the supervisor to touch upon topics of common interest, such as the employee's hobbies, family, and current events. Casual discussion of familiar subjects should encourage him to begin talking, and can help the supervisor learn more about the individual he is counseling. Initially, while the supervisor is attempting to evaluate the attitude of the subordinate, he should be careful not to reveal his own attitudes or opinions. Doing so may cause the subordinate to respond with information he believes the supervisor wants to hear, rather than speaking his own mind.

While attempting to establish rapport, the supervisor should not dominate the conversation. Encouraging the subordinate to talk and participate actively in the interview makes him feel he is helping himself. By asking questions that require more than simple yes or no answers, the supervisor can gain further insight into the subordinate's problems. Questions that require explanations provide valuable information about the subordinate's personality, beliefs, and reactions. Responses to non-specific questions not only help clarify problems but may also provide valuable clues to workable solutions.

Once the employee begins to talk, he should be permitted to express his thoughts freely, in his own words, and with as few interruptions as possible. The supervisor should talk only when the employee is unable to continue. If the conversation becomes mired in confusion or unnecessary detail, a slight prompting by the supervisor can restore the flow of information. A question or comment is sometimes all that is needed to bring the conversation back on track.

A potential pitfall in counseling is to provide too much assistance. The overly helpful supervisor is likely to encourage a sense of dependence rather than self-reliance in the employee. The security supervisor who takes the subordinate's problems into his own hands actually performs a disservice. A supervisor may correctly conclude that a worker's problem is best solved by a particular set of actions, but the key is to lead the worker to his own discovery of those actions. The confidence gained by discovering the answer to his own problem will stiffen the employee's resolve to carry out corrective measures.

If nothing else is accomplished during the interview, the employee should at least leave the session feeling that some positive step has been taken. A counseling session that closes with the subordinate believing he is no nearer to a solution than he was at the outset is not only a waste of time, but can also be counterproductive. Even if the employee only comes closer to understanding the nature of his problem, this in itself represents progress.

A security supervisor is sometimes unable to recommend a solution to a problem because its resolution lies beyond his expertise or authority. A supervisor must recognize his own limitations and be prepared to turn to others for assistance. Problems that are psychiatric, financial, or religious in nature are clearly beyond the domain of the security supervisor. Referring subordinates to specialists or specialized agencies for additional assistance is an acceptable and potentially beneficial course of action. It frees the supervisor to concentrate on counseling that solves work-related problems, and it keeps the supervisor from becoming overly involved in matters beyond his sphere of responsibility.

Referral to an outside source, however, should not be seen as an excuse for the supervisor to wash his hands of the subordinate and his problem. When making a referral, the supervisor should follow up to be sure the employee's problem is being addressed. A display of interest assures the subordinate the supervisor genuinely cares about him.

A skilled security supervisor can usually differentiate between problems and symptoms. A counseling session should concentrate on the core of a problem, not on surface manifestations. An employee may permit his attention to be drawn away from the main issue by focusing on extraneous symptoms of a problem. When this happens, a supervisor needs to filter out the irrelevant factors and bring the issue back into focus.

Once the problem has been identified to the satisfaction of the supervisor and subordinate, a course of action should be discussed and agreed upon. For remedial action to succeed, the subordinate must act in specific, tangible ways. Tangible actions, for example, might be for the subordinate to write to his creditors; to reduce by fifty percent the number of absences from work in the next month; or to enroll in an alcohol abuse prevention program. A corrective course of action that is specific, and therefore observable, permits the supervisor to evaluate the subordinate's progress. It also helps to provide a time frame for the completion of corrective measures.

A written record of the counseling session can greatly facilitate the supervisor's follow-up. While it may not be desirable to take notes during a counseling session, it is important to record its main points as soon as possible after an interview. A brief follow-up report should include a description of the problem discussed, the course of action proposed and agreed upon, and the decision of the subordinate to act according to a schedule.

Most importantly, confidentiality is an essential condition of interviewing. Details obtained from a subordinate, whether included in a follow-up report or not, should be considered privileged information. It takes only one indiscreet comment in the presence of an outsider to poison the relationship between subordinate and supervisor. An established, successful counseling program can be destroyed the instant the employee perceives that private discussions have become public knowledge.

PART IV

Dealing with Non-Security Personnel

Resource or hindrance—organizational employees who do not specifically work for security can fall into either category. The job of providing security for an organization is vastly complicated if employees fight security measures or do not cooperate with them. Simple lack of awareness about security concerns is frequently the cause of non-security employees being a hindrance rather than a help to security. Therefore, a large part of any security manager's job is likely to be the enlistment of cooperation with security by the organization's personnel. Security awareness programs can do much to shape favorable attitudes among employees. Alert employees with positive attitudes about security may be an organization's best defense against internal crime and a useful sensor for detecting vulnerabilities.

Since the personnel are a key part of successful security, personnel selection by departments other than security can have great impact on the loss prevention efforts of the organization. If applicants' backgrounds are not carefully examined, the organization may inadvertently import trouble. Security department involvement in background screening may be appropriate, or as an alternative, security can provide training in proper pre-employment screening to personnel who will be hiring other employees.

Outgoing personnel can also aid security efforts if tapped through exit interviews. Before leaving, such individuals can often give valuable insight into existing and potential security weaknesses.

CHAPTER 21

Shaping Attitudes: A New Approach to Loss Prevention
Roger Griffin, CPP
Vice President
Commercial Service Systems, Inc.

Security executives and security practitioners have a serious responsibility in shaping employee attitudes and ethics about loss prevention. Much can be done to influence the behavior of fellow employees, and security professionals are beginning to see the logic behind investing time and energy to promote security awareness as an important part of employee training.

One definition holds that ethics is the science of the ideal human character and morality is the quality of that which conforms to right ideals or principles of human conduct. In security, we must teach conformity in the positive sense of the word, and we must deal with conduct that is destructive to the organizations we serve and to society as a whole.

An increasingly important question is "How do we deal with individuals whose conduct is destructive or potentially destructive to the organization?" A law enforcement agency is entitled to claim total success each time an investigation results in the conviction of a criminal. An industrial security organization is entitled to the same kind of credit when those results are obtained, but their responsibility goes beyond that.

The mission of law enforcement is the successful prosecution of criminals. The mission of security, on the other hand, is the protection of personnel and assets. The prosecution of employees is relevant, then, only as it applies to creating a deterrent against destructive conduct by other employees.

The chairman of the board of any company has a responsibility as a corporate citizen to see that criminals are punished. The head of a company is more interested, however, in how prosecution reduces losses than simply in how many people are prosecuted.

All employees who commit crimes should be prosecuted whenever

Reprinted with permission of the American Society for Industrial Security, from *Security Management,* January 1983, pp. 49.
Taken from a speech given before the San Francisco Chapter of ASIS.

possible. Many practical problems are involved in prosecution, not the least of which is the difficulty in developing court quality evidence. In many cases it is physically impossible to develop the required evidence or impractical to do so due to lack of time, manpower, or financial resources. For these reasons, apprehending and prosecuting employees guilty of destructive conduct is not the number one priority of the industrial security community.

This concept is rather well recognized. The increasing frequency with which "loss prevention" is substituted for "security" in the literature on the subject and in the titles of the executives and departments that administer these programs indicates that the first priority is prevention rather than apprehension and punishment.

THE ART OF LOSS PREVENTION

Recently, loss prevention has become much more scientific. An abundance of impressive hardware now exists to assist security professionals in their task. But currently, and perhaps for a long time to come, loss prevention is and will remain more of an art than a science. That art is principally the ability to influence, in a positive way, the behavior of other human beings.

After-the-fact apprehension and enforcement are no longer sufficient as security measures. This kind of effort is commendable, but it is reactive rather than preventive. Security is losing ground to crime because companies never have enough security/loss prevention personnel to handle each problem or potential problem individually. As costs increase, it becomes more and more difficult to justify the expenditures required to solve problems through investigation and prosecution. The need for a systems approach to loss prevention becomes clear.

Within a systematic approach, developing techniques for altering employees' attitudes about integrity in the work environment becomes an important element of the loss prevention program.

In the 1980s, industry's problems are serious enough that many business strategies will be completely revised and the loss prevention executive will have opportunities to exercise ingenuity. Leaders in the field of loss prevention can now take the initiative in establishing standards of ethics and conduct for the employees of their companies.

These same loss prevention leaders will have to create the innovations required to make those standards meaningful among the work force at large and to sell the need for those standards to management.

MANAGEMENT AND LABOR

One of the main obstacles blocking the implementation of this proposition is the divisive nature of the relationship between management and labor.

The history of this conflict is complex. The problem was created, in part at least, by the robber baron mentality, which resulted in the exploitation of labor. The organized labor movement solved many of the early problems, but the selfish, often unreasonable positions taken by labor unions over the years have widened the chasm between the work force and management. When the leaders of both management and labor infer through their positions and statements that they do not have a common goal more important than the specific desires of either side, inevitably the attitudes of individuals on both sides become polarized as well.

UNIVERSITY OF MINNESOTA STUDY

A recent study by the Sociology Department of the University of Minnesota entitled "Theft by Employees in Work Organizations" focuses on causes and patterns in employee theft. The observations and conclusions in the report are based on research involving 35 corporations, 5,000 of their employees, and 24 labor unions and employee associations.

The first chapter outlines the state of theoretical and research knowledge on the topic of employee theft. Surprisingly, very little material is available on the subject. The authors do offer some limited conclusions, however, drawn from the research material that was available. First, the roots of the deviant behavior detrimental to the interests of the employer are to a great extent an integral part of the work experience. In other words, deviant behavior such as theft is to be expected in almost every type of work place.

Also, the employee's perception of the quality of the work environment is a significant factor affecting the decision to become involved in theft and counterproductive activity. The recurring theme of job dissatisfaction pervades these studies as an explanation of the occurrence of deviant acts against the work organizations.

Finally, informal rules of the work group to a large extent regulate both the amount and type of deviant behavior. This implies that every work force has its own informal rules and that those rules have a greater impact on employee conduct than the official rules of the organization they work for.

The Minnesota study suggests that understanding this process of social control is essential to coping with employee theft problems. Employee theft is not a random event, but a response to the social and environmental factors present within the work setting.

That this body of subtle rules exerts such an important influence on workers is a sobering thought for many managers, but it may be an opportunity as well. Informed management does not attempt to destroy the unofficial communications grapevine existing between workers. Rather, that grapevine is used to communicate in a way not possible using normal channels. The same innovative approach should be taken with regard to this other natural phenomenon in the work force. It should be studied and understood and converted to positive uses.

The Minnesota study gives some interesting insights into understanding what actually goes on inside the work force. The authors took a unique approach in attempting to determine how much theft takes place. Instead of attempting to refine the standard methods of assessing inventory shrinkage, they went directly to the employees. They sent questionnaires to the home addresses of the employees to be queried and received almost 5,000 replies, which represented responses from 51% of those to whom the questionnaire was mailed. The employees of nine retail store organizations, ten electronic manufacturing firms, and sixteen general hospitals were surveyed.

Studies of this type are important because they produce factual data, which both loss prevention personnel and upper management can use to good advantage. Exhibit 21–1 contains a compilation of the involvement in dishonest activity reported by the employees surveyed in response to the questionnaire they received in the mail.

These self-reported survey statistics are no doubt on the conservative side, and yet 60% of the retail employees reported they had been involved in some kind of dishonest behavior. 40% of the manufacturing employees reported dishonest behavior, as did 45% of the hospital employees.

The Minnesota group asked the question, "What are the things that affect an employee's involvement in behavior directed against the work organization?" They isolated four variables:

- *The personal attributes or standards of the individual employee.* Certain employees would never be dishonest no matter how great the opportunity to steal without getting caught, just as certain employees will always take advantage of any weakness in the system.
- *The employee's occupational position within the organization:* The position the person occupies and the work he or she does will obviously limit his or her opportunity for dishonesty.
- *Relative levels of job satisfaction:* disgruntled employees are surely a greater risk.
- *The employees' perceptions of various social controls deterring theft activity:* Peer pressure is a constant force either for conformance or nonconformance.

LOSS PREVENTION POLICY

A number of policy implications are suggested by this type of research. An organization, through ineffectual monitoring of less serious forms of workplace deviance, may be tacitly encouraging employee theft since employees seem to take their behavioral clues from management's reaction to all forms of rule-breaking activity.

ITEMS	Daily	Weekly	Monthly	Yearly	Once	Total
Retail Sector						
Misuse discount privilege	1.2%	5.5%	21.7%	16.0%	12.8%	57.2%*
Take store merchandise	.3	.8	2.3	2.5	5.9	11.8
Get paid for more hours than worked	.0	.5	1.5	2.3	4.7	9.0
Damage merchandise	—	.1	.4	.7	1.1	2.3
Excess expense reimbursement	.4	.2	.9	1.5	1.2	4.2
Purposely underring purchases	.1	.4	2.1	1.0	1.9	5.5
Unauthorized taking of money	.1	.0	.4	.4	1.1	2.0
Manufacturing Sector						
Take precious metals	.1	.1	.5	1.0	1.4	3.1
Take raw materials	.1	.3	3.5	9.7	7.3	20.9
Get paid for more hours than worked	.2	.5	2.9	4.8	3.7	12.1
Excess expense reimbursement	.1	.6	1.4	5.5	2.4	10.0
Take company tools and equipment	—	.1	1.1	6.9	8.6	16.7
Take finished products	—	—	.4	2.2	3.9	6.5
Hospital Sector						
Take hospital supplies	.2	1.0	9.4	13.3	13.0	36.9
Take or use medications	.1	.5	2.0	3.7	3.5	9.8
Get paid for more hours than worked	.2	.6	2.2	2.4	4.0	9.4
Excess expense reimbursement	.1	.0	.3	.5	.9	1.8
Take tools or equipment	.0	.1	.5	3.3	4.1	8.0

*Reported as possibly due to ambiguities in the way the discount privilege is defined by various companies.

Exhibit 21–1. Percent of involvement.

While prosecution is expensive and time-consuming, failing to prosecute an employee sends a clear message to other workers that the greatest penalty for theft is being fired.

Ironically, the high theft employee frequently exhibits a trait employers look for in prospective employees—a desire to achieve. Often, the subject of an investigation is a management trainee. In some cases theft by these people can be attributed to frustration in the achievement of their goals. Disgruntled employees tend to be more easily tempted to commit dishonest acts.

When the likelihood of being discovered is great, employee theft decreases. The employee's perception of the punishment or sanction to be imposed is also an important factor. Interestingly, the informal reactions of fellow workers appear to be more influential in reducing theft than the official reaction of the employer.

These findings of the Minnesota research team confirm the notion that preemployment screening of prospective employees continues to be an important theft control strategy. Not only does the procedure screen out the "bad apples," it also conveys the message to those ultimately hired that the organization is interested in a work force with integrity.

The most encouraging finding of the study is that organizational policies and practices *can* have an impact on the amount of employee theft. Less theft is found in organizations in which theft control has been incorporated as a goal of the inventory control system. If individuals with inventory control responsibilities make conscious efforts to watch for irregularities and then check into why they may be occurring, the result would be a reduction in the number of thefts.

Loss prevention cannot function in a vacuum. Loss prevention executives must constantly strive to integrate their goals into the overall goals of the organization and to exercise ingenuity in capturing the interest and cooperation of other employees.

Employee conduct cannot be taken for granted . . . and that conduct can be influenced in a positive way by establishing standards. Studies of the type referred to here can have important policy implications depending upon the degree of credibility people involved in loss prevention find in them. As the problem of employee theft increases, more security executives will probably be persuaded that preventative measures can play an important role in their efforts to secure company assets.

CHAPTER 22

Motivating the Other 99%
John C. Cholewa III, CPP
Special Agent
General Telephone Company
of Wisconsin

Security Management readers recognize that security is an extremely important aspect of any organization. The security department knows it can add to an organization's "bottom line" by decreasing expenses which would normally occur as a result of internal and external theft, sabotage, vandalism, and lawsuits among other threats. Too, the security department knows that it is, in fact, actively involved in maintaining the viability of the organization and that the absence of a security function could be devastating. Statistics on the massive and varied threats to which organizations are exposed all support this knowledge. For example:

- The US Department of Commerce estimates that retail merchants lost approximately $8 billion to shoplifters during calendar year 1976.[1]
- The US Chamber of Commerce estimates that computer frauds cost the nation in excess of $100 million per year.[2]
- Dun & Bradstreet reports that employee thievery can be blamed in whole or part for 30% of all business failures.[3]
- Cumulatively since 1968, terrorists have exacted hundreds of millions of dollars in ransoms and have killed over 1,100 executives.[4]

Obviously these data represent only the tip of the iceberg. The intent of this

Reprinted with permission of the American Society for Industrial Security, from *Security Management*, May 1979, pp. 52.

[1] Michael Minto, " 'The Brotherhood' Professional Shoplifting Ring: How They Operate," *Security Industry & Product News,* Volume 7 Number 3 (March, 1978), p. 18.
[2] August Bequai, "Legal Problems in Prosecuting Computer Crime," *Security Management,* Volume 21 Number 4 (July, 1977), p. 26.
[3] R. J. Bargert, "Check for the Thief Within," *Security Industry & Product News,* Volume 7 Number 3 (March, 1978), p. 25.
[4] Lloyd W. Singer & Jan Reber, "A New Way to Face Terrorists—A Crisis Management System," *Security Management,* Volume 21 Number 5 (September, 1977), p. 6.

article, however, is not to document the need for security within organizations, but rather to examine the potential for greater effectiveness of security departments through the motivation of those organizational employees who are not formally affiliated with the security department.

Viewing the organization as a whole from the vantage point of the security department, we can readily identify three distinct groups of individuals. Referring to Exhibit 22–1, we see the following:

- "Organizational Employees," a set which is comprised of all members of the organization.
- "Top Management," a subset consisting only of organizational members who fill the top management positions within the organization.
- "Security," a second subset made up of all organizational members who are part of the formal security function.

Historically, the primary (and sometimes the only) motivational efforts by security managers have been directed toward top management and security department personnel. This is understandable. If top management can not be motivated to support the security function, protecting organizational resources effectively will be extremely difficult, if not impossible. Obviously, if the security personnel themselves are not properly motivated, the effectiveness of the security function will suffer greatly.

What is happening when we concentrate on top management and security personnel? If we are doing a good job, we are creating an atmosphere in which top management and departmental personnel view the security function as being important and deserving of active support. Motivational efforts have caused the top management team to recognize the importance of the security function within the organization, and those same efforts have transformed the security department members into well-motivated employees.

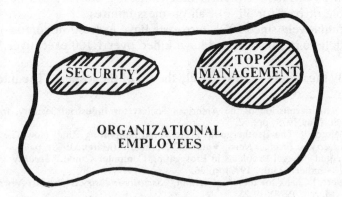

Exhibit 22–1. The organization.

By limiting our motivational efforts to those two groups and ignoring the remainder of the organization's employees means we are focusing attention on approximately 1% of the total organizational population. The remaining 99% of the employees are not being motivated to support the security function, in which case the security department is forced to fight its "battle" alone. Such a situation is, however, unnecessary in any organization.

Many security departments are aware of the need to make allies of employees throughout their companies. No doubt many departments are highly successful in doing so. Many security departments also realize that the first step toward motivating employees to support security efforts is education. Letting employees know that a formal security function exists in the organization, and making sure they are aware of their own personal responsibilities regarding organizational security is a necessary first step toward gaining their support. However, although initial and continuing security education is an extremely important step in the motivational process, it is only the beginning.

Before examining potential methods of motivating employees, a review of motivation theory is in order to help us understand why motivational efforts may succeed or fail. Motivation theories are proposed by many theorists, each with his own ideas concerning why people act in certain ways. Some, such as Maslow and Herzberg, are well known while others are less frequently cited. I would like to concentrate on another theorist—Victor Vroom—who developed a model to predict behavior based on Expectancy Theory. I chose this model over others because real-world testing has done much to validate the thinking about it.[5] The model is regarded highly by current motivation researchers for its ease of implementation and emphasis on individual differences.[6]

I offer a simplified version of Vroom's Expectancy Model, which will serve my purpose of providing insight into why individuals act in certain ways. The model guides the manager in the effort to motivate people—whether top managers, subordinates in the security department or the remainder of the organization's employees.

$$F = \sum_{i=1}^{n} (E_i \times V_i)$$

F is the force to act.

E is the expectancy or probability that a given outcome will result from a given action.

V is the valance or desirability of the outcome to the individual acting.

[5]J. Richard Hackman & Lyman W. Porter, "Expectancy Theory Predictions of Work Effectiveness," *Motivation and Work Behavior* by Richard M. Steers & Lyman W. Porter (New York: McGraw-Hill, 1975), pp. 200–208.

[6]Richard M. Hodgetts, *Management: Theory, Process and Practice* (Philadelphia: W. B. Saunders, 1975), pp. 329–330.

(Values for E vary from 0.0 to 1.0. Values for V range from -1.0 to $+1.0$).[7]

The model shows that the force to act in a given manner is a function (or result) of the desirability (V) of the perceived outcomes to the person who is deciding whether to act or not, and of the perceived probabilities (E) that the action will in fact result in the perceived outcomes.

Generally before acting, people do not consciously calculate all the possible outcomes of their action, what the probability of each of those possible outcomes is and how desirable each outcome would be. Nor do they go through the mathematics to determine whether or not they should proceed with a given action. But most people do consider their alternatives in some rational and logical manner. Vroom's model simply attempts to explain the decision-making process people go through in quantitative terms.

To picture how this model might work we could look at two individuals—a gardener and an assemblyline worker. Suppose both employees would like an increase in pay and both believe that doing more work will result in that increase. To achieve the desired outcome, they both consider going to work one hour early. As the outcome is highly desirable to them, we will assign a V value of $+0.8$ for both individuals. As for the E value (the perceived probability that going to work an hour early will enable them to do more work), we will assign a value of 0.9 to the gardener. He is almost certain that if he goes to work an hour early he will accomplish more work. As for the assemblyline worker, he recognizes that if he goes to work early he will very probably not accomplish any more work. His co-workers will not be there and the line will not be running. So we will assign an E value of 0.1 to him. If we then compute the force to act (F) for each worker we see that the gardener has a high F value of 0.72, whereas the assemblyline worker has a low value of 0.08.

Assemblyline Worker—	Gardener—
$F = E \times V$	$F = E \times V$
$F = 0.1 \times 0.8$	$F = 0.9 \times 0.8$
$F = 0.08$	$F = 0.72$

Clearly, the gardener would be more highly motivated to go to work early than would the assemblyline worker. Of course, that example is very much simplified. Each worker would perceive more than one outcome from going to work early. Each of those additional perceived outcomes would have its own E and V values. The strength of the force to act would be the result of multiplying each E value by its respective V value and then adding all of these together. To demonstrate how additional perceived outcomes could affect the worker's motivation, we could look at just one additional

---

[7]Victor H. Vroom, "An Outline of a Cognitive Model," in *Motivation and Work Behavior* by Richard M. Steers & Lyman W. Porter (New York: McGraw-Hill, 1975), pp. 185–189.

outcome resulting from the assemblyline worker going to work early. He might believe that his peers would react negatively to his reporting to work early. He might be ridiculed or ostracized for such an action. In fact, he might be so certain of a negative reaction that we would assign a value of 0.9 to E in that case. He would probably view the reaction of his co-workers as very undesirable, therefore we assign a V value of -0.9. Doing the mathematics we see that his force to act (F) is now -0.73 as opposed to the former value of 0.08.

Assemblyline Worker
$F = i = 12\ (E_i \times V_i)$
$F = (0.1 \times 0.8)$ 1st outcome $+ (0.9 \times -0.9)$ 2nd outcome
$F = (0.08)$ 1st outcome $+ (-0.81)$ 2nd outcome
$F = -0.73$

Previously he was not motivated to go to work early, whereas he is now strongly motivated *not* to go to work early.

The value of this model to the manager lies in the fact that a subordinate's motivation to act in a certain manner may be altered. This may be accomplished by causing changes in outcomes he perceives as the result of acting in that manner and by causing changes in his perception of the probability that the act will result in a given outcome.

Returning to the question of how to motivate employees to support the security function, we find that Vroom's model can be of assistance. First, let us examine the conditions that would prompt employees to support the security function actively. Through dealings with individuals who regularly support investigative, law enforcement and intelligence efforts—informants and sources—we have come to realize, that different things motivate different people to offer their support. Some see their assistance as a civic duty, others do it for money, others see it as a means of harming a competitor, still others do it for revenge.[8] In security we sometimes find managers relying on the money motive to elicit support. The money motive is fine for top management because having the organization make a profit is their goal. If the security manager can sell top management on the idea that the security department can contribute to the "bottom line," the security function will be supported. This example fits nicely into Vroom's model. If the act of supporting the security function is perceived as having a high probability (E) of resulting in an outcome (increased profits), and if increased profits is a highly desirable outcome (V) to top management, the force to act (support the security function) will be great.

In some security education/motivation programs the security department also appeals to the money motive in an effort to get the support of

[8]Paul B. Weston & Kenneth M. Wells, *Criminal Investigation,* 2d ed. (New Jersey: Prentice-Hall, 1974), p. 98.

organizational employees.[9] While nothing is inherently wrong with that approach, it certainly will not be as effective with general employees as it was with top management. Why? There are a number of reasons.

First, most employees are considerably less concerned with the organization's profit picture than its top management. You can tell the employees the better the organization fares financially the better they will fare themselves, and vice versa. The problem is employees seldom see a direct relationship between their personal financial situations and that of the company. Therefore the argument that the money they help save the company will show up in paychecks will not be a very strong motivator for those individuals.

Then, we have the question of perceptions. Referring to Vroom's model once again, we can see that pay increases would be highly desirable to the employees, resulting in a high V value. When we say that increased organizational profits (resulting in part from employee support of the security function) will result in increased pay, the employees will subconsciously assign their E values to that statement. If they believe very strongly that supporting the security function will result in pay increases, they will assign a high E value. That, combined with the high V value, will result in a high level of motivation to support the security function. (That is, assuming no other perceived outcomes of supporting the security function would drastically alter the overall force to do so.) But, in most cases, employees will be skeptical of the notion that greater profits, regardless of their source, will go into pay increases. They find it far easier to believe that increased profits will be shared among top management in the form of bonuses and profit-sharing plans.

I do not intend to say that money cannot be a motivator for employees vis-à-vis the security function, because it *can* be if we so desire. All we have to do is change employees' expectancy that money will accrue to them as a direct result of supporting the security function. In that way, we would use money as a motivator.

In general, Vroom's model tells us we must do the following four things to motivate employees to support the security effort, regardless of the types of motivators we intend to employ:

1.   Identify potential outcomes which the majority of employees would consider desirable. These desirable outcomes are many—monetary reward, recognition by superiors, recognition by peers, time off, a bigger desk, or perhaps a private office.
2.   From that list of "desirable outcomes," select those the organization would be willing to provide.
3.   See that the employees are aware of the nature of the outcomes (rewards) for supporting the security function.

---

[9]Lawrence F. Clark, "Security Education for All Employees," *Security Management,* Volume 22 Number 3 (March, 1978), p. 44.

4.   Take steps to ensure that employees believe the promised outcomes will occur as a result of their giving support to the security function.

According to Vroom's model, if the employees perceive a high probability (E) that a desirable outcome (V) will result from supporting the security function, their inclination or force to act (F) will be high and they can be expected to provide the desired support.

Determining just which outcomes are considered desirable by the employees should not be an overwhelming task. In many cases we already know. Employees may have told us directly or indirectly through the informal information network, or we may have learned by observing their actions and reactions to various situations.

Seeing that the employees know the outcomes will come about as a result of their actions is the responsibility of the security department and top management. Numerous ways can be used to accomplish the task. Certainly most individuals would perceive a complimentary write-up in the organization's newsletter as desirable. If such write-ups result each time an employee significantly supports the security function, it will not take long before everyone catches on. When a member of the management team presents a $500 check to Mr. X because he reported a strange truck and men in the holding yard and prevented the loss of $30,000 worth of material, other employees will soon catch on. Similarly, if employees know the top level security manager writes letters of commendation for inclusion in the personnel records of deserving employees, an increase in support will probably not be far behind.

These examples are just a few of the many ways to provide desirable outcomes for employees who support security efforts. Many organizations already reward employees supporting the organization in some way—suggestion programs are a prime example. The objective is to transfer that method of motivating employees to the security department's efforts. Vroom's model shows why such methods work and offers guidance for implementation of those methods. It can be used as an analytical tool to determine why present reward programs may or may not be having the desired result.

Security is an increasingly important function within organizations, and it is one which will suffer without support from all members of the organization. Security is people, so all employees must be motivated to support security actively.

CHAPTER 23

Four Steps to Security Awareness

Marshall M. Meyer, CPP
President
Security Associates, Inc.

Security losses in a business vary in direct proportion to attitudes and levels of honesty among employees. One way to ensure that employees feel their company is concerned with both their safety and the security of the company's products and facilities is through a security awareness program.

Any guideline for a security awareness program can only be that—a guide. Each person responsible for constructing a viable program must consider the circumstances specific to his or her company that affect each step in the proposed program. Relevant concerns include: the size of the work force; the cyclical nature of the work load; the location, whether urban or rural; the type of product manufactured; the area crime rate; the source of facility personnel; and the facility's history of incidents and security violations.

Tailoring the security awareness program outlined here to a specific facility should enable the security director to enhance security, diminish losses, and improve employee morale.

Four major steps make up the program: orientation, use of visible deterrents, a continuing training program, and management support.

INITIAL ORIENTATION

The initial security orientation is considered vital since the first impressions of a company's attitudes toward security are often the most important. Essential to an effective orientation program is, of course, competent new employees. Hiring individuals qualified to perform the tasks for which they are employed is the first step in creating an effective security awareness

Reprinted with permission of the American Society for Industrial Security, from *Security Management,* June 1982, pp. 32.

program. The personnel manager must attempt to hire not only the most qualified individual for the job, but also the one he or she believes would be the most honest and conscientious. The goal should be obtaining honest employees at the outset and then instilling in them a sense of cooperation throughout their term of employment.

Each employee should be introduced to the security program by a member of the security management team in cooperation with the personnel department. This orientation can be given in small groups or to an individual, but should be accomplished within the first week of employment. The following are among the items that should be discussed in depth:

- The purpose of security, with particular emphasis on the requirements of the facility.
- What security means to the new employee. Here the message should be emphasized that good security on the job provides for long-range, economic benefits at home.
- How the employee can help support the existing protective effort.
- The value management places on security and safety awareness.

Orientation sessions also present an opportunity to provide the applicant with important information about established rules and procedures. For example, items such as the following should be reviewed.

- Identification cards and whether they must be worn at all times during working hours.
- Package-pass procedures—who may issue a valid pass and the purpose of the package pass.
- Location of emergency fire doors, evacuation routes, and what is expected of employees during emergency situations. (Here, let employees know the security department is not only concerned with corporate security, but also with the personal safety of the employees.)
- Authorized employee entrances, emphasizing those restrictions that are strictly enforced and monitored.
- Inspections of personal vehicles entering or exiting the facility, lunch pails or sack inspections, and locker inspections—when they occur and why.

Generally, the orientation should cover only those fundamentals necessary for the new employee to adjust smoothly to the job and understand the company's attitude toward security. Further rules and regulations should be included in an employee handbook, even if this is nothing more than a single typed page. Employees should be given handbooks at the orientation session so they can read the section relating to security requirements and ask questions while someone from the security department is available to answer them.

New employees can be required to sign a document saying they have read and understood the security requirements as outlined in the handbook. This procedure enhances the importance of the security function and demonstrates what is expected of an employee.

An employee who has attended an effective security program will frequently report co-workers if they commit an act that is dishonest or against the best interests of the company. However, selling the security program requires technique. The sincerity of the speaker is essential to success. Downgrading a rule or regulation by saying something like, "Higher management wants this enforced, but we really don't pay too much attention to it, so just be careful," will prevent employees from taking the security orientation, or the security program, seriously.

VISIBLE DETERRENTS

Employee attitudes are affected by the examples set by management, so visible support for security from management is all important. Making the security program visible and actively involving management at all levels of the facility's loss prevention program are two ways of giving employees a strong impression of security.

For example, the plant manager and his staff should wear identification cards if this is a policy of the facility. The plant manager and his staff should stop at the guard post to be checked, lock their office doors, clear their desks, and do all other things expected or required by the rules of the facility.

The most visible security feature, of course, is the uniformed guard force. It is essential that these individuals present a respectable image. Uniforms should bear distinctive markings to facilitate identification, and neatness in dress should be stressed. Guards must show all employees the same degree of respect they would to the plant manager and his staff. In turn, they should receive equal consideration. Most employees realize guards have a job to do and respect those who are effective in the performance of their duties.

The second most visible security feature is the hardware used to protect the facility. The deterrent value of these features is dependent on the following:

- Proper location. All sensitive and critical areas should be posted as restricted areas and provided with whatever additional security features are necessary to provide adequate protection.
- A program of inspection and maintenance for all physical security features. Such a program will help control costly deterioration and visibly demonstrate the importance management places on security.

Management's insistence that all employees adhere to regulations, rules, and procedures is vital to maintaining employee morale and respect for security goals. Just as important, however, are the security controls employees encounter every day, such as access controls, lock door policies, clean desk policies, vehicle inspections, package inspections, visitor controls, parking controls, clock key rounds, scrap metal controls, trash removal programs, tool crib controls, expendable supply controls, inventory procedures, and internal audits.

Management must not only be responsible for planning, supervising, and directing activities of the awareness program, but these staff members must be willing to become involved in making the program work. Supervisors, officials, and foremen must be trained in their personal responsibilities to the security program. Middle management should be required to enforce regulations and report violations, with no favoritism extended to friends or relatives.

PROGRAM TOOLS

The use of visual aids, such as movies, film strips, or posters, can be useful in putting a security awareness program together. Numerous films concerning security and safety may be obtained from:

> Factory Mutual Engineering Association
> 510 Walnut Street, 11th floor
> Philadelphia, PA 19106
> (215) 922-8080

> Department of the Treasury
> Bureau of Alcohol, Tobacco, and Firearms
> Washington, DC 20226

> Environmental Defense Fund, Inc.
> 1525 18th Street, NW
> Washington, DC 20036

> Ohio Insurance Institute
> PO Box 632
> Columbus, OH 43216

Additional information is available from the National Referral Center in the Library of Congress. This is a free referral service that directs those who have questions concerning any subject to organizations that can provide information. The National Referral Center is located on the fifth floor of the Library of Congress, Thomas Jefferson Building, Second Street and Independence Avenue, SW, Washington, DC. Correspondence should be addressed to:

Library of Congress
Science and Technology Division
National Referral Center
Washington, DC 20540
(202) 287-5670

In larger installations, newsletters or monthly bulletins describing the company's loss prevention program should be distributed to all employees. The subject of the bulletin should be printed in large type and the bulletin signed by the security director. The information should be fresh and topical and features should be changed monthly. Variations in style, such as narrative or checklist, should attract the attention of a large segment of the employees and thus enhance the value of existing security/safety programs.

A good security program should take advantage of all media available to enhance its effectiveness. Keeping employees aware of safety rules for the home as well as the office can help employees realize that management has a deep interest in them personally, as well as in protecting the company's assets.

CONTINUATION OF THE EMPLOYEE AWARENESS TRAINING PROGRAM

The training an employee receives during orientation is critical as it gives him or her a proper attitude about security. However, the continued training of employees is also essential. Once employees have been informed of their responsibilities, it is anticipated they will comply with what is expected of them. However, some employees need to be frequently reminded of their responsibilities, and review of these principles is useful for all employees. Thus, security awareness programs should be ongoing.

All employees, regardless of position within the company, should receive semiannual security briefings. These briefings should re-emphasize security requirements, policies, and individual responsibilities. This is the primary method of educating and training management and other employees in the basics of assets protection.

Another way to keep employees aware of a company's security program is to form an employee council to support the work of the awareness program. Such a security and safety group can provide the security awareness program with continuous support. At least one representative should be designated from each department. If that individual is absent, an alternate should attend meetings in his or her place. This arrangement allows the security department to develop two deputies in each department to interpret and implement procedures and educate staff members. The employee committee thus created can help solve security problems that may arise. If the council learns as much as possible about the protection of the company, it will be able to supplement security efforts at the department level.

Specific goals of the security and safety group and the continuing security awareness program should include:

- Increased communication between security staff and employees.
- Increased understanding and interpretation of security requirements for staff members of all departments.
- The development of departmental strategy and accountability to gain voluntary employee compliance of rules and policies established by the administration.
- The development of centralized support for security measures from all employees.
- A review of existing problems and a search for workable corrective measures.

An agenda should be prepared prior to each meeting of the council or group and distributed to the members.

At the meetings, security supervisors should point out patterns of troublesome incidents that are taking place and the *modus operandi* in each case. This approach can be effective if it receives the full backing of the group. Ideally, any feedback from these discussions should result in the implementation of vigorous action to eliminate lapses in security.

Members of the security and safety council have the following responsibilities in their own departments:

- To conduct meetings with other department members to foster good security habits.
- To inform and interpret the security role for employees to gain their support.
- To act as deputies for the security staff and to encourage supervisors to do the same in their work areas.

MANAGEMENT AWARENESS TEAM

In addition to an employee safety and security council, involve management in the security awareness program. Management support should be active, especially as the awareness program is being developed. A management awareness team can be asked to identify the facility's specific security requirements and problems and to formulate policies and procedures for regulating the security awareness program. This committee should include representatives from every department and all levels of management. The number of representatives should correspond to the size of the facility's work force, but should also be a manageable size.

Each committee member should be assigned a particular responsibility. The committee chairman, preferably a security management official or personnel manager responsible for security, should report directly to the operations manager in matters related to the committee's work. Committee members' assignments should include, but not be limited to, the following:

- providing guidance to those who conduct initial security orientations for new employees.
- overseeing the facility's continuing awareness training program.
- overseeing the facility's security maintenance program.
- overseeing the company's program for monitoring and/or enforcing security regulations, procedures, and policies.
- overseeing the facility's program to ensure that management officials are fulfilling their assigned security responsibilities.

The result of the management committee's work, a written document with specific security instructions, should be incorporated into the facility's formal awareness program.

After their security suggestions have been incorporated into the awareness program, the management committee should continue to conduct meetings on a regular basis. They should also continue to collect information relevant to changing security needs and the effectiveness of the individual elements and activities of the program.

With good organization and the strong support of management, a security awareness program can generate profits by reducing losses, increasing profits, and permitting management to use its time and resources in productive activities.

CHAPTER 24

Checking References: It's Worth the Investment
Marshall M. Meyer, CPP
President
Security Associates, Inc.

Richard Burke, a top aide to Senator Edward Kennedy, claimed to be the victim of a shooting, a break-in, and numerous death threats. Three weeks after he resigned from his post, Burke admitted the whole episode had been a hoax and that he had also falsified information on the employment application and resumé he submitted to the senator. Despite the fact that he had access to highly sensitive information, Burke's credentials were never checked.

Janet Cooke, a *Washington Post* reporter, eventually admitted the story that earned her a Pulitzer Prize was fictitious. Citing newsroom pressures as the reason for her deception, Cooke failed to mention that she had also supplied false information on her job application and resumé. The *Post* never checked Cooke's credentials.

In times of economic stress and high unemployment, personnel managers find that an increased number of job applicants lie about their backgrounds. While dishonesty can occur in good or bad times, the absolute need for employment causes more individuals to feel desperate. To land a job or position of any worth, applicants must make themselves look good.

Some psychologists believe that embellishing credentials, falsifying resumés, exaggerating job experience, and perpetrating hoaxes on potential employers is rampant. Delusions of grandeur and strong incentives—money, promotion, fame, authority—coupled with the anonymity possible in a transient society has led more and more people down the path of pretense.

According to statistics compiled by the Department of Commerce, thirty percent of all business failures result from the dishonest acts of employees. Since the future of any business is molded by its people, each employee must be selected with the same care used to acquire new machinery or plan a new site. An applicant walks in as an unknown quantity in-

Reprinted with permission of the American Society for Industrial Security, from *Security Management*, March 1983, pp. 10.

troduced only by favorable statements. To make a sound employment decision, details of previous employment must be checked out. Patterns of past performance are usually a reliable guide to the kind of future an applicant may be expected to develop with a new employer.

Some companies spend thousands to advertise job openings, hoping to attract the best qualified applicants. But they spend very little, if anything at all, to screen the final candidates. Poor employee selection procedures eventually erode an organization's profits by increasing the cost of hiring, training, and terminating employees. In a very short time, a dishonest employee can cause company losses, disrupt a smooth-running operation, or affect the morale of an entire staff.

The most cost-effective part of the hiring process is preemployment screening. Many vital facts about an applicant can only be developed and verified through investigation. The expense of an error in judgment is much greater than the small cost of learning these important facts.

While cost may be a factor in an employer's decision to limit screening, more frequently employers shy away from this practice because they fear litigation. Extensive litigation in recent years has made organizations cautious about employment practices that might make them vulnerable to charges of discrimination. Consequently, many employers mistakenly believe the traditional methods of screening and selection are not permitted under the law.

The uniform guidelines on employee selection, adopted in 1978 by the Equal Employment Opportunity Commission, the Civil Service Commission, and the Department of Labor, do not prohibit any specific personnel selection procedure, including reference checking, preemployment investigations, and tests. All selection procedures, however, must meet the requirements of all applicable laws.

A number of federal and state laws do affect the way employers gather and use information on prospective employees. Title VII of the Civil Rights Act of 1964 bans all discrimination in employment because of race, color, religion, sex, or national origin (see Exhibit 24–1). This act applies to all employers with fifteen or more employees and covers all terms and conditions of employment. It holds the employer responsible for any discrimination that goes on within an organization, regardless of who does the hiring, interviewing, and final employment decision-making. Title VII is administered and enforced by the Equal Employment Opportunity Commission.

This law directly affects a company's ability to access an applicant's arrest records. A case in point is *Gregory vs. Linton Systems, Inc.* (US District Court for the Central District of California, Docket #68-1744-1H).

Gregory, a black male, prepared an application for employment and was offered a job with Linton Systems, Inc. Subsequent to the offer, he was required to fill out a security questionnaire. Gregory's responses to this form showed he had been arrested on fourteen separate occasions on charges more serious than simple traffic violations. The offer of employment was withdrawn on the basis that it was standard company policy not to hire persons with multiple arrests.

YOU CAN	YOU CANNOT

NAME & ADDRESS

Ask applicants to write their name and address on an application.	Ask an applicant, whose name has been changed, for his or her original name.
Ask applicants if a complaint has been sworn against them, if they were ever indicted for or convicted of a crime and, if so, under what name.	

BIRTHPLACE

	Inquire into the birthplace of an applicant, a spouse, parent, or other close relative if outside the United States.
	Ask applicants to disclose their ancestry or place of national origin.

AGE

Ask an applicant's age, but only if the information is a bona fide occupational qualification, or if the data is necessary to comply with state or federal minimum age laws.	Ask an applicant's age if it is not relevant to the job. Generally, do not ask to see a birth certificate.

RELIGION

As a general rule, an applicant may be told, "This is a six-day-a-week job and employees are required to work Monday through Saturday."	Ask an applicant's religion, or ask for the name of his church, parish, pastor, or the religious holidays observed.

RACE OR COLOR

	Ask about an applicant's color or race or require applicants to submit a photograph with their applications.

CITIZENSHIP

Ask an applicant if he or she is a US citizen or if he or she intends to become one.	Inquire whether an applicant, spouse, or parents are naturalized or nativeborn citizens, or ask for dates when they became citizens.
	Require an applicant to produce naturalization or first papers.

YOU CAN	YOU CANNOT

EDUCATION & EXPERIENCE

Ask an applicant about schooling, both academic and vocational. Inquire into the work experience of the applicant.	

CHARACTER

Inquire into applicant's character.	

Exhibit 24–1. Anti-discrimination rules.

YOU CAN *(cont.)*	YOU CANNOT *(cont.)*

RELATIVES

Ask for names, addresses, and relationships of persons to be notified in case of accident. Inquire into the US location of a relative's place of business.	Inquire about a relative's place of business if it is outside the U.S. Ask where an applicant's spouse, parents or other relatives reside. Ask a male applicant about the maiden name of his wife or mother.

MILITARY EXPERIENCE

Inquire into an applicant's military experience in the US armed forces or state militia. *After hiring,* you can ask to see discharge papers.	Inquire into the applicant's foreign military experience. Require an applicant, before employment, to produce armed forces discharge papers. (They show birthplace, date of birth, etc.)

MEMBERSHIPS

Ask an applicant about membership in organizations, the nature of which does not disclose race, religion, or national origin. Ask if an applicant belongs to an organization advocating the overthrow of the US government.	Ask an applicant to disclose membership in organizations that could indicate religion, race, or national origin.

SEX

Male or female sex may be a question on the application generally only after an official agency has indicated that gender constitutes a bona fide qualification for the job (washroom attendant, model, actor).	

Exhibit 24–1 *(continued)*

Gregory brought suit, charging violation of Title VII of the Civil Rights Act. In rendering its decision, the court first made it clear that the question of race did not enter into the employment decision. It did note the following, however:

- Multiple arrests with no convictions are not, by themselves, an indication of job performance. Previous arrests do not indicate that a worker would be less honest or less efficient than any other employee.
- Historically, more blacks than whites have been subjected to arrest. Therefore, using multiple arrests alone as the grounds for rejection of employment discriminates against blacks. Such discrimination cannot be justified or excused by any business requirement.

The employer was restrained from obtaining information about prior arrests listed on the application form that had not resulted in convictions. The court was of the opinion that such information would be used in an illegal and discriminatory way.

The final enjoinder by the court is confusing. It states, in effect, that the employer could seek arrest information from public records, but it does not clarify how this information could be used.

Other well-publicized laws forbid job discrimination based on age, union affiliation, or physical disability. In the near future, military records may be considered irrelevant. Pressures are being exerted on the Department of Defense to refuse to disclose why an individual left the military.

In addition, courts have consistently found that a poor reputation within the community, marital status, financial difficulties, homosexuality, childcare problems, contraceptive practices, height and weight, or bad parenting cannot be used as a reason for withholding employment offers, unless the employer can prove a definite relationship between the trait in question and job performance. Other information is discriminatory in certain instances. Establishing the educational level achieved by an applicant establishes qualifications. However, the Supreme Court has stated that a high school education as a condition of employment is discriminatory and illegal when this requirement disqualifies minorities at a substantially higher rate than others, and when no evidence shows that a high school education is needed to perform the job.

In the same vein, English language requirements cannot be used to bar the employment of people not fluent in English if the language is not an important job requirement. Other questions that could be considered discriminatory include physical requirements, experience requirements, availability for weekend work, friends or relatives working for the company, and appearance. These questions can be asked, however, when the employer can show that the information is job related.

The Fair Credit Reporting Act (FCRA) sets guidelines and regulates the activities of organizations (consumer reporting agencies) that compile background reports on individuals and then submit these reports to a client. The intent of the law is to ensure that the information collected is timely, accurate, and given only to those persons who need further details to make credit or employment decisions (see Exhibit 24–2).

When it was first made law in 1970, FCRA caused most companies then using consumer reporting agencies to discontinue this practice. In some cases, companies stopped using all types of screening even though screening, per se, was still legal and acceptable. To clarify, employers using consumer reporting agencies can screen employees, investigate potential applicants, and obtain records and make inquiries concerning applicants for employment—as long as certain guidelines are followed (see Exhibit 24–3). These guidelines include notifying applicants in advance that they will be investigated, notifying applicants if they do not receive the job because of derogatory information disclosed in the investigation, and giving applicants an

Action by Applicant or Employee	Action by Employer	Fair Credit Reporting Act Requirement
1. Applies for (a) employment, (b) retention, (c) promotion, or (d) reassignment.	1. Conducts background investigation with own staff.	1. None
2. Same as 1.	2. Orders a consumer report.	2. None
3. Same as 1.	3. Orders an investigative consumer report.	3. Employer must: (a) inform the applicant, in writing, not later than three days after requesting the report, that a report has been or may be requested, and (b) that applicant has the right to request information on the scope and nature of the report.
4. Applicant, in writing, requests information as to scope and nature of an investigative consumer report requested on him.	4. None	4. Employer must: provide the requested information, in writing, within one to five days after the request, or two to five days after the report is ordered.
5. None	5. Conducts background investigation with own staff.	5. None
6. None	6. Orders consumer report.	6. None
7. None	7. Orders investigative consumer report.	7. None
8. Same as 1.	8. Rejects application because of information from own investigators.	8. None
9. Same as 1.	9. Rejects application because of information contained in either a consumer report or an investigative consumer report.	9. Employer must: (a) Inform applicant of fact that rejection was based on information contained in such a report, and (b) provide the name and address of the Consumer Reporting Agency involved.

Exhibit 24–2. Summary of Fair Credit Reporting Act requirements. Reprinted with permission. Copyright © 1974 by the Merritt Company.

10. None	10. Takes adverse action on an employee's employment relying on information contained in a consumer report or an investigative consumer report.	10. Employer must: give same information as under 9. (NOTE: This requirement is not clear from the language of the act—15 USC 1681m (a)—but is the interpretation of the Federal Trade Commission.)

Exhibit 24–2 *(continued)*

opportunity to review the information that eliminated them from consideration. The employer must also tell the applicant the name of the agency to contact for further information.

The consumer reporting agency must be concerned, of course, with the accuracy of the information reported to the client. If the applicant claims the information is not true, the agency is obligated by law to recheck the validity of the data. The agency does not need to divulge the source of the information, only its contents.

In addition, the standards set by FCRA limit the types of records that can be presented and the kind of information that can be retained on file. Certain exceptions to the act should also be noted:

- If the individual being considered for employment earns over $20,000 annually, the Fair Credit Reporting Act does not apply. Other standards and Title VII do apply.
- Employers who check their own personnel are not considered consumer reporting agencies. Therefore, any employment checking done by the company itself need not follow the standards set by FCRA. All other EEO standards do apply, however.

Individual states have also set guidelines for preemployment screening practices. In 1977, the Department of Justice authorized the fifty states to prepare legal statutes or executive orders affecting an employer's right to access criminal records of employees or potential employees. A number of states complied, and 1979 several states passed laws that permitted certain classes of employers to obtain certain types of information (see Exhibit 24–4). In general, the statutes fall into one of the following categories:

- *Access to both convictions and arrests:* an employer who is authorized by state law or executive order may, upon request, obtain both the arrest and conviction records of an applicant or employee.
- *Access to convictions only:* limits the information available to employers to convictions only, and this information is released only on certain conditions. Almost all states require the employer to have a good reason for needing either conviction or arrest records or both.

PRE-NOTIFICATION

Example 1: Statement on Application Form

"Your application for employment with [name of company] will be expedited. However, as part of our normal employment processing, a routine inquiry may be made on the facts stated in your application. This inquiry normally concerns an applicant's character, general reputation, personal characteristics, mode of living, and other factors that will aid in our evaluation. Further information on the nature and scope of such inquiry, if one is made, is available upon written request."

Example 2: Statement on Application Form

"Thank you for considering a career with [name of company]. In order to provide our employees with opportunities for advancement, a routine inquiry is generally made concerning character, general reputation, personal characteristics, and factors considered to be of importance to your future growth with us. Public Law 91-508 requires that we advise you that such routine inquiries may be made. Upon written request, information on the nature and scope of the inquiry, if one is made, will be provided."

Example 3: Statement acknowledging receipt of resumés, employment summaries, applications, or other employment data sent by mail

"Thank you for your recent application for employment with [name of company]. Public Law 91-508 requires that we advise you that a routine inquiry may be made to provide applicable information concerning character, education, personal characteristics, and mode of living, as well as other data that will be used to evaluate your [application, request, etc.]. Should an inquiry be made, additional information on the scope and nature of the findings will be provided, upon written request."

Example 4: Statement to be used when application is retained for future consideration

"Your application for employment with [name of company] will be referred to our personnel director for review, and considered in the future. As part of our normal procedure for processing any new applicants for employment, a routine inquiry may be made of the facts stated in your application. This inquiry normally concerns information relating to an applicant's character, general reputation, personal characteristics, mode of living, and certain other factors that will aid in evaluating your potential as an employee. If you are employed, we may inquire about certain facts outlined in your application. If such an inquiry is made, now or at some future date should you become employed with us, the results of such inquiry are available to you upon written request."

Example 5: Statement with option for refusal

"Because of the nature of our employment practices, all applicants for employment with [name of company] are required to permit a routine inquiry on the facts and information provided in their applications [or summaries, resumés, etc.]. This inquiry will normally pertain to an applicant's general reputation, personal characteristics, mode of living, and such other factors useful in our evaluation. Should you become employed with our firm, we may, depending on certain business practices, consider an inquiry of this type at a future date during your employment with our company. In any instance when an inquiry is made, now or in the future, the scope and nature of such inquiry will be made available to you upon written request. Should you feel that you do not wish such an inquiry to be made (even though it is required by our employment practices and we are required under Public Law 91-508 to provide you with details of such inquiry on your request,) you may decline to have such inquiry made by advising your

Exhibit 24-3. Sample formats for pre-notification and post-notification required by the Fair Credit Reporting Act.

interviewer. However, if you decline to have such inquiry made, we cannot guarantee that your application for employment will be given appropriate consideration."

Example 6: Statement notifying a current employee of investigation

"As a routine part of our employment practices, your file will be reviewed and certain routine inquiries may be made. This inquiry normally concerns information on an individual's character, general reputation, personal characteristics, mode of living, and other factors which will aid in our review. If such an inquiry is made, further information on the nature and scope of such inquiry will be made available to you upon written request. (If a prior inquiry was made under the provisions of the FCRA, indicate that this review updates previous inquiries. If no prior inquiry was made under ths Act, include a comment such as: PL 91-508 requires employers to notify applicants or employees of inquiries made in connection with their employment or promotion. We are making such inquiries of selected employees. The inquiry normally will consist of . . . and other factors that will aid in our review.)"

Example 7: Statement replying to an employee request for advancement

"Your request for [upgrading, promotion] has been received. This request will be given due consideration. However, as part of our normal employment procedures, a routine inquiry may be made on the facts stated on your application. This inquiry normally concerns information on an employee's character, general reputation, personal characteristics, mode of living, and other factors that will aid in our review. Upon written request, assuming an inquiry is made, the results will be made available to you in accordance with Public Law 91-508."

POST-NOTIFICATION

Example 8: Letter response to an applicant's request for additional information

"This letter is in response to your request for information concerning an inquiry or report made in connection with your application for employment with [name of company].

_____No report was requested in connection with your application.

_____The report was requested. These reports are routine procedures which include such general identification information as residence verification, marital status, and/or other data considered of importance to the evaluation of your (application—   ).

_____Upon receipt of this form signed by you, appropriate arrangements will be made for you to review the report. Public Law 91-508 requires that requests for the review of such report be made in writing. Verbal requests cannot be honored.

Please complete the enclosed form and return it to this office within five days. (You may wish to enclose a self-addressed envelope.) At that time, your request for examination of the report will be honored."

Very truly yours,

_____
Signature

Example 9: Release to be mailed with Example 8

"I, the undersigned, having applied for employment with [name of company] on [date] hereby request that I be permitted to review the report made on me, on the date and time specified below. I understand that failure to appear for this appointment to resolve any dispute that may be contained in the report may preclude my right to examine this file. I understand that the reporting agency may make a reasonable charge for reviewing its files, and such charge is [name price], payable in advance. A review of a file may be made only during regular working hours [state times]. If I so desire, after proper identification and pre-payment of the examining fee, I may be apprised by summary of the file contents by tele-

Exhibit 24–3 *(continued)*

phone. This alternative, however, can only be arranged when the reporting agency is fully satisfied that the information is being transmitted to the proper party. I further understand that upon completion of my review of the report, I may discuss any discrepancies that may then be re-verified or if they can not be re-verified, stricken from the report. If the information contained in the report is disputable, I may submit a statement to the reporting agency, who will notify all subsequent users of reports concerning me and enclose a copy of this statement."

Applicant's Request for Time and Date for Review of File
"I wish to examine the report on [day], [date] 19____, at [time], am/pm. I am authorized to bring one other person with me at the time I have requested above, and I will bring [full name], [address], [relationship]. I may be reached by telephone at _____ to confirm the appointment.
Requestor's name (PLEASE PRINT) _____
Requestor's signature _____
Requestor's home address _____ _____
Requestor's date of birth (for confirmation) _____
Note to Requestor: Please return this form in the enclosed self-addressed envelope within five days, giving us at least five full working days to arrange your appointment time."

Example 10: Statement notifying an applicant he or she has been denied employment although investigation was favorable
"Thank you for your inquiry about your application for employment received by [letter, phone] on [date]. Although a report was obtained that complied with the provisions of Public Law 91-508, the contents of the report in no way affected our employment decision. (You may wish to elaborate on your reasons for the denial of employment to the applicant.) Since our decision was not based on the investigative report, there is no obligation to reveal the contents of the report. (You may also desire to elaborate on future possible consideration of the applicant.)"

Example 11: Statement notifying an applicant that he or she has been denied employment because of false or missing facts
"We are sorry to inform you that based on certain inquiries made in accordance with our statement to you [on your application, by letter], we cannot consider you for employment. Certain facts stated by you were found to be inaccurate based on the findings of our investigative service. Should you desire to review the report, please let us know within five days and appropriate arrangements will be made."

Example 12: Statement notifying an applicant that his or her application will be considered in the future
"Your application for a position in our firm has been reviewed. We find, however, that at this time your qualifications and experience are not required. We appreciate the time you took to apply for a position with [name of company] and we assure you we will keep you in mind should a suitable position become available. (The decision to not employ the individual has been based on other than the investigative consumer report, either wholly or partially, and no other comment pertaining to compliance with FCRA is required.)"

Example 13: An alternative to Example 12
"During a routine inquiry, which you were advised might be made at the time you applied for employment with our firm, it was found that certain statements made in your application [could not be verified, were found to be inaccurate, were not as you stated]. Based on these findings, we must advise you that at this time you cannot be considered for employment. (Should the applicant, upon receiving this information, request a review of the file or report, the form letter in Examples 8 and 9 should be sent to him or her.)"

Exhibit 24–3 *(continued)*

SPECIAL CONSIDERATIONS:
A. Under Sections 605 and 613, public record information for employment purposes, when it has been updated, need not be reported to the applicant even
though the applicant is denied the position based on the report.
B. Whenever employment is denied, either wholly or in part, because of the
information contained in a consumer report, the applicant is entitled, if he so
requests in writing, to have this information. However, the source of such
information need not be given to him. Sources of consumer data, including
prior employers, are to be protected from disclosure.

Exhibit 24–3 *(continued)*

Access to Both Convictions and Arrest	Access To Convictions Only	Access Upon Review	Access Flatly Banned	No Laws On Access
Florida	Colorado	Alabama	Alaska	Idaho
Illinois	Connnecticut	Arizona	Arkansas	Indiana
Kentucky	Georgia	Hawaii	California	Michigan
Minnesota	Maine	Kansas	Delaware	Mississippi
Montana	New Mexico	Louisiana	Dist. Col.	Missouri
Nebraska	Tennessee	Maryland	Iowa	New Jersey
Nevada	Washington	Massachu-	New York	North Dakota
Pennsylvania		setts	North	Ohio
Virgin Islands		New Hamp-	Carolina	Oklahoma
West Virginia		shire	Oregon	Puerto Rico
		South	Rhode	Texas
		Carolina	Island	Vermont
		South	Virginia	Wisconsin
		Dakota	Wyoming	
		Utah		

Exhibit 24–4.   A summary of state laws on access to criminal records.
(As of March 1983).

• *Access upon review:* while basically similar to the previous condition,
added criteria must be met by the employer before conviction records
are released. Generally, arrest records are withheld. In Maryland, for
example, an employer may petition the Secretary for Public Safety and
Correction asking for approval to obtain criminal conviction data on a
prospective or current employee. To receive this information, either
the public welfare or the business itself must be adversely affected if
the information is not released.
• *Access flatly banned:* these states refuse to allow any employer to obtain
criminal history information, either arrest or conviction records.
• *No laws on access:* these states may or may not allow access depending
on who is making the request, the reason for the request, and any other
factors deemed appropriate by law enforcement officials. Although
these states do not have laws on access, the chance that an employer
will receive information is greater in these states than in states where
access is controlled by statute.

Most police agencies have always been free to release arrest or conviction records to private employers if they so choose. The danger is that

the information may be incorrect, and the department that released the records may be open to legal suits.

The value of background information has been reduced further by employers who fear litigation if they provide details about a dishonest or incompetent employee. As suppliers of information, according to the law, employers must not deliberately or maliciously give false information about a former employee.

To summarize, employers can seek information about applicants, interpret and use the information for employment selection, and share the results of reference checks with another employer. The purpose of the legal restraint is not to eliminate reference checking, but to make sure the criteria used in employment decision-making are pertinent and do not discriminate. The following measures can ensure compliance:

- Be consistent and apply standards of employment uniformly.
- Make sure the information used in employment decision-making is job related. Avoid unnecessary requirements such as excessive physical or educational prerequisites.
- Document in writing all hiring decisions to show the choice was made on relevant information.
- Obey the Fair Credit Reporting Act when using outside investigative agencies. If an applicant is not hired because of information contained in preemployment reports, notify the applicant of this fact. The reporting agency should then disclose the contents of its report to the applicant.
- Use public records, such as court cases, litigation proceedings, bankruptcy hearings, and workers' compensation records. However, all these records must be obtained and used properly.

When fair practices are used, reference checking is not an infringement of privacy. It is, instead, a sound tool for evaluating individuals that can provide greater objectivity for employers and greater fairness for job applicants.

In recent years, employers have left themselves open to another form of liability by refusing to investigate a potential employee's background. The legal principles of "vicarious responsibility" or "respondent superior" place the responsibility for what employees do or fail to do on the employer. If an individual with a history of violence injures another while on the job, the employer will probably become involved in litigation. Courts have held that employers cannot dismiss their responsibilities by claiming they did not know of the employee's violent propensities.

When considering reference checking, then, employers must find a middle ground between what EEO guidelines will allow and what the courts consider reasonable employment screening practices. Companies that have restricted their investigations of prospective employees may be placing their organizations in jeopardy. Adequate screening of employees is not based on some absolute standard. It should, however, be in keeping with the responsibilities of the job being filled. Some jobs expose both fellow employees and the public to greater risk if the employee later proves unreliable, and it is these types of jobs that require a more detailed check of a candidate's personal and work history.

Because of the many ramifications of the hiring process, a clearly written company policy on employment procedures is invaluable, especially in companies with many facilities where a local manager or supervisor hires and often fires employees. Unfortunately, in most companies, the security manager is left out of the hiring process. The security aspects of hiring become the function of the personnel department, and the security professional is called on only to provide occasional suggestions.

As a result, all persons responsible for hiring must understand that they cannot just arbitrarily hire someone without also accepting responsibility for the conduct of that employee. Every manager and supervisor must understand the company's employment policies and the law so they can check references adequately and protect against litigation.

In most cases, reference checking is accomplished by phone or by letter. The following suggestions can help ensure that the results of either method provide useful information gathered within the limits of the law.

CALLING A REFERENCE

The most expeditious way to verify an applicant's employment history is by calling references. If certain techniques are followed, the process is relatively easy. Exceptions occur when the reference is hard of hearing, has a language problem, is antagonistic, does not particularly like the applicant, or is busy at the time of the call. The interviewer should be aware of any problems that might arise and be prepared to offer alternatives.

How the interviewer opens the conversation may determine whether the reception will be friendly or antagonistic. Always state why the call is being made, and ask "Is it convenient for you to talk at this time?" If the answer is a flat no, suggest or ask for a time when it is convenient for the reference to talk.

Emphasize that the applicant (use his or her full name) has given this person as a reference, and the interview should be conducted as soon as possible. Infer, but do not threaten, that the applicant's job may be at stake unless the interview is completed in a timely way. Never get nasty, overbearing, authoritative, threatening, or demanding.

Throw-off references (individuals not named by the applicant) are usually the best sources because they are likely to provide more factual information. Never tell a throw-off reference that he or she has been given as a reference. Simply state "(name the applicant) has applied for a position of trust and confidence with (name the company). We understand you know him or her and probably can provide information that would be helpful in evaluating that candidate." Never lie about the reason for the call.

Depending on the responses from the reference, proceed with the questioning. Never interrupt even to clarify an answer. Regardless of what the reference says, allow him or her to speak without interruption. Always be calm and receptive regardless of the nature of the response.

Make one or two word notes of items that need elaboration. Return to these points only after the questioning is finished. Keep in mind that the compliments given by a reference are just as important as any adverse information. They can offset data provided by a prejudiced individual and give a more fair evaluation of the applicant's capabilities.

In most cases, people need to be encouraged to respond. To get a full answer to a question, ask it more than once and in several ways. Always make the questions simple, direct, and to the point.

Never allow the reference to end the conversation before getting all the relevant information. Remember, however, that one reference may not know everything about an applicant. Therefore, ask for names of additional throw-off references who can provide missing information or who can document adverse statements.

Always thank the reference for their cooperation, even when he or she has been less than helpful or candid. Never be facetious or nasty.

Keep handwritten notes in the investigative file, even after preparing a final report of the interview. If information supplied seems to be malicious or without foundation, indicate this perception in the report. Never accept such information at face value. It must be confirmed to be of any use.

WRITTEN REFERENCES

A specially designed form should be used when an applicant's references are checked by written request (see Exhibit 24–5). Normally, at least two of three references supplied by the applicant should be contacted. The reference form should accompany a cover letter rquesting the cooperation of the reference (see Exhibit 24–6). Always include a company self-addressed, stamped envelope with the request.

Keep a record of all correspondence on the applicant in a log. The log should contain at least the date letters were sent, the address of the recipient, the name of the applicant and a control number (CN 101-1 in Exhibit 24–5). This control number should appear on all forms sent out for this applicant, so if information comes back unsigned, the reference can still be identified.

When the forms are returned, the information should be reviewed for accuracy. Any discrepancies with data supplied by the applicant or any derogatory statements should be brought immediately to the attention of the person responsible for the hiring decision.

You have been given as a reference by the person listed below who has applied for a position of trust and confidence with this firm. Your cooperation in completing the form so that we may evaluate the applicant would be sincerely appreciated and will be held in strictest confidence.

June 10, 1982: _____

_____

APPLICANT'S NAME

_____

ADDRESS
1. Length of time you have known applicant _____(Years)
   _____(Friend)_____(Relative) Other:_____
2. Marital Status _____Number of Children_____Is Spouse Employed?
   _____If yes, where?_____
   _____

3. How long has applicant resided at this address? _____(Years)_____ (Months)
4. Is applicant in good health? _____
5. How would you describe their personality?—Pleasant (   ) Amiable (   )
   Outgoing (   ) Friendly (   ) Other _____
   Member of any clubs or organizations? _____
   Reputation in the neighborhood? _____
   To your knowledge, has applicant ever been in trouble? _____
   Last place of employment _____
   Would you recommend for a position of trust and confidence? _____
   Please elaborate on reverse providing additional information.

May we thank you in advance for your important assistance.

PLEASE REPLY TO:
The Steel Company
11918 Blank Street   _____
Baltimore, MD 21207   REPLIER'S SIGNATURE

PER: P. H. Brown, Manager   _____
     (301) 427-7105   DATE

A self-addressed, stamped envelope is enclosed.

Exhibit 24–5.   You have been given as a reference.

                                        Date:
Dear Reference,
  You have been given as a reference by _____
  The importance of responding to this inquiry cannot be emphasized strongly enough.
  It is our company policy to protect our customers as well as our employees, and all information you provide will be treated in full confidence and seen only by our employment supervisors.
  May we thank you in advance for your cooperation in this important request.

                                        Sincerely yours,

Exhibit 24–6.   Cover letter asking for a written reference.

If the reference supplies incomplete or inaccurate information, the applicant should be asked to clarify his or her statements. The applicant may need to supply additional references, who should also be interviewed. Serious discrepancies that cannot be clarified may warrant termination or other management action. The applicant should also be contacted again should a reference fail to respond within a suitable length of time, normally fifteen days.

Because more detailed information can be gathered by phone, at least one reference given by the applicant should be contacted this way. The same form that is mailed to other references can be used as a checklist during this interview. Ask for the names of additional people who might know the applicant. Few references supplied by the applicant will offer negative information. However, certain statements, when considered in light of other available data, may indicate some gaps in the information supplied on an application.

EDUCATIONAL RECORDS

The "Family Educational Rights and Privacy Act of 1974" prohibits anyone other than the applicant from receiving educational information. Therefore, a signed waiver form must be completed by the applicant before an employer can have access to this data (see Exhibit 24–7).

Usually only the last school attended by the applicant for one full year is verified. If no school was attended for a full year, check the two attended most recently. Verify all the information supplied by the applicant—social security number, date and place of birth, full name when attending the school—and make sure the applicant signs and dates the form.

Use the same procedures for contacting other references by mail. If no word is received fifteen days after the original request was mailed, a second inquiry should be sent. If the school still fails to respond, contact the applicant and suggest he or she call the school to advise the registrar that the information is needed as a condition of employment. If action to clarify false information is not taken within thirty to sixty days, it may not be used by the employer to terminate or discharge the employee.

Rather than invest the time and training needed for adequate in-house reference checking, some firms turn to outside agencies to investigate applicants or employees being considered for promotion. In these cases, the constraints on "consumer reporting agencies" outlined earlier do apply. However, no law precludes an outside service from reporting information uncovered during its investigation even if that information is outside the framework of the questions that can be asked by an interviewer or on an application form.

Other forms of background checks, such as the polygraph and paper and pencil testing, have been used effectively by some companies. The Equal

TO: (1)   Brook Senior High   1969-73

                EDUCATIONAL INSTITUTION   YEARS ATTENDED

    (2)   Community College of Ohio   1973-74

                EDUCATIONAL INSTITUTION   YEARS ATTENDED

In accordance with the "Family Educational Rights and Privacy Act of 1974", I, the undersigned, hereby authorize the individual or firm that shall present the original or a photocopy of this release in person or by mail, to receive any and all information relating to my attendance as a student at the above-named educational facility.

Information may be released in written or verbal form to the requestor, and should include at least the following: my academic standing; my major subjects of study; my attendance record; any extracurricular activities in which I was involved; any record of disciplinary problems during the course of my attendance; my years of attendance; and other information of assistance in evaluating me for a position of trust and confidence.

I hereby now and forever hold harmless and preclude any legal action against any person, firm, corporation, public or private institution that may have custody of my educational records released on this authorization.

(The following is to be filled out by applicant)

401-09-4182	John Robert Smith
SOCIAL SECURITY NUMBER	FULL NAME (PRINTED)
June 24, 1955	1241 E. Barton St., Baltimore, MD 21207
DATE OF BIRTH	ADDRESS
Dearborn, Ohio	John Robert Smith
PLACE OF BIRTH	SIGNATURE
John Robert Smith	June 10, 1982
FULL NAME WHILE IN ATTENDANCE	DATE SIGNED

(If Female & Married—Give Maiden Name)

PLEASE REPLY TO: The Steel Company, 11918 Blank St., Balto., MD 21207
                Per: P. H. Brown, Manager   (301) 427-7105

IDENTITY OF BEARER OR REQUESTING FIRM
(THIS FORM MAY BE REPRODUCED)

Exhibit 24–7. Authorization for release of educational records.

Employment Opportunity Commission, the EEO enforcement agencies, and a number of state agencies that oversee fair employment practices have issued guidelines designed to ensure that all applicants taking such tests are treated equally. The federal enforcement agencies do not, however, recognize any one certification of validity.

Today, background checks of potential employees have become increasingly important as a regular part of any security program. Protecting company assets by ferreting out dishonest individuals before they become employees should be an important part of personnel activities.

No company would purchase new machinery without researching the performance of that model. Reference checking should be viewed in the same way. By following the guidelines outlined here, reference checks can be done—and done effectively.

CHAPTER 25

Exit Interviews as a Loss Prevention Technique

G. A. Lapides*
Western Regional Security Manager
McKesson & Robbins Inc.

The generally accepted theory of exit interviews is that employees about to leave a company might be able to help the company identify problems contributing to employee turnover. An employee's experiences and reasons for leaving could suggest needed changes or courses of action that would improve morale, better the working conditions, and/or increase efficiency. Departing employees are more likely to speak openly about their job and their likes and dislikes about the employer than are continuing employees. From this information, improvements can be made.

Over the years, exit interviews have been divided into two categories: those conducted with employees who are leaving voluntarily, and those conducted with employees who are terminated. This latter category is further divided into two groups: persons terminated because of dishonesty or violations of company rules, and persons terminated because they are incompetent or unsuited to the job. Exit interviews with employees leaving voluntarily are easier to conduct and more fruitful. However, to obtain more complete data, an exit interview program should include all employees leaving the company.

While the exit interview originated as a responsibility of the personnel department, it can be used by anyone within the company. Nevertheless, it is usually better to have a member of management other than the employee's direct supervisor perform the exit interview. Most employees tend to be less candid with their direct supervisors because they are concerned that what they say may have an effect on their employment references. Also, an interview conducted by someone they don't know can make the process more objective.

The benefits obtained from exit interviews vary according to the skill

---

*G. A. Lapides is presently Director of Security at Microdata Corporation.
Reprinted with permission of the American Society for Industrial Security, from *Security Management*, May 1979, pp. 36.

of the interviewer and content of the interview. Questions can be tailored to meet the needs of special deparments or to gain specific information. Most companies using an exit interview in a structured manner do obtain some useful information. Whether or not the results are used is another matter.

Basically exit interviewing as it is used today is a tool for identifying those factors relating to employee turnover, morale and efficiency. In my opinion, exit interviews can and should be used as a loss prevention technique. If certain questions are added concerning security procedures and dishonest or illegal activities, the exit interview could be expanded into a useful information gathering tool for the identification of loss vulnerabilities.

If companies are concerned about loss prevention, then they appear to be overlooking what could be an effective source of information about loss. In companies already conducting exit interviews, testing the usefulness of exit interviews for security can be done by simply expanding the current questions to include security questions. Those companies with on-site security or personnel departments can conduct effective face-to-face exit interviews with little additional cost.

Businesses without one or both of these departments have a more difficult problem, but alternatives are possible. One is to develop a list of questions and/or topics for discussion and supply this list to the management representative assigned to perform exit interviews at a particular site. A second alternative is to devise a post employment questionnaire on security and mail the questionnaire to all previous employees. Based on the results of other mail questionnaire studies though, the number of replies would be disappointing. The lack of an opportunity to follow-up and probe the responses would also limit the amount of reliable data that could be gathered.

Recently, thirty-seven security administrators employed by manufacturing and distribution firms in Illinois were surveyed by the author. Confidential questionnaires sent to these managers asked if their companies used exit interviews and if the interviews were used as a security tool. They were asked to suggest questions and procedures that could be used during a session of this type and to comment on the possible benefits to the security department.

The results showed that *not one* of the companies responding used exit interviews as a security tool. All respondents agreed, however, that security exit interviews could be of benefit to their companies. Less than half of the managers responding reported that their personnel or employee relations department did use exit interviews, but only one company said that questions related to security were asked during those conferences.

All the security administrators surveyed suggested that the most reliable method of conducting security exit interviews would be private and confidential face-to-face interviews. The opinion was almost evenly split, however, regarding who should conduct the interview, with nearly half favoring security personnel. The other half expressed concern about the impact of such a practice on working relationships with their personnel departments. These managers indicated that the security department should provide the questions or topics but should allow the personnel department to conduct the interview. Almost all respondents in this survey felt that all terminating employees should be interviewed to insure the usefulness and accuracy of the data.

Finally, all agreed that the manner in which the interview was conducted and the questions asked were more important than the person assigned to perform the task.

Generally, the results of the survey indicated that certain prerequisites are necessary for the conducting of an adequate security exit interview.

- The interview should be conducted on a face-to-face basis.
- The interview should be conducted on the last day of employment.
- Adequate interview preparation by the questioner, including a review of the employee's personnel file and discussion with the subject's immediate supervisor, is necessary.
- The interview should be conducted in private in an impersonal and objective manner.
- The employee being interviewed should be assured of the confidentiality of information.
- The interview should be structured and standardized so that generally all employees are asked the same questions.
- The interview should have previously defined objectives and subjects for discussion.
- Procedures must be established for the analysis, interpretation and feedback of the information to the appropriate manager. Specific applications of the findings should be discussed.

The responding managers suggested the following questions as appropriate for the security exit interview.

- Are there any problems you know of that security should be aware of?
- Do you have any comments about our security program, or ideas of ways it could be improved?
- Have you ever observed anyone taking merchandise?
- Do you have any information concerning thefts, theft-rings, or dishonest employees?
- What is your opinion of the security program here?
- Do employees respect the security program?
- If you had to find a way to steal anything, how do you think it could be done?

In security exit interviews, as in any type of interview, answers received and comments made can be influenced by a person's attitudes, prejudices, and personality. Answers from employees are also influenced by the reason they are leaving and may not always be the truth. Interpretation and evaluation, along with standard interview techniques, are the major keys to the proper use of the information obtained. Questioners are, in reality, performing one kind of attitude survey and are looking for patterns of information.

After a number of interviews are performed and the information is analyzed, specific problems may come to light, or a direction to proceed to reduce losses may be evident. If conducted properly and if gathered the data is analyzed, interpreted properly and used, security exit interviews can be one of the better and least expensive loss prevention tools.

PART V

Outside Resources

Sometimes the expertise or the manpower for a security assignment is not available on staff. In that event, assistance from outside the organization may be sought. Using outside help effectively requires a judicious approach. Consultants of every description can be found, but their qualifications and methods of operation vary considerably. Selection of the right consultant is obviously important, as is establishment of a clear working relationship.

Just as the choice of security consultants must be made with care, so should the selection of contract guard services be handled circumspectly. Whether to use contract guards instead of proprietary officers is a question that should be evaluated in light of the specifics of a given site and organization. Pros and cons are associated with either alternative. If the choice is to contract the services, setting the bid specifications, evaluating the bidders and their bids, and arranging fulfillment of the contract will be more successful if approached from an informed standpoint. As with the security program, contracted services should be reviewed regularly. Changes in the facility, the circumstances for which the service was hired, or other factors may alter the requirements or may eliminate the need to use outside assistance at all.

CHAPTER 26

How to Choose and Use Consultants
Mary Alice Kmet
ASIS Staff Writer

"A consultant is nothing more than an unemployed executive with a brief-case."

This jaundiced view of the consulting profession is one rationale used by some managers who hesitate to employ consultants. A few still feel that calling in a consultant reflects badly on their own management abilities. Others view with skepticism the lack of standards in the field which allows almost anyone to hang out a consulting shingle.

The Association of Consulting Management Engineers offers a more enlightened definition of consulting services:

". . . an organized effort by specially trained and experienced persons to help management solve problems and improve operations through the application of objective judgement based on specialized knowledge and skill, and the systematic analysis of facts."

This definition, while more specific, still leaves room for a variety of interpretations. In his book *The Management Consultant,* Alfred Hunt says: "To a large extent, consulting reflects the thinking, personality and style of the practitioner. It's practice is largely unstructured."

Undoubtedly, the open-ended nature of consulting is an important attraction for many who choose this profession. However, it also places a responsibility on the manager who must select, direct and evaluate consulting services. While efforts at certification and licensing are being made by professional consulting associations and state legislatures, finding the right consultant for a specific job is still largely a matter of trial and error. The experiences of three security professionals who regularly employ consultants show that successful security consultant/client relationships can be established despite the many variables.

"I call in a consultant on anything that requires a special expertise we

Reprinted with permission of the American Society for Industrial Security, from *Security Management,* September 1980, pp. 150.

don't have on staff and can't acquire rapidly," says Don W. Walker, Corporate Director of Security, GENESCO Inc. He uses consultants for their technical know-how in developing bid specifications, and "when I want to get an objective opinion of something that I have been close to." He feels this outsider's view based on a broad knowledge of other industries helps management assess the value of an internal program.

James N. Atkinson, Director of Corporate Security, Johnson and Johnson, uses consultants "when I don't have time to do it myself." He calls in outside experts to perform physical security surveys, to provide executive protection, and to develop technical specifications for security systems. "Consultants permit a small corporate staff to do a professional job," he says.

Richard H. Krueger*, Manager-Corporate Security, Digital Equipment Corporation, agrees with this evaluation. "I use consultants to augment my own staff," he says, "to fill in the peaks." He staffs "for the valleys" and adds specialists when the need arises. In addition to these special instances which arise on short notice, Krueger sets aside reserves for consulting services he knows he will need in the future. Once again, these services often involve security installation projects.

For all three men, judgement plays a large part in the selection of a particular consultant. "I have twenty-eight years of experience in the field, and I know many consultants personally," says Atkinson. "If I'm not sure who to use, I'll try several, evaluate their performance, and then select one to use consistently."

Walker also bases his decision on his knowledge of people in the field. "I rely on their reputation and my past experience with them," he says. "If something new comes up, I go back to the people I have used and ask them to suggest someone."

Krueger is the only one of the three who routinely keeps some consultants on retainer. "When the timeliness of wanting them around is a factor," he'll arrange to have the consultant available on short notice. But, he admits, the theory that the company will spend less because the consultant is on retainer has not panned out. "It's more for convenience than for cost savings," he adds.

Digital Equipment has devised a "standard consultant agreement" because the company as a whole uses many consultants. Krueger augments this basic agreement with specifics applicable to each security assignment. Both Walker and Atkinson negotiate contracts on a case by case basis. Because he often uses consultants in emergencies, Atkinson makes some agreements verbally. He feels comfortable with this arrangement because of the level of trust and confidence he has established with the consultants he uses regularly. "I don't view contracts as vital documents," he says. "In an emergency, we don't have time for formality."

All three also employ a variety of options in the statement of fees.

---

*Richard H. Krueger is presently Director of Security at SMR Corporation.

Walker usually agrees to a daily rate plus expenses. Atkinson frequently sets an upper limit—"not to exceed x number of dollars," he explains. In other cases, Atkinson is able to predict a more exact fee. "If I'm sending someone to Italy to do a physical security survey, I can figure it will take five days to do it, and five days to write the report. I can get the airfare from here to Italy, multiply the consulting fee by the number of days and compute the charge."

In the majority of cases, Krueger finds that a flat fee is stated and then broken down by how much time each consultant will spend on the job. For example, if three consultants are working on a project, consultant A may be worth $50 an hour, consultant B worth $60, and consultant C worth $70. The fee would be stated in terms of how much time each consultant would spend on the assignment. "Consultants are worth different rates," he notes. "They don't come out of cookie cutters."

The nature of the assignment plays a large part in the level of supervision deemed necessary by each security manager. "I either work very closely with them, or leave them alone," says Walker. "If they are asked to give an objective look at one of my projects, they work independently. If the security staff is working with them, we meet daily to give guidance and make suggestions."

In most cases, Krueger sets a completion date and benchmarks along the way when the consultant's progress can be reviewed. "They know what we want as an end product. We leave it to them to decide how to climb the mountain," he says.

In evaluating the consultant's performance, Atkinson monitors the quality and timeliness of the consultant's work, and reviews the validity of the recommendations. He discusses the performance of the consultant with the other employees and managers who were involved in the project. Walker also relies on a "group assessment" when measuring the value of the end result. He makes an initial evaluation and then solicits feedback from others who worked with the consultant.

Because his company uses consultants regularly, Krueger feels that the presence of a security consultant "does not strike fear into the hearts of the employees." As a result the recommendations made by a consultant do not hold more or less weight than recommendations made by any other employee. Security oversees a two-phase program to follow up on the consultant's findings. The first phase, implementation, sees that those sections which are accepted are actually put into effect. In the second phase, maintenance, security makes sure that the programs are continued.

Atkinson admits that management is not always receptive to every recommendation made by a consultant. "Each company in the corporation feels their autonomy is very precious. They may find ten to twenty percent of the report unacceptable." With the remaining recommendations, Atkinson and the company arrive at a consensus on what should be done, and set a schedule for completion. The security department periodically audits the agreement by checking on the progress of the company.

In all three cases, these managers have established a relationship with consultants that has worked well over the years. Despite efforts to standardize such parts of the relationship as the statement of fees or a contract, the consultant/client partnership is still highly subjective. Fred Tompkins, Systems Consultant for Calculon Corporation, contends that few consultants actually fit the description of a true consultant. "Most are contractors who come in and do the work for a corporation." In his view, "a consultant should act as a devil's advocate, a catalyst to get the internal organization to do their own work."

Walker agrees with this opinion. "I don't believe in having a consultant routinely dropping in each week," he says. "If you need consultants around all the time, then you're not administering your own department."

Atkinson also warns about the wide variance in the credentials of security consultants. "Heaven help the innocent company that doesn't have a security director to hire a consultant," he says. "There are damn few good consultants."

Nonetheless, companies seem to be using consultants more and more. Atkinson, Krueger and Walker all report that they will continue to use consulting services. "There is a definite place in security for consultants," says Walker. "Basically, I believe in using every resource available to me," he adds, "and consultants are an excellent resource."

Engage A Management Consultant WHEN:

- Internal staff lacks a specialized skill required for the project or problem.
- Improvement opportunities are recognized but time and people are not available to tackle them.
- An objective evaluation of current situation is indicated to plan for the future.
- The development and growth of people can be stimulated with professional help.
- New management concepts and techniques appear necessary.
- A catalyst is needed to guide organization planning and strategies.
- Other groups or agencies will be influenced by findings of objective or expert analysis.

From Association Management Scope, No. 1—1980 Series, published by Lawrence-Leiter and Company, Management Consultants, Kansas City, KS. Used with permission.

CHAPTER 27

Drawing on Outside Expertise
Samuel C. Sciacca
Lead Engineer and Business Manager
Security Systems Engineering Group
Gilbert/Commonwealth

Today's protection executives have a wide range of tasks to perform in the course of their duties. They are called upon to secure facilities, manage a guard force, curb alcohol/drug abuse, and plan for disaster control. However, one of the most time-consuming and complex jobs they face is the planning, procurement and implementation of a physical security system for a major facility.

Typically, this job requires the security manager to perform a site survey, prepare a written report and budget estimate for management, evaluate equipment vendors' offerings, provide direction to the engineering staff, and prepare new security operational procedures that reflect the various elements of the new system. Often, this executive also must spend a great deal of time retraining in-house personnel in state-of-the-art equipment and techniques. These efforts can interfere with the other security responsibilities of the department and may lead to a less than satisfactory solution to the design problem.

One way to avoid these conflicts is to use a security systems engineering consultant. Security engineering consultants can be part of a small specialized firm or a large multidiscipline company. They deal with equipment and techniques on a day-to-day basis, and keep abreast of new developments in the field. Additionally, the wide range of experience gained by consultants can help them screen the many different concepts that might be compatible with a specific site or company policy.

Engineering consultants have a working knowledge of what is required to combine access control, CCTV, and intrusion detection equipment to provide a total system approach rather than individual piecemeal subsystems. A consulting firm must also be aware of technical developments that could affect equipment, construction, or maintenance costs.

Reprinted with permission of the American Society for Industrial Security, from *Security Management*, September 1982, pp. 73.

In the *Protection of Assets Manual,* Richard Healy and Timothy Walsh give three reasons for obtaining the assistance of a consultant:

- to obtain expert advice,
- to save money, or
- to obtain an objective viewpoint.

These three elements are vital to the implementation of a sound security program. The following discussion details three aspects of a client/consultant relationship.

PLANNING

The consultant begins his job by interviewing the security director (client) and his or her staff to determine the objectives of the new system. Each job is viewed as a unique problem requiring its own solution. For example, nuclear and liquefied natural gas plant security systems must comply with federal codes. Retail store systems are designed basically to curb theft. Department of Defense and Department of Energy facilities, among other concerns, require protection against sabotage. Through an initial interview, the consultant learns what design specifications the security system must meet to fulfill the client's objectives.

The interviewing process continues with the operations personnel in the client's company. The consultant must become familiar with the facilities' operational characteristics to assess the effect of various security elements. The third group that must be contacted in the interviewing process is facility engineering. From this group the consultant learns of specific site construction practices or codes, hazardous areas, material standards, and other parameters that can affect the design of the system. Once these three groups have discussed their concerns, the consultant consolidates the data to determine any conflicts. At this point, the second step of the planning begins— the site survey.

Supported by the information derived from the interviews, the consultant surveys the actual site. If perimeter intrusion detection is required, he studies existing structures (such as fences and walls) for soundness and suitability for sensor application. The consultant views the site terrain and considers how it might affect system selection. He notes other aspects of the engineering sketches such as lighting, power, conduits, and junction boxes, and tentatively identifies what security equipment and/or procedures might be applicable.

With this data, the consultant prepares a report to the client. The report begins with a discussion of those security elements requested by the client. He addresses each element, commenting on its adequacy, ease of installation, and consistency with the overall security plan. If the objective is to meet federal codes, the report can also indicate how the company is satisfying the code requirements and what position the client can take when questioned by an inspector.

The report then addresses any alternatives the consultant might recommend. For example, the client may have indicated that low level light silicon intensifier target (SIT) or intensified silicon intensifer target (ISIT) cameras are desirable. The report will discuss this request but may also suggest alternatives such as an ultricon camera and some additional lighting. If alternatives are suggested, the report will identify the advantages of the new option (lower cost, reduced maintenance, etc.).

The last part of the report is the budget estimate. Using techniques recognized in the industry the consultant approximates costs for material and labor.

This report is an extremely useful tool for the protection executive. He can now present his position to corporate management and support it with a professional, objective document. This backup serves to disseminate security policies in a uniform manner to the other departments, as well as apprising them of the ramifications of various alternatives.

IMPLEMENTATION

Once corporate management decides to proceed with the program, the engineering consultant begins the second phase of work. This phase is divided primarily into two parts: the procurement specification and the construction specification.

The procurement specification describes, in generic terms, the equipment to be purchased. This document must be generic to encourage competitive bidding among suppliers. The consultant is in an excellent position to describe equipment in this way because he designs many systems in the course of a year and is aware of the variety of offerings in the security equipment field. Also, he has dealt with most, if not all, of the suppliers at one time or another, knows the strengths and weaknesses of each one, and prepares the procurement specification with these facts in mind. For large complex systems, the specification will also address quality assurance, spare parts, acceptance testing, and quality control. These additions can ensure that the products supplied meet the most critical standards of reliability consistent with the vital functions they perform.

The construction specification provides the blueprints for the installation work. It addresses the various engineering disciplines required in the work package, such as:

- *Civil*—This portion of the specification deals with concrete foundations, excavation, fence work, conduit trenching, and other structural concerns.

- *Mechanical*—This engineering discipline deals with the nuts and bolts of the installation, approved material types, mounting methods, and construction practices.
- *Architectural*—Regardless of whether an existing building is being modified or a new facility is being constructed, the consultant provides complete architectural plans dealing with finished surfaces, room layouts, bullet resistant structures, and the use of space. Architectural engineers work closely with mechanical engineers.
- *Electrical*—The electrical section of the specification describes the construction and installation of equipment according to applicable electrical codes—such as the National Electrical Code and codes prepared by Underwriters Laboratories or Factory Mutual—and sound engineering practice.

In addition to the written portion of the construction specification, the consultant prepares a complete set of construction drawings. Together these two elements provide a total bid package ready to be sent to various contractors for proposals.

The consultant continues his services by assisting the client in bid evaluation, primarily concerning the procurement specification. The consultant and client examine each offering for technical compliance, as well as quality, durability, and maintenance. The consultant's close relationship with the suppliers is particularly useful here. He can recognize the advantages and disadvantages of various products and can advise the client accordingly. In addition, the lowest priced proposal may not be the most cost-effective one. Total life cycle cost analyses must be considered so the client can make an informed decision in selecting components. After the contracts are awarded, the consultant will witness factory acceptance tests, prepare quality assurance and quality control reports, monitor vendors for contractual compliance, and witness the field acceptance test.

At the construction site, the consultant can supervise and monitor the installing contractor. Working with the client's engineering staff, he can make field changes on site, avoiding rework at a later date.

The consultant can also act in the client's interest during any financial disputes with the contractor. If, for example, the contractor hits an unexpected obstacle (such as an underground pipe) during trenching that was not identified during the bidding process, he may rightfully request additional funds to work around the problem. The consultant can verify that any such claims are fair, thus protecting the client from excessive charges.

The knowledge a consultant can bring to the planning, scheduling, and monitoring of a security system project is essential to the success of a design project. Additionally, he is supported by the many services available through the engineering firm. Granted, some clients can draw on in-house experience in construction monitoring, electrical design, drafting, or other phases of such a project. In these cases the client does not need to retain the consultant for the full project duration. The protection executive may need outside help only to provide the survey and report. Once the decision is made to proceed, an in-house engineering staff can provide all further support. Most consultants are extremely flexible in the nature of their assignment. They will serve in whatever capacity the client requires, whether it be only a site survey, the preparation of a report, or full project responsibility.

CONTRACTUAL AGREEMENTS

Most engineering consultants will work under a number of contractual agreements depending on the size of the job, the scope of work, and the duration of the assignment. While the client is free to negotiate any arrangement that is suitable to both parties, most contracts will be one of the following forms:

- *Lump Sum*—In this type of contract, the client agrees to pay the consultant a sum of money for the work done. This agreement is effective for jobs with a clear definition of the work to be undertaken. However, alterations to the job requirement will necessitate a change in the contract. Also, if the scope of the job is not clear or the job is too large and complex, the consultant might include contingencies in his proposal.
- *Cost Plus Fixed Fee*—In this contract, the client agrees to reimburse the consultant for his direct labor and expenses plus a lump sum figure that is pure profit. The advantage of this type of agreement for the client is that he only pays for the labor and materials expended on the job. This type of contract also requires a well-defined work assignment so the consultant can estimate the required effort with some degree of confidence.
- *Time and materials*—When a project is largely undefined, a time and materials contract is desirable. In this contract, the client agrees to pay the consultant for direct labor with a multiplier to cover overhead and profit. Expenses are reimbursed at actual cost. The client is free to increase or decrease the work assignment without changing the contract. The consultant is not held to a firm estimate and, therefore, does not need to include contingencies. This type of contract can be modified to include a ceiling figure that limits the financial commitment on the part of the client.

As a protection executive, it is your responsibility to see that your security program is conceived, developed, and implemented in a cost-effective and beneficial manner. If in-house technical expertise and state-of-the-art knowledge are available to you, your project is well on its way to success. If, however, you find you need assistance in any aspect of the program, look at a security engineering consultant. He offers whatever level of effort you need for the efficient and timely realization of your security objectives.

CHOOSING A QUALIFIED CONSULTANT

You plan to implement a comprehensive security program, and you have decided to retain an engineering consultant for the design. But which firm? Obviously, whether or not the system ultimately meets your needs and specifications depends on the capabilities and qualifications of the consultant you choose. Consider using the following procedures to find the consultant best suited to your needs.

Before releasing a request for proposal, ask the prospective consultants to submit a statement of qualifications and experience. This document will help you decide if the consultant's background meets your specific needs. Government agencies, usually request forms SF 254 and SF 255, which indicate past experience, include a company profile, and name the project staff. Most consulting firms keep updated copies of these forms on file and you can request a copy.

Once you have received the firm's qualifications, examine them carefully. The consultants should have technical experience in the security equipment you want for your system. Also, consider the size of your project. Obviously, a consultant who has designed systems for nuclear power plants has a great deal of experience in sophisticated security programs. However, he may be no more suitable than a small, three-man firm if you need to secure a warehouse or office. Large projects such as refineries, power plants, industrial facilities, and military operations require people who are intimately familiar with the unique problems associated with a project of that magnitude.

Equally important is the consultant's security staff. Check to see that sufficient experience is present in the group. Consider, too, the depth of the staff. If one key person quits will there be someone to fill his position or will your project suffer?

Finally, determine the financial soundness of the firm. Do not confuse company size with superiority in this department. A small company with years of demonstrated performance can be as effective as a large multidisciplinary firm.

If any questions remain about the suitability of a certain company, arrange to discuss the matter with the prospective consultant. Most firms are more than willing to expound on their capabilities. You, on the other hand, can meet the people who will play an important role in the success of your project. Introductory meetings with prospective consultants allow you to determine whether or not you will be able to work comfortably with each firm—an important consideration in any project.

MANAGING AN ENGINEERING CONSULTANT IN
YOUR SECURITY PROJECT

Once you decide to use an engineering consultant for your security project, you must keep a few points in mind. You must control both the project and your consultant's efforts from initial design to installation. In this way, you ensure that the finished product will fall within your objectives and budget. The following steps can assist you in achieving your goals:

- From the project's beginning establish official lines of communication, both written and verbal. Ideally, they should be between you, or your project manager, and the consultant's project manager. Attention to this detail will ensure that the direction and information the consultant receives is consistent with your policies.
- Establish a transmitting procedure for letters, reports, drawings, and other materials. The procedure should include a form that indicates the transmittal number, date, contents, and action required. Sensitive or proprietary transmittals should require a receipt.
- Establish milestones with the consultant and require progress meetings. Typically, meetings are useful whenever the consultant completes such major efforts as the site survey, first draft report, or construction specifications. These meetings will give you an opportunity to review the progress of your security program through the various stages of development, thus allowing you to fine tune or modify your system before installation. Avoid regularly scheduled meetings (weekly or biweekly, for example) as they tend to be unnecessary and increase the consultant's costs.
- Clearly identify the scope of work the consultant is to perform. The scope of work should be part of the contract and include a list of the materials (reports, drawings, specifications) the consultant must provide. Document any changes in the assignment made by you and/or your staff, and request an estimate of the cost before giving the go ahead.
- Outline the objectives of your program to the consultant. Is the system to be designed for theft control, intrusion detection, sabotage, compliance to government codes, or another specific objective?
- Be candid with your consultant. Tell him your security objectives, policies, reservations, and doubts. If you know your allocated budget for the system, advise the consultant so the system designed does not exceed this amount.
- If you have equipment preferences or dislikes, make this known. However, be prepared to listen to the consultant if a more suitable alternative is possible.
- Remember that during the contract period the consultant essentially

works for you. Delegate responsibility and exercise authority as you would with your own staff, to ensure that the consultant's work satisfies your need for his services.

CHAPTER 28

Choosing Contract or Proprietary Security
Joseph Cohen
Region Operational Director
Allied Security

The rising increase in crime in the United States poses many problems for today's businesses. Many companies have taken the position that law enforcement alone cannot handle this increase and have looked to the private security sector for aid in reducing their exposure to crime. When choosing between contract or proprietary security, the management of these companies must question their specific requirements, needs and desires. The intelligent selection of contract security or proprietary security is essential, prompting the need for an in-depth look at these two alternatives.

Contract security can be defined as an outside contractual agency whose purpose and scope is to provide a substantial measure of security for the contracting company. The contractual agency provides this service through the use of security officers and investigators, hired, trained, supervised and managed by the contract company.

In the evaluation process management must look at the advantages and disadvantages of contract security. First, consider the advantages.

Performance Contract: A performance contract gives the contracting company a strong level to insure a certain performance level from the contract company. Requiring written performance standards for the security officers, supervisors and management of the contract agency will aid in insuring the maintenance of those standards, or the loss of the contract. The reason for the performance contract, not as a penalty for the contract agency but as insurance for the contractor, should be clearly understood by all.

Security Expertise: Security expertise is the prime reason many companies look to contract agencies for their security needs. The motive is cost containment. With a contract service, many companies share the cost of the security experts, and one company may need experts in several facets of the

Reprinted with permission of the American Society for Industrial Security, from *Security Management*, October 1979, pp. 26.

field. If a company had to hire security experts for each aspect of security, the cost would be prohibitive for all but the largest companies.

Specific Insurance: Because individual insurance for security officers is very costly, many companies feel they cannot afford to add this expense to the rising costs of their general insurance premiums. As in the case of the security experts, the cost is shared if a company hires a contract security agency. Without this insurance coverage, however, a company could be financially ruined by just one civil suit.

Fewer Administrative Burdens: If the security officers are contracted through an outside agency, a company will have fewer administrative burdens concerning personnel documentation, supervision, unemployment or workman's compensation cases and hearings, and training.

Personnel Requirements: Many companies have fluctuating personnel requirements because of regular increases or decreases in production or business. If a company uses a contract agency, it can increase or decrease the number of security officers with the fluctuation of business without the cost of unemployment compensation in slow periods or advertising, personnel and training costs in peak periods.

Lower Costs: The advantage cited most frequently by companies who choose contract security is cost. The total payroll cost of security is substantially reduced since direct secondary costs are virtually eliminated. For example, expensive fringe benefits such as sick time, vacations, overtime, social security insurance, unemployment insurance, general liability insurance and retirement pensions in addition to the cost of uniforms, training, supervision, and personnel are lowered. The wages of the security officers are not regulated by what other employees of the company are paid. Consequently, lower wages generally result for the security officers in comparison with the wages of unionized employees.

No Absenteeism: A company that contracts the security work to an agency eliminates the problems of absenteeism among security employees because of sickness or vacations. As a result, fewer problems arise for the management of the company while insuring that the required number of security employees will be on hand consistently.

No Union Problems: Not having to deal with unions is another reason often cited by companies for choosing contract security. The contract agency assumes all collective bargaining responsibilities if the security personnel are members of a union, eliminating the problem of not having security personnel during labor disputes involving company employees. In most cases, the employees of contract security companies are nonunion and, therefore, not subject to strikes or other labor actions that could adversely affect the security of a contracting company.

Impartiality: An advantage of significant importance is the one of impartiality. Contract security officers can be more consistent and impartial in enforcing company rules and regulations because they are outsiders. The officers are also less likely to be drawn into a compromising situation because of friendships with company employees.

No Disciplinary Problems: When a company contracts with an agency, the responsibility of controlling discipline and keeping of disciplinary records become the responsibility of the agency. Controlling discipline can be very time-consuming, can result in substantial costs in man-hours for record-keeping and hearings, and can be a burden to management.

No Reassignment or Termination Problems: The administrative problems and cost of reassignment or termination are completely handled and absorbed by the contract agency. This factor particularly interests many companies evaluating the need for a contract agency.

The many advantages of contract security can be a major factor in the decision-making process. Other advantages can be noted, but those listed previously are general in nature and apply to most security situations.

Next, consider the disadvantages of contract security.

No Loyalty to the Contracting Company: Fostering employee loyalty is a difficult task. Loyalty can be encouraged by the contracting company if it maintains control over the officers who work at the contracting facility and regulates who gets raises when. If the security officers know that raises and promotions come from the contracting company, their loyalties will lie there.

Lack of or Inadequate Training: The contracting company must specify its requirements for training and check to insure the security officers are receiving that training. Ask the contract security company for a copy of their training material and for documentation that shows the security officers have received the training. Observe the training facilities and check the instructors used by the contract agency to insure their ability to provide quality training.

Lack of or Inadequate Supervision: The contracting company should stipulate the amount of supervision required from the security agency and should check to see it is being maintained. The contracting company can require that supervisors sign the report of the daily security officer and indicate the amount of time spent with that person. Specific reports concerning the topics discussed or the items inspected by the supervisor should be directed to the representative of the contracting company. Remember the quality of those contacts depends upon the quality of the supervisor. A contracting company should investigate the training received by supervisors to know if it has been complete and competent. Documentation is extremely important—know what you are paying for and make sure you get it.

Low Wages: A contracting company *can* and *should* specify the wages the security officers are to be paid. (A contracting company that wants a security officer to look like Paul Newman and have the law enforcement background of J. Edgar Hoover but is willing to pay only the minimum wage will get an officer that looks like J. Edgar Hoover and has the law enforcement background of Paul Newman.) A contracting company, in giving the keys of its facility to a security officer, should be realistic about the caliber of the individual, determined in part by the wages paid to that individual. Every contracting manager should ask, "Could I be criticized by my superiors or am I remiss in my responsibilities for leaving the facility in the hands of a security officer making the minimum wage?"

Poor Performance and Poor Quality People: A contracting company, if it wishes may select the security officers who are assigned to its facility by evaluating the candidates before they come to work (require the personnel folders of the candidates and interview the candidates personally). A contracting company has as much control over this process as it would if it were hiring the security officer for their own payroll. Another point—the wage paid to the security officer is of prime importance in attracting the caliber and quality of the security personnel required at the facility.

No Immediate Control Over the Security Officer: A contracting company can have as much or as little control over the security officer as desired, depending on how involved the company wants to be. If a contracting company accepts whatever it is given by the contract security agency, it must live with what it accepts.

While the disadvantages of contract security are serious, careful selection of a contract agency, with diligent maintenance of standards and vigilant management of those standards, will yield an effective security posture defined by a quality contract. If a contracting company sets standards in selection, training, supervision, and wages, and if they diligently monitor to insure that these standards and requirements are maintained, then the disadvantages of contract security can be eliminated. As with any service or product, an adequate quality assurance program is mandatory for success.

The other choice for a security setting, other than a contract security company is to have a proprietary security department within a company. A definition of proprietary security is that the operational and monetary responsibilities of security are administered and managed within the company itself. In addition, all *liability* for the security department and the actions of its employees are accepted by the management of a company. The advantages of a proprietary security department will be discussed in the following paragraphs.

Company Image: The chief advantage of proprietary security mentioned by most security experts is that of company image. The security officers are linked to the company by distinctive uniforms and patches that indicate a company's identity. The company has the opportunity to select uniforms and equipment that reflect the image of the company.

Loyalty: The idea that an individual will become more loyal to the organization as he or she becomes a part of the total company, sharing in all the benefits and problems of the company was also mentioned frequently.

Control: Direct control of the security officers is high on the list of advantages. A direct chain of command is needed for the flow of information both up and down that chain. Proprietary security provides the opportunity for more open and direct lines of communication between management and the security force.

Personnel Selection: Another advantage is the opportunity to select personally the people to be working in the security force. Selecting individuals with the background most desired by the company is closely linked to the image of the company projected by security. Personnel selection does not require a significant background in the security atmosphere. Rather, a knowledge of the job market and of personnel procedures provide the critical edge.

Training: Proprietary security offers the opportunity to select and direct the specific training the security officers will go through. Therefore, the effectiveness of the training can be monitored and additional areas of training based on security's effectiveness can be identified. Closely related to training is job performance evaluations in which the company's management can analyze the capabilities and short-comings of the security employees, and can implement measures to keep the security force at peak performance.

Familiarity: Another advantage of having proprietary security officers is the familiarity the officers gain with employees and management. The immediate identification of employees, because of familiarity and longevity, is once again aligned with image. All people like to be recognized.

As with contract security, a look at the disadvantages of proprietary security must be carefully considered to evaluate the choice effectively. The most recognized disadvantages are:

- Much higher administrative costs
- Higher wage and benefit costs
- Uniform and equipment costs
- Higher training costs
- Absenteeism cost
- Scheduling and manpower problems
- Inflexibility of manpower needs on an immediate basis
- Fraternization or collusion with other company employees
- Unionization or collective bargaining

The two main disadvantages seem to be much higher costs and unionization of the security personnel. In a proprietary program, these two items cannot be eliminated, and in today's economic climate they are extremely negative disadvantages.

The deciding factors in choosing between contract security and proprietary security are a matter of very personal needs, wants and desires, as well as serious economic evaluations and management responsibilities.

CHAPTER 29

Asking the Right Questions
William G. Butler
Security Manager, Illinois Facilities
Baxter Travenol Laboratories, Inc.

Selecting a contract security service is much like selecting a new car. A number of options must be considered. First, is a new car really needed or can the old model be repaired? Has sufficient financing been arranged?

If you decide to invest in a new car, you then must shop around and look for the best deal possible. Many factors must be taken into account, such as size, ride, comfort, service requirements, insurance costs, and the availability of parts. Before making a final choice, you may consider many styles, makes, models, colors and accessories—keeping in mind that the more special features you feel you need the more the car will cost. You can buy the cheapest, stripped down model if it will satisfy your needs, but don't expect the power, ride, comfort, and features found in more expensive cars.

Similar items should be considered before a firm selects a contract security service. The security manager faces a real challenge if he or she intends to get the most for the money being spent. The best approach is to give yourself time, know what you want, shop around, and consider the options in a businesslike manner—remembering that whether you are buying a consumer product or security services you will get what you pay for.

All decisions about the use of contract security services must be based on actual security needs. The security needs of the organization should be reviewed continuously, keeping in mind the goal of improving the performance of and support for security at all levels. If the security need only requires a basic night watchman, then hire a night watchman. If, however, the need requires specialized control programs, such as escorts, alarm response, investigations, safety checks, traffic control, inspections, key control, equipment monitoring, mobile patrols, report writing, public contract, coordination with law enforcement agencies, or a host of other specific duties, then intelligent, capable security officers must be hired.

Are there quick and easy methods to determine an organization's se-

Reprinted with permission of the American Society for Industrial Security, from *Security Management*, May 1981, pp. 50.

curity needs? Maybe, in very small firms, but in larger companies, this job becomes difficult and complex. Many firms do not know exactly what their losses are, nor do they have a way of finding out. One of the best ways to determine security needs is through a survey conducted by qualified outside experts or by the organization's security officials. Frequently, recommendations made by an outside agency carry more weight with the firm's top management because the contract group is thought to be less self-serving and less biased than the firm's own security personnel. But, regardless of who conducts it, the security survey should help to focus the views of top management on actual security needs and encourage them to commit support and funds to prevention programs.

These executives must also be convinced that leaving security needs unattended will result in excessive losses. They must be ready to adopt a plan for handling the security needs, since the company's hard earned money will be used to pay for them. Security will never be anything other than what the firm's executives want after considering the company's vulnerabilities, and what they are willing to pay for.

Once the need for security has been firmly established, and money has been committed for the implementation of prevention programs, then goals and objectives for the department must be defined. Most firms want their security staff to accomplish the following two goals:

- Improve the quality of the overall security service.
- Upgrade the performance, reliability, and effectiveness of each security officer.

These goals are difficult to achieve, but they can be attained, and a contract security agency should be willing to work closely with the client to help reach them. A commitment by *both* parties to objectives such as the ones that follow will help insure that the goals are met.

- Reduce security officer turnover.
- Effectively screen guard applicants.
- Upgrade guard training.
- Reduce unnecessary expenses.
- Eliminate dishonest practices by security personnel.
- Add job enrichment features to the guard's duties.
- Reduce security officer turnover.
- Effectively screen guard applicants.
- Upgrade guard training.
- Reduce unnecessary costs and expenses.
- Eliminate dishonest practices by security personnel.
- Add job enrichment features to the guard's duties.
- Provide clear-cut lines of communication within the guard's organizational structure.

- Set office performance standards and hold the officers to them.
- Provide orientation sessions on both the agency and the client company.
- Promote the credibility of security at every opportunity.

The tasks assigned to security not only establish the guard posts and duties, but also set standards of performance. The responsible jobs often assigned to security personnel can be handled by contract security services with good planning and forethought to job enrichment. Yes, hiring a firm that can provide professional officers may cost more, but the returns will be worth every penny considering the losses prevented, the problems solved, and the accidents avoided.

Preliminary planning for the actual bidding on a security contract should begin three to four months before the date you want a new service to start. A firm already employing a contract security service should disregard that commitment when studying needs, goals, and objectives. The feasibility of switching to an in-house security force should also be considered, but the decision on which type of security to use should be made before the account is opened for bids. When you are ready to contact outside firms, set a limit on the number of agencies you invite to bid on the account. No other agencies should be given an invitation to bid or given a copy of the bid package.

You should have the bids of at least three reputable security agencies that are genuinely interested in the business to compare during the selection process.

If you are using a contract agency currently, be honest with them. Tell them what you are doing, offer to let them bid competitively, but don't tell them who they will be bidding against. If you are dissatisfied with the service they are providing, give them notice that their services will not be required following the expiration of the current contract, and tell them that you do not wish them to bid on the account. Be sure to examine your agreement closely to ensure that you satisfy all the provisions regarding cancellation.

Security managers can use information collected from many sources when preparing a bid package or when narrowing the list of possible agencies down to those you will invite to bid. Sending out questionnaires to other security managers, talking to local security practitioners, visiting companies with similar problems, and studying the operations of local security agencies can all be useful tools. In addition, you may wish to ask employees about current security practices, contact local law enforcement agencies, and read security reports or other publications. The value of the information should be weighed against the security goals and objectives that you have established for your organization.

The actual bid package is a document of great importance, although it is not used as widely as it should be. A good bid package will provide a wealth of information to the bidding companies about your operation and your requirements, at the same time giving them a clear picture of your security needs. It also allows you to compare apples to apples during the selection process. The following list includes some of the specific data that should be in a bid package.

DATES

- State the date when the current contract expires.
- Give the period to be covered by the new contract.
- Tell when bids are due (give at least three weeks and specify the number of copies needed).
- Announce when and how the award will be made.

HOURS AND SECURITY POSTS

- Outline weekly hours and explain complexities.
- Show the location of all posts with hours coverage is needed.
- State grade structures, if applicable.
- Define command and control channels.

PAY SCALE

- Fix the exact pay scale or range for each officer grade (don't leave this up to the agency). If several scales are being considered, then state that fact and ask for a quote on each scale.
- Describe the merit pay increase system if used. List levels and propose a schedule of when merit pay can be awarded and the amounts involved.
- List other pay and rate charges the agency will be allowed to make. State conditions, time periods and other specifics.
- List holidays that will be allowed. (Billing rates for holidays may vary if the agency employees are members of a union.)
- List overtime billing rates which will be allowed. (If time and one-half is paid for overtime the billing rate should not exceed 1.42 times the standard hourly billing rate. Double time billing rate should not exceed 1.92 times the standard hourly rate.)

EQUIPMENT AND UNIFORM SPECIFICS

- Identify what equipment you want the agency to provide such as radios, vehicles, traffic control equipment, or foul weather gear.
- State the type and number of uniforms to be issued to each officer. (You might even want to request photographs of the uniforms used by the agency.)

- List the equipment and materials your firm will provide. (An example might be a special badge or patch you want the guards to wear.)
- Identify the forms and reports you want the agency to provide.

TRAINING

- State the number of hours of training you want given to new employees with specifics about where and how the training will be presented.
- Define conditions under which the client may be billed for training hours.
- Give information on weapons and firearms training, if applicable.
- Identify special subjects to be presented including when and where the courses should be given.

FIXED COST ANALYSIS

- Ask the agency to list costs and other expenses used to determine billing rates.
- Require lists of any overhead and burden expenses that might be helpful when comparing bids.

CLIENT LIST

- Ask the bidding agencies to list all clients in the local area with the name and telephone number of a contact.
- Ask for the names of other clients not necessarily in the locale with hours and guard service requirements similar to yours.

HIRING RESTRICTIONS

- Require that the agency refrain from hiring former employees of your company and assigning them to your account for at least six months after the employees' termination.
- Require that you be allowed to approve all applicants and brief new security officers prior to their assignment to your facility.
- Require that relatives of your employees not be employed by the agency.
- Ask the agency to state any exception policies or reciprocal restrictions they require for the protection of their employees.

EQUAL EMPLOYMENT OPPORTUNITY (EEO) COMPLIANCE

- Set compliance standards and point out that the contract will contain a contractor's certification of compliance.
- List Equal Employment Opportunity Commission provisions that are applicable and state any unusual requirements.

SELECTION STANDARDS FOR SECURITY OFFICERS

- State if physical examinations will be required.
- List any special physical demands or requirements for the job such as excessive lifting, standing, or walking.
- Include any education, language, writing, sight, or hearing standards required.
- Describe posts that could be staffed by a handicapped person.

WORK PERFORMANCE STANDRDS

- Describe a typical job performed by security personnel.
- Reserve the right to dismiss from the account any security officer whose work performance is unsatisfactory.
- Attach a copy of the company work rules and regulations and underscore the most important security policies and procedures.

SPECIFICS TO BE INCLUDED IN BID SUBMISSION

- Ask for a list of billing policies.
- Ask for a copy of the agency's insurance coverage. (Demand a copy of the policy, not just a certificate, so that you can examine the exclusions.)
- Have the agency provide information on their local managers including background, training, and experience.

SPECIAL CONSIDERATIONS

- Remind the agency that the contract will contain a 30-day cancellation clause to protect both parties.
- List problems the agency should especially work to avoid, such as improper scheduling, a high turnover rate, inadequate supervision, and problems with payroll.

- Establish firm policies concerning the use of the polygraph, continuity of post coverage, agency supervision techniques, and scheduling changes. Do not include penalties for non-performance. (You have the best penalty of all at your disposal—the 30-day cancellation clause.)

BID SELECTION

- Point out that the bid will not necessarily be awarded to the lowest bidder.
- Reserve the right to award the contract based upon your company's judgment.
- Inform the bidders that all bids will be acknowledged and those agencies not selected will be informed *only* of this fact. (No reasons for non-selection need to be given.)

Once the bid package is prepared, you are ready to contact firms for their bids. Only allow those agencies that are truly capable of performing the services you need to bid on the account. Do not invite bidders simply because of their reputation, their pricing, or their performance with others. Check out the company yourself, looking at such factors as their financial status, union affiliation, internal policies, philosophies, pay scales, benefits, problem solving capabilities, and willingness to adapt to your security needs. Avoid the trap of getting bids from the same agencies year after year and then contracting with the same agency each time.

When comparing one security agency to another, ten critical points must be considered. These points do not include important concerns such as EEO compliance, union affiliation, uniforms, benefit packages, pay scales, and billing rates. They do, however, attempt to objectively compare different security agencies according to their administration and personnel philosophies. These points are:

- *Retention of good people:* The agency must be able to attract, hire, train, equip and assign mature personnel to the guard force. A low turnover rate, achieved through the proper selection and fair treatment of quality personnel, should be a basic management goal.
- *Employment of qualified personnel:* The client must examine the agency's ability to maintain an alert, stable, efficient, and qualified guard force whose members are sharp in appearance, proud of their work, and familiar with all of the client's standard operating procedures.
- *Maintaining high officer morale and solving pay problems:* The agency must be genuinely sensitive to guard morale problems and be able to pay their personnel the correct amount on time.
- *Providing staff for extended periods of time:* The agency must be able to prove their ability to properly staff and schedule guard personnel

on all shifts for the posts established by the client, including both week-days and weekends.

- *Positive guard attitude:* Both the client and the agency must have a way to monitor the attitude of the officers and measure their ability to convey company security policies and procedures to employees, guests, contractors and visitors in a polite and courteous manner.
- *Responsiveness to change:* Agencies must be able to cope with changes requested by the company, and prove their ability to implement those changes with a minimum of confusion and resentment from the officers or company employees.
- *Interest in the client:* The agency must demonstrate a continuing interest in the company's efforts to protect its people and assets.
- *Control and supervision of officers:* Agency managers must consistently follow effective control procedures, including good methods of communication and modern supervisory techniques.
- *Responsiveness to the desires of company management:* The agency must be responsive to the company's views on security, and be able to project that view to all individuals.
- *Accuracy of billing records:* This last yardstick measures the agency's ability to accurately account for all hours of service provided. Correct billing invoices must agree with the hours actually worked. Agency fees should be reasonable, with 62% to 70% of the fee returned to the officers in direct compensation. This percentage should be discussed with the agency prior to contract negotiations and later made a part of the agreement.

A good bid package will help make the evaluation process less painful. The task of comparing bids is difficult, and several persons from departments outside security, such as purchasing, accounting, employee relations, legal, or safety, should be asked to participate.

The guard pay scales and billing rates contained in each agency's bid may need to be expanded or condensed in order to make accurate comparisons. The company purchasing or accounting departments can be especially helpful in this step.

The three most important factors to consider when comparing contract agencies are perhaps the most difficult to evaluate. They are the reputation of the agency, the quality of the local management, and the employee relations within the agency and between the agency and the company.

Other considerations can be rated more easily. One system assigns a number from one to ten to each item enabling the company to arithmetically rank each of the bidding agencies. A sample of a bid analysis checklist follows. However, this list may contain subjects unimportant to some companies while omitting others that are critical. When developing a similar checklist to meet specific company needs, the security manager should remember to make the topics as objective as possible, including only those items that can actually be checked and rated.

BID PACKAGE

- Provided all requested information
- Professional quality of submission

RATES

- Average rate based on all charges (Multiply the score by ten in order to weight this entry.)
- Standard time rates
- Overtime and holiday rates
- Equipment fees
- Percent of fees paid to security officers
- Security officer pay scales
- Overhead cost considerations
- Hidden fees for items such as consulting fees and equipment costs

GUARD SELECTION AND TRAINING

- Pre-employment screening
- Qualification testing
- Compliance with company employment restrictions
- Quality of initial training
- Willingness to allow company representatives to participate in training
- Classroom and on-the-job training
- Follow-up training
- Ability to retain quality personnel
- Methods for attracting applicants
- Costs absorbed by agency
- Personnel sources

AGENCY CONSIDERATIONS

- Size and financial stability
- History (and prospects) of guard pay problems
- Quality and philosophy of service
- Current contracts in the area
- Ability to do investigations and security surveys

- Reputation for ethical business practices
- Personnel management methods
- Willingness to customize service to meet company needs
- Experience with similar accounts
- Responsiveness and follow-through on needs
- Modern personnel management policies
- Knowledge of federal, state and local laws

ADMINISTRATIVE SUPPORT AND/OR SERVICE

- Union considerations (relationships and potential problems)
- Agency publications (standing orders, regulations, etc.)
- Records, reports, logs, and other forms
- Methods for paying guards
- Uniforms and equipment
- Insurance (including provisions covering the protection of client and quality of the policy)
- Employee benefit package
- Ability to comply with company stipulations
- Contract obligations in the area

SECURITY OPERATIONS

- Published standards of guard performance
- Communications techniques
- Company controls allowed
- Agency internal control measures
- Flexibility
- Ability to effectively handle day-to-day operations
- Company interests respected and satisfied
- Emergency response capability
- Expertise in operations
- Policy and procedure assistance
- Post orders
- Care for client equipment
- Controls, inspections and follow-up actions
- 12-hour work limit

MANAGEMENT AND SUPERVISION

- Location of local office and availability of agency managers
- Quality and reliability of guard supervision

- Responsiveness
- Compatibility with company representatives
- On-site supervision
- Established performance criteria
- Inspections, visits and technical assistance provided to company
- Quality of management group
- Attitude and character

RISKS

- Ability to cope with start up problems
- Ability to sustain operations after start up
- Growth capability
- Possibility of rate increases
- Responsiveness to changes requested by client
- Ability to supply what company wants
- Willingness to retain selected personnel from the agency previously used by the company
- Quality of service
- Ability to react quickly to changes
- Emergency planning
- Vulnerability to key personnel losses

INTANGIBLE FACTORS

- Response to requested uniform modifications
- Comments from other clients
- Guard morale
- Strike and labor dispute support to company
- Willingness to give client control of overall security operations
- Long-range planning in keeping with client needs
- Respect for client policies and procedures
- Techniques used to prevent fraternization
- Guard dismissal procedures
- Care, maintenance and quality of equipment provided
- Requirement for company to become involved in internal agency matters
- EEO compliance
- Ability to solve technical and personnel problems
- Use of polygraph in keeping with company's views

OTHER

- Experience in locale
- Image in local labor market
- Accuracy in billing invoices

- Clerical support availability
- Ability to supply extra guards when needed
- Capability to perform special investigations
- Computer availability
- Patrol vehicle reliability
- Cost for and quality of special equipment
- Willingness to share information on common problems
- Ability and willingness to repair or replace lost or damaged company equipment

This rating system allows the company to look at many aspects of the service the agency can provide. A contractual agreement based on this extensive research will help prevent the occurence of surprises not covered in the contract. Paying attention to the terms and conditions that finally go into the contract is the best way to get good security services from the agency you select. Award the contract to the bidder you trust only after each party *understands* what the other part is obligated to do.

Selecting a qualified security agency to perform contract security is not much more complicated than selecting a new car. Just take your time, do a little shopping, know what you are looking for and base your decision on common sense and good judgment.

PART VI

Legal Concerns of Security Management

In an increasingly litigious world, nearly anything an organization does can expose it to legal problems. The security operation is no exception. Security is intended to protect the assets of the organization, not endanger them. Therefore, legal pitfalls are wisely recognized and avoided.

Understanding of the legal grounds for private security personnel's authority is a fundamental responsibility for all security managers. Familiarity with the civil and criminal liabilities attached to security activities is equally important for security professionals. Such liability arises not only from the actions of proprietary security employees but also sometimes from those of contractual service personnel as well.

Although apprehension is an infrequent duty for security personnel, proper handling of the task calls for knowledge of legal requirements. Similarly, investigations conducted for security purposes must meet fairly strict criteria if their findings are to hold up in court.

Still another aspect of the security manager's job that carries legal implications is the conduct of security operations during labor disputes. In the course of protecting the organization's property, security personnel can inadvertently cause charges of unfair labor practices. While a law degree is not a prerequisite for most security executives, awareness of the ways in which security operations can jeopardize an organization legally is.

CHAPTER 30

The Legal Basis of Authority
David L. Steeno
Assistant Professor
Western Illinois University

Private security, as a profession, developed in response to the need for protection and security in excess of that provided by public law enforcement. While many private security personnel perform functions similar to public law enforcement officers, they generally have no more formal authority than an average citizen. Basically, because the security officer acts on behalf of the person, business, corporation, or other entity that hires him, that entity's basic right to protect persons and property is transferred to the security officer.

In addition, the authority of private security personnel is derived indirectly from various sources of law—tort, contract, and criminal law, as well as constitutional law and administrative law. The following examples and cases relevant to each type of law show the legal basis for the security officer's authority.

TORT LAW

Tort law regulates civil relationships between people, and is the primary source for the authority of security personnel.[1] The law of torts is found in statutes and judge-developed common law. It differs from criminal law in that it involves a private party seeking individual relief for an injury. Tort law allows a person who has been injured or damaged by another to sue that person in civil court to obtain compensation for the injuries received.

The authority of private security personnel is affected in a negative way by tort law. The law restricts the security officer's activity because a lawsuit

From *Physical Security: Practices and Technology* by Charles Schnabolk, published by Butterworth Publishers, 1983. Also published in *Security Management,* May 1982, pp. 50.
[1]Bird, W. J., Kakalik, J. S., and Wildhorn, S., et al., *The Law and the Private Police* (Santa Monica, CA: The Rand Corporation), December, 1971, Vol. IV, p. 7.

may be brought against the officer for some act or failure to act that might result in injury. Tort law sets limits on the activity of security personnel by defining, through case precedent, the boundaries of reasonable conduct.

Tort liability may be imposed for an intentional or a negligent act. In some circumstances liability for a tort can be imposed even though an individual is without fault. Imposing liability without fault is called strict liability and generally does not apply to the actions of security personnel.

CRIMINAL LAW

A crime is any act or failure to act that injures the public at large and that is prohibited and punishable by law. The state brings action against a perpetrator in the form of a criminal prosecution to protect the interests of society.[2] Unlike tort law, in criminal law the perpetrator is answerable to society and not to any individual. Like tort law, criminal law acts only as a deterrent to improper conduct and defines conduct parameters for the security officer.

An action by an individual can result in both criminal and civil liability. For example, assault, battery, criminal defamation, and criminal damage to property are torts as well as crimes. The injured party can bring a civil suit against the wrongdoer and the state can bring a separate criminal prosecution against the same offender.

CONTRACT LAW

A contract is an agreement between two or more competent persons. It consists of a promise or set of promises that can be enforced by the law or recognized by the law as a duty.[3] Under the agreement, each party promises to perform some act or to refrain from performing some act in reliance upon, and in consideration of, the other party's promise to perform or to refrain from performing some act.

A contract may be express or implied, oral or written. An express contract is one in which the agreement between the parties has been indicated in words—oral or written. However, if the promises of the parties are inferred from their conduct or acts alone, without spoken or written words, the contract is said to be implied.

A contract is breached when, without legal excuse, a party either fails to perform or performs in a manner not in accord with the terms of the

[2]Prosser, W. L., *Handbook of the Law of Torts*, Fourth Edition. (St. Paul, MN: West Publishing Company), 1971, p. 7.
[3]Calamari, J. D. and Perillo, J. M., *The Law of Contracts*, (St. Paul, MN: West Publishing Company), 1970, p. 1.

agreement. A court can remedy the breach by requiring the breaching party to perform or by awarding monetary damages to the innocent party.

Contractual arrangements can limit the authority of the security officer. In contracts betwen a business enterprise and a contract guard service, the business could create standards of conduct for agency guards more restrictive than those permitted by law. For example, the business enterprise could indicate in the contract that guards must be unarmed even though by local law the guards could carry weapons.

Guard service contracts typically determine the respective liabilities of the business entities should someone be injured by an action of the guard.[4] Such agreements cannot prevent an entity from being sued by a third party, but can determine which entity will ultimately assume the cost of any judgments.

By protecting the interests of union employees, labor contracts may also restrict the type of action security personnel can take against union members. For example, collective bargaining contracts might limit inspections of employee packages or set conditions for the interrogation of employees.[5]

CONSTITUTIONAL LAW

The United States Constitution sets forth the basic rights of all individuals. In doing so, it places limitations on the conduct of the government and its officers, including police officers; security officers who have been commissioned by a government agency and thereby given similar authority to a police officer; and anyone who is acting for, or in conjunction with, either the police officer or the commissioned security officer.

With the notable exception of private security officers in California,[6] constitutional restrictions apply only to government officers and not to private citizens.[7] However, the courts are beginning to look closely at the purpose of non-commissioned private security officers. If their activities are judged to be similar to those of the public police and performed with the same ultimate purpose (e.g., prosecution of the offender), constitutional restrictions could be applied to security officers as well.

The mere licensing of private security personnel by a state regulatory agency is not "state action" and does not bring the acts of a non-commis-

---

[4]See Annotation, "Liability of One Contracting for Private Police or Security Services for Acts of Personnel Supplied," 38 ALR 3d 1332 (1971).

[5]For a further discussion of this area, see Bilek, A. J., Klotter, J. C., and Federal, R. K., *Legal Aspects of Private Security*, (Cincinnati, OH: Anderson Publishing Company), 1981, pp. 169–173.

[6]In *People v. Zelinski*, 594 P. 2d 100 (1979), the California Supreme Court applied the State of California Constitution to a private search that had been performed pursuant to a statutorily authorized citizen arrest.

[7]*Burdeau v. McDowell*, 256 US 456 (1921).

sioned security officer within the scope of the United States Constitution.[8] State licensing laws are generally intended to regulate some form of business and, with few exceptions, do not confer any type of police authority on the licensed person.

The United States Constitution is applicable to the activities of security personnel if they have been commissioned as some type of special officer. In these cases, the parts of the Constitution most applicable are: the Fourth Amendment's prohibition against unreasonable searches and seizures; the Fifth Amendment's guarantee against compelled testimony; the Sixth Amendment's right to legal assistance in criminal proceedings; and the Fourteenth Amendment's guarantee of due process.[9]

In 1914, the United States Supreme Court provided a remedy for the violation of an individual's constitutional rights by government officers. In the case of *Weeks v. United States*[10] the court adopted an exclusionary evidence rule. The court held that evidence obtained by federal officers through unconstitutional methods rendered the evidence inadmissible in a federal criminal prosecution. This exclusionary rule was made applicable in 1961 in the case of *Mapp v. Ohio*.[11]

Shortly after the *Weeks* decision, the court formulated an equally important corollary in holding that any indirect product of an illegal search was also inadmissible in a criminal proceeding.[12] This decision was clarified by the court years later when it used the "fruits of the poisonous tree" metaphor

---

[8]*Weyandt v. Mason's Store, Inc.*, 279 F. Supp. 283 (W. D. Pa. 1968).

[9]*Fourth Amendment:* "The right of the people to be secure in their persons, houses, papers, and effects, against unreasonable searches and seizures, shall not be violated, and no Warrants shall issue, but upon probable cause, supported by Oath or affirmation, and particularly describing the place to be searched, and the persons or things to be seized."

Fifth Amendment: "No person shall be held to answer to a capital, or otherwise infamous crime, unless on a presentment or indictment of a Grand Jury, except in cases arising in the land or naval forces, or in the Militia, when in actual service in time of war or public danger; nor shall any person be subject for the same offense to be twice put in jeopardy of life or limb; not shall be compelled in any criminal case to be a witness against himself, nor be deprived of life, liberty, or property, without due process of law; nor shall private property be taken for public use, without just compensation."

Sixth Amendment: "In all criminal prosecutions, the accused shall enjoy the right to a speedy and public trial, by an impartial jury of the State and district wherein the crime shall have been committed, which district shall have been previously ascertained by law, and to be informed of the nature and cause of the accusation; to be confronted with the witnesses against him; to have compulsory process for obtaining Witnesses in his favor, and to have the Assistance of Counsel for his defense."

Fourteenth Amendment, Section I: "All persons born or naturalized in the United States and subject to the jurisdiction thereof, are citizens of the United States and of the State wherein they reside. No State shall make or enforce any law which shall abridge the privileges or immunities of citizens of the United States; nor shall any State deprive any person of life, liberty, or property, without due process of law; nor deny to any person within its jurisdiction the equal protection of the laws."

[10]232 US 383 (1914).

[11]367 US 643 (1961).

[12]*Silverthorne Lumber Co. v. United States*, 251 US 385 (1920).

in holding that any tangible evidence gathered as a result of illegally obtained information was subject to exclusion.[13]

Constitutional restrictions and the exclusionary rule do not apply to private persons as a general rule. However, as with most rules of law, there are exceptions. Two recent cases concerning the exclusion of evidence are significant.

The first case is *People v. Zelinski,*[14] which concerns an arrest by store detectives in a retail store in California. In the course of a search by private security personnel, a vial containing heroin was discovered. The police later took custody of the vial and the defendant was charged with unlawful possession of heroin. The California Supreme Court concluded that the narcotics evidence was obtained illegally by the store detectives and excluded the evidence from the criminal trial. The court quoted from an earlier California case. The judges in the case held that a citizen effecting an arrest was only authorized to take offensive weapons from the arrestee, not to conduct a search for contraband incidental to the arrest or to seize such contraband.

The court in *Zelinski* noted that the rationale for the rule limiting searches by private persons is that, without statutory authorization, private citizens are not permitted to take property from other private citizens. Private citizens are permitted to retrieve only those items in plain view. The court also based its decision on the California State Constitution, Article I, Section 13, which provides in part that, "The right of the people to be secure in their persons, houses, papers, and effects against unreasonable seizures and searches may not be violated. . . ."

Shortly after the *Zelinski* decision, a District of Columbia trial court suppressed evidence in *United States v. Lima.*[15] The judge ruled that a private store detective had illegally obtained evidence and he excluded that evidence. The language of the trial court suppression order was similar to the wording in the *Zelinski* decision and resulted in some commentators predicting the exclusionary rule would soon be applied to security officers across the United States.[16]

The *Lima* case began with the filing of an information for petit larceny resulting from a shoplifting incident in the District of Columbia. The trial court granted a defense motion to exclude the evidence on the basis of an illegal search by the licensed store detective. The trial judge determined that those who are regularly employed as retail store security guards are subject to the Fourth Amendment prohibition against unreasonable searches and seizures.

Eventually, the full Court of Appeals heard the government's appeal

---

[13]*Nardone v. United States,* 302 US 379 (1937); 308 US 338 (1939).
[14]Footnote 6.
[15]*US v. Lima,* DC Superior Court, 47 LW 2696 (April 16, 1979).
[16]Euller, S., "Private Security in the Courtroom: the Exclusionary Rule Applies," *Security Management,* Vol. 24, No. 3, March, 1980, pp. 38–42.

of the suppression order and reversed the trial court's decision.[17] The Court of Appeals in *Lima* said that searches and seizures by private security employees traditionally have been viewed as searches and seizures conducted by private citizens and therefore not within Constitutional proscriptions. However, if a security officer has powers akin to a regular police officer and is appointed by a government official, these "trappings" of state authority are sufficient to trigger Fourth Amendment restrictions. Determining what is sufficient government involvement to trigger application of the Fourth Amendment, however, can be decided on a case-by-case basis.[18]

The Court of Appeals in *Lima,* then, reaffirmed the general principles that the federal Constitution does not apply to actions of private citizens, and the licensing of a security officer does not automatically transform that person into an agent of the state. At present, the California exclusionary rule articulated in *Zelinski* remains the first and only instance where a state supreme court has applied exclusion across the board to private security personnel. In general, evidence obtained illegally by private security personnel is admissible in court, although in isolated instances courts have excluded evidence because of some peculiar circumstances involved in the case.[19]

Zelinski also illustrates a key concept about constitutional law. Even though the United States Supreme Court may rule that the federal Constitution does not require some action, a state court may apply the provisions of its state constitution to require the same action. Security personnel in that state, then, are obliged to comply with that state decision.

ADMINISTRATIVE LAW

Administrative law is the section of civil law that deals with the creation and activities of federal and state independent agencies and executive departments.[20]

The private security business is frequently regulated by state and local statutes, ordinances, rules, and regulations. While these laws may be concerned with the qualification, hiring, and training of security personnel, they generally do not confer any special authority on the personnel who are licensed.[21] In some jurisdictions, special police powers are given to licensed security personnel under certain, specified circumstances. The method by which a private citizen becomes vested with special police powers is called

---

[17]*US v. Lima,* DC Court of Appeals, 48 LW 2668 (March 12, 1980).
[18]*Ibid.*
[19]See, for example, *Level v. Swinewki,* 93 N.W. 2d 281 (Mich. 1958); *Williams v. Williams,* 221 N.E. 2d 622 (Ohio 1966).
[20]See Walsh, T. J., and Healy, R. J., *Protection of Assets Manual* (Santa Monica, CA: The Merritt Company), 1979, Part III, Administrative Law, pp. 21–45.
[21]See *Private Police,* Report of the Task Force on Private Security, National Advisory Committee on Criminal Justice Standards and Goals (Washington, DC), 1976, pp. 381–387.

"deputization." A commission does not confer upon the private citizen all of the public peace officer's powers, but does subject the commissioned security officer to the constitutional obligations and limitations placed upon the public officer.

CHAPTER 31

The Legal Basis of Liability
David L. Steeno
Assistant Professor
Western Illinois University

Security personnel are subject to both civil and criminal liabilities. These concepts are not mutually exclusive, and the same action could result in both types of liability. In this article, however, the two types of liability will be discussed separately.

CIVIL LIABILITY

The basic civil liability that pertains to the security industry is found in tort law. A tort is a civil wrong; it results from a violation of a duty owed to another that causes a compensable injury. In some instances the tort may result in a court-issued injunction prohibiting the continuation of some kind of tortious activity.

Torts are classified as intentional, negligent, or strict liability. The individual who commits the tort is called the tortfeasor. The tortfeasor is the defendant in a civil suit and is liable for damages because he acted with an unreasonable intention or because he failed to exercise reasonable care.[1] A tortfeasor may be a person, a corporation, an association, or some other entity. The person who was injured by the action of the tortfeasor is called the plaintiff.

A plaintiff may recover general and special damages in a negligence action as compensation for the injury resulting from the defendant's failure

From *Physical Security: Practices and Technology* by Charles Schnabolk, published by Butterworth Publishers, 1983. The information in this chapter was compiled substantially by David Steeno, assistant professor at Western Illinois University, Macomb, IL. Also published in *Security Management*, December 1982, pp. 10 and January 1983, pp. 29.
[1]Steeno, D. L., "Be Sure Your Security Is Legally Secure," *Security World*, Vol. 18, No. 6, June, 1981, p. 35.

to exercise reasonable care. General damages are awarded on the basis of the "enlightened consciences" of the jurors and cover the plantiff's pain and suffering, loss of limbs, disfigurement, or mental grief. Special damages include present and future medical expenses and loss of income.

Punitive damages (also called exemplary damages in some jurisdictions) are designed to deter and punish the tortfeasor for his intent to injure. Since negligence does not involve such an intention, punitive damages are generally not awarded in negligence cases. However, punitive damages are sometimes awarded for gross (as distinguished from "simple") negligence because of the defendant's outrageous conduct. In gross negligence cases, the defendant is judged to have acted in such total disregard for the safety of others that the punishment is the same as that for intentional acts.

In the past few years, judicial and legislative sanctions against the security industry have increased.[2] This increase is due in part to the exceptional growth of the industry, rising expectations of the public, the quality of security services, the increase in the number of new laws and lawyers, and the availability of liability insurance. Also, individuals are more sophisticated in their knowledge of legal matters, and more aware of their rights. Juries have awarded substantial judgments, and new theories of liability, which have improved a plaintiff's chances of obtaining a recovery in a civil suit, are being developed.[3]

Two evolving theories of liability specifically affect the security industry. The first concerns the willingness of courts to impose a legal duty of protection. A duty of protection has been extended to motel/hotel owners and landlords, for example, holding them liable for failure to protect guests and tenants adequately from foreseeable criminal activity.

Historically, a landlord's responsibility to a tenant was primarily to keep the premises in a reasonably safe condition through maintenance and repair. The landlord had no duty to police the areas under his control.

Recently, however, the question has been raised as to whether a landlord must protect those persons legally on the premises from foreseeable criminal activity. Historically, landlords were not held liable for criminal attacks on tenants because of the causation requirement of tort liability. It was accepted tort theory that a crime was an intentional act of a third party. Intentional acts are usually considered to be unforeseeable events because one cannot predict what another person will do in any particular circumstances. However, in some circumstances a landlord may be held civilly liable for injuries occurring to his tenants that result from an intentional act of another.

For example, in *Klein v. 1500 Massachusetts Avenue Apartment Corporation.*[4] a tenant was criminally assaulted in a common hallway of an

---

[2]Barry, R. L., "Loss Prevention for the Loss Preventors," *Security Management,* Vol. 23, No. 3, March, 1979, p. 22

[3]Steeno, p. 35.

[4]*Kline v. 1500 Massachusetts Avenue Apartment Corporation,* 439 F.2d 477.

apartment house. The landlord was aware of prior criminal activity against his tenants and their property. He was also aware of conditions that made it likely that further criminal attacks would occur. Despite such information, the landlord decreased the amount of security provided in the apartment complex. The *Klein* court held that the landlord's failure to provide adequate security in light of the knowledge he possessed made him liable for the resulting injuries to the tenant.

Some jurisdictions are resisting efforts to extend liability to the landlord in such situations.[5] However, the concept of landlord liability for a failure to protect is gaining acceptance. A New Jersey court, for example, has imposed liability reasoning that a landlord's implied warranty of habitability obliges him to furnish reasonable safeguards to protect tenants from foreseeable criminal activity on the premises. However, any approach to landlord liability is based on the premise that the acts of the criminal must be reasonably foreseeable based on the landlord's actual or constructive knowledge of prior crimes occurring on the premises.

A similar duty of protection has been extended to innkeepers. The case against a Howard Johnson's motel brought by singer Connie Francis after she was raped in her motel room was especially interesting because of the theory in the case. Her civil suit alleged that the attack against her was due to the motel's failure to provide adequate locks on the sliding glass door leading to her room. The jury decision awarding her over one million dollars alerted the hotel/motel industry to their exposure in this type of case. Although intentional acts of third parties have traditionally absolved liability because such acts were considered unforeseeable, such acts may not relieve liability where the act of the third party was reasonably foreseeable under circumstances within the defendant's knowledge.

The second evolutionary theory is the concept of a nondelegable duty. Previously, liability could be avoided in certain instances by delegating a duty to another. A frequently invoked method of delegation was to hire an independent contractor.

Under the principles of agency law,[6] an independent contractor relationship relieves the one who hired the independent contractor of liability because no control is exercised over the activities of the contractor. Thus, a motel owner, for example, could employ a security agency to protect the motel. If an incident occurred that resulted in an injury, the motel owner would claim he was not responsible for the injury because the duty to provide protection had been given to the guard service.

---

[5]Compare Stalmack, J. M. "The Illinois Landlord's Obligation To Protect Persons On His Premises Against the Criminal Activities Of Third Persons," *Illinois Bar Journal*, June, 1980, pp. 668–675, with *Holley v. Mt. Zion Terrace Apartments, Inc.*, 382 So. 2d 98 (FL App. 1980) where the Florida Court of Appeals upheld the theory of liability for failure to protect tenants against foreseeable criminal activity.

[6]Principles of agency are discussed in the material dealing with respondeat superior under vicarious liability.

Under the concept of a nondelegable duty, however, the motel owner would remain liable. Some duties rightfully belong to certain individuals, according to the courts, and the law will not permit these individuals to escape liability by delegating the duty to someone else. The law will allow a delegation of authority, but not of responsibility, for the performance of a legal duty.[7] Contract provisions that attempt to delegate such duties to others are not enforced by the courts and have not relieved individuals of civil liability.

Four other types of civil liabilities affect security personnel: negligence, intentional torts, vicarious liability, and strict liability.

NEGLIGENCE

Negligence is the absence of due care or due diligence. It is the failure to act as a reasonable and prudent person would have acted under the same or similar circumstances. A person who is negligent has failed to conduct himself with appropriate regard for the safety and rights of others.

In a negligence case, the plaintiff is responsible for demonstrating through a preponderance (more than fifty percent) of the evidence that there was:

- an act or failure to act (an omission) by the defendant
- a legal duty owed to the plaintiff by the defendant
- a breach of duty by the defendant
- a foreseeable injury to plaintiff
- damages

Where the law has imposed a legal obligation or duty upon the defendant, the jury must determine if the defendant's conduct was reasonable under the circumstances. If the defendant is judged to have breached his duty, the jury must decide the amount of damages necessary to compensate the plaintiff.

Security personnel have been held liable for negligence by failing to exercise due care in the use of firearms, motor vehicles, and force. Any time a security officer fails to use reasonable care and this failure causes damage, he can be held liable for his negligence. This negligent act or failure to act also exposes his employer to civil liability.

Supervisors are especially vulnerable to three types of civil exposure: negligent supervision of personnel, negligent training, and negligent supervision. The supervisor is liable when his negligence was a substantial factor in bringing about the plaintiff's injury. The Restatement of Torts, Second, Section 307 states that, "[I]t is negligence to use an instrumentality, whether

---

[7]Prosser, W. L., *Handbook of the Law of Torts*. Fourth Edition, West Publishing Company (St. Paul, Minnesota), 1971, p. 470.

a human being or a thing, which the actor knows, or should know, to be incompetent, inappropriate or defective and that its use involves an unreasonable risk of harm to others.''

INTENTIONAL TORTS

Intentional torts occur when a person acts in a manner designed to bring about an intended result. In other words, the tortfeasor intended the consequences of his act or at least intended to perform the act that caused damage to the plaintiff.

Because the tortfeasor has committed a willful wrong, the law may seek to punish the wrongdoer by imposing punitive damages over and above the compensatory damages available in a negligence action. The following list, though not exhaustive, defines the intentional torts of most concern to the security professional.

Assault: an unauthorized act that results in the fear of imminent harmful or offensive contact. No physical contact occurs, but the actor causes the plaintiff to fear immediate physical contact. The plaintiff must have become apprehensive as a result of the defendant's gesture. In most cases, words alone are not sufficient to create a reasonable fear of harm.

Battery: a harmful or offensive contact with the plaintiff in which the defendant intentionally touches the plaintiff physically or touches some object immediately associated with the plaintiff, such as a cane used by the plaintiff for walking. Such contact must be nonconsensual and not privileged. For example, a merchant has a common law privilege to recover his property reasonably and this privilege would be an acceptable defense in an action brought against the merchant for battery. However, if the merchant's action was unreasonable, the privilege would not apply and the merchant could be held liable for battery. Any illegal search by a security officer will probably be considered battery. If the plaintiff consented to the search, however, a claim of battery would not be upheld.

False imprisonment or false arrest: an unlawful detention or confinement of the plaintiff within fixed boundaries. Any unauthorized restraint gives reason to bring action for false imprisonment. Such restraint can be imposed by physical contact or by intimidation that suggests to the plaintiff that physical force will be used if escape is attempted.

False imprisonment is a wrongful detention for a private purpose, with no intention to bring the detainee before a court. False arrest is a wrongful detention by someone presumed to have the legal authority to enforce the law.

For recovery, the plaintiff must prove the restraint was against his or her will. If the plaintiff agrees of his own choice to surrender freedom of motion, by voluntarily accompanying the defendant to clear himself of an accusation for example, no imprisonment can be claimed. However, consent given on the basis of force, duress, or fraud is not valid.

An action for false imprisonment is one of the torts most frequently brought against security personnel. The following cases illustrate actions that result in suits of this type.

In the first case, a store employee suspected a customer of having hidden a can of flea spray on his person. The employee stopped the customer in the middle of an aisle and loudly demanded to know what had happened to the can. Eventually the employee called the customer a thief in front of some thirty customers, who watched as the employee searched the customer, then grabbed him and marched him to the manager's office. The office was at the front of the store where other customers observed the commotion.

No can of flea spray was ever found on the customer's person. The customer sued the store for assault and battery, slander, and false imprisonment. He recovered $10,000 in compensatory damages and $30,000 in punitive damages.[8]

A second case involved an employee interrogation. A corporate employee was called into the manager's office and accused of theft. She was told she could not leave until she signed a confession. After additional threats and forcible detention for five hours, she signed a statement admitting the theft. The court held these actions constituted false imprisonment. One person can detain another in a reasonable manner for investigative purpose if he legitimately suspects a theft is being committed. However, he cannot allege probable cause as a defense for detention if the offense occurred previously and the detention was not for investigation but to obtain a confession.[9]

Another employee detention case involved the investigation by bank personnel of a suspected theft of money a bank customer claimed to have deposited. Bank officials forcibly detained the suspected employee for more than two hours. After threats of prosecution and offers to drop the matter if the employee confessed, the employee agreed to write a confession. The employee later refused to supply the confession, and the customer eventually discovered she was in error. The bank employee recovered $30,000 in damages from the bank for false imprisonment.[10]

In addition to illustrating the tort of false imprisonment, these cases point out that the tort can occur even if an employee is interviewed at his or her place of employment while "on company time." The test is not whether an employee is being paid for the time involved (although payment can help to demonstrate that the interview was voluntary), but whether the employee

---

[8]*Great Atlantic and Pacific Tea Co. v. Paul*, 261 A.2d 731 (MD 1970).
[9]*Moffatt v. Buffums' Inc.*, 69 P.2d 424 (CA 1937).
[10]*Parrott v. Bank of America Nat. Trust and Sav. Assoc.*, 217 P.2d 89 (CA 1950). Annotation, 35 ALR 2d 263.

was free to leave the site of the interview. If the employer's actions or words restrict the individual's liberty, then imprisonment exists.[11]

Generally, the advising of Miranda rights is not required prior to an interview by an employer.[12] However, in a union environment the employee has the right, upon his request, to have a union representative present during an investigatory interview. The employer cannot deny the union member's request to have a union representative present during any interview the employee reasonably believes could result in disciplinary action against him. A failure to honor such a request "interferes with, restrains, and coerces the individual right of the employee to engage in concerted activities for mutual aid or protection."[13]

The employer does not have to offer to bring a union representative in but is required to honor such requests if they are made. If the request is made, the employer has the option to continue or terminate the interview, and he may point out this option to the employee. Finally, if a union representative is present during the interview, the representative's role is to assist the employee by clarifying facts or by suggesting names of others who could help. The representative cannot be a legal advisor to the employee or attempt to answer questions for the employee.

Defamation: any form of unprivileged communication to a third party without the consent of the plaintiff that injures the reputation of the plaintiff in the eyes of the community. Slander is the oral defamation of another (other than over the radio or television), and libel is defamation by the written word. The defendant may be able to defend against the tort if the statements made were true, privileged, or given with the consent of the plaintiff. Punitive damages are awarded where the communication was malicious (called "publication") or where the words themselves are slanderous.

Suggesting to another that the plaintiff committed a criminal offense is slander per se. In such cases, the plaintiff does not need to demonstrate actual damages. For example, a security officer who yells, "Stop thief!" across a crowded room while pointing to a particular person is liable potentially for defamation as long as a third person witnesses the incident.

Certain communications are considered to be privileged either absolutely or partially. A former employer has a qualified privilege to respond to requests for information about former employees from a prospective

---

[11]For an excellent discussion of generally accepted techniques of employee theft investigation, see Barefoot, J., *Employee Theft Investigation,* Security World Publishing Company, Inc. (Los Angeles, CA), 1979.

[12]Caveat: some jurisdictions by "local custom" and not by case of statutory law require the advisement of warnings by private security personnel prior to interrogation. Local officials in a few jurisdictions may refuse to handle a private case where private security personnel failed to comply with local law. Thus, it behooves the security officer to contact local prosecutors, police officials, and judges to determine the local custom.

[13]*NLRB v. Weingarten, Inc.,* 420 US 251 (1975) and *International Ladies' Garment Workers' Union v. Quality Manufacturing Company et al.,* 420 US 276 (1975).

employer. If such requests are answered in "good faith" (that is with reasonable grounds for the response), the employer is protected from liability even if the communication later turns out to be incorrect. However, due to the threat of litigation, many employers have become reluctant to test their qualified privilege in court by responding to requests for employment information.

Generally, truth is an absolute defense to defamation actions. This statement must be qualified, however, by adding, "provided that it is published with good motives and for justifiable ends."[14] Truth is neither a defense to criminal defamation,[15] nor an absolute defense to the civil tort in every jurisdiction. Some states have statutes that render a defendant liable for a true statement published for malicious motives.[16] Even where such statutes have been ruled unconstitutional because they violate the First Amendment's guarantee of freedom of the press, [17] liability claims have been awarded for the publication of true statements because they are an invasion of privacy or intentionally interfere with a beneficial employment contract.[18]

Malicious prosecution: cases in which the defendant initiates criminal proceedings, although the proceedings indicate the plaintiff is innocent. The proceedings also must show a lack of probable cause for starting the proceeding and malice on the part of the defendant. Malice is defined as instituting or continuing criminal proceeding for reasons other than to bring the offender to justice. Examples of malice include prosecutions brought by defendants to extort money, collect debts, or force the performance of contractual agreements.

Although probable cause is not a defense against charges of false imprisonment in most jurisdictions, it is a defense to the tort of malicious prosecution.

An individual may be liable for either instigating or continuing a criminal prosecution. However, an individual cannot be held liable unless he takes an active part in instigating or encouraging the prosecution. There is no liability for merely reporting the facts to police officials who may exercise their right to pursue the charges further. If criminal prosecution resulted from the defendant's persuasion, or his incomplete or biased statement of the facts, however he may be liable if such statements were the deciding factor in the decision to prosecute.[19]

---

[14]Prosser, p. 797.
[15]For example, Illinois Revised Statutes, Chapter 38, Section 27-1 provides: "A person commits criminal defamation when, with intent to defame another, living or dead, he communicates by any means to any person matter which tends to provoke a breach of the peace." Section 27-2 states: "In all prosecutions for criminal defamation, the truth, when communicated with good motives, and for justifiable ends, shall be an affirmative defense."
[16]Prosser, p. 797.
[17]*Farnsworth v. Tribune Co.,* 253 NE 2d 408 (IL 1969).
[18]Prosser, p. 802–818; 927–949.
[19]*Smith v. Allied Supermarkets,* 524 SW 2d 848 (MO 1975).

Invasion of privacy: an unjustified intrusion into another's reasonable expectations of privacy. The tort identifies four situations that are reasons to bring action:

- the misuse of a plaintiff's name or picture for commercial advantage,
- the placing of another in a false light,
- the public disclosure of private facts, and
- an intrusion into the seclusion of another.

Typically, a security officer commits this tort when he engages in an illegal search, such as an unauthorized inspection of employees' packages. The tort may also occur if electronic surveillance or visual surveillance of individuals takes place. Remote observation of individuals trying on clothes in fitting rooms has given rise to a number of cases alleging an invasion of privacy. However, other cases on record indicate if signs are posted outside the fitting rooms giving sufficient notice to customers that the rooms are subject to surveillance, a person's justified expectation of privacy, and reasonable observations could be made without incurring liability for invasion of privacy.

Overzealous surveillance by private detectives may lead to invasion of privacy charges.[20] In one case, a woman brought action against an insurance carrier and a private detective agency. She claimed she was constantly shadowed by detectives after she filed a personal injury action against the insurer. Generally, the filing of a civil suit implicitly waives the right of privacy, because the defendant (the insurance carrier in this case) has a right to investigate by reasonably unobtrusive methods. However, in this case the court held that the methods used violated the plaintiff's right to privacy. The court said:

> "After finally discovering the identity of the defendants on August 13, her attorney contacted the attorneys for the defendants and informed them of her condition and that their conduct had almost made her lose her mind, and defendant's attorney stated he would request his client to discontinue these activities; nevertheless, the surveillance continued in as aggravated form as before, and plaintiff was forced to undergo electroconvulsive shock treatment from August through November. The conduct of the defendants in shadowing, snooping, spying and eavesdropping upon plaintiff was done in a vicious and malicious manner not reasonably limited and designed to obtain information needed for the defense of plaintiff's lawsuit against Bell but deliberately in a way calculated to frighten and torment her. Plaintiff's neighbors also noticed the espionage and thereby gained the impression that she was engaged in some wrongful activity and began to discontinue any association with her. The shock and injury to her nervous system is permanent."[21]

---

[20]*Nader v. General Motors Corp.*, 255 NE 2d 765 (1970).
[21]*Pinkerton National Detective Agency, Inc., v. Stevens*, 132 SE 2d 119 (GA 1963).

Of increasing concern to security personnel are actions that involve possible tort liability for invasion of privacy, including reference checks, background investigations, and the use of truth detection devices.[22]

Trespass and conversion: an unauthorized, intentional, or physical invasion of a plaintiff's real property, or remaining on land after permission has been rescinded constitutes trespassing. The wrongful taking of a plaintiff's personal property is called conversion and subjects the tortfeasor to civil liability when it intentionally interferes with the plaintiff's use or right of possession.

Intentional infliction of mental distress: a defendant intentionally causes physical injury or mental suffering through the use of highly aggravating words or conduct. Early tort cases refused to recognize mental injury because these injuries were too difficult to prove and damages too difficult to determine. However, cases of extreme misconduct eventually underscored the need for recourse when intentional conduct was calculated to cause, and ultimately did cause, serious mental distress.

One of the leading cases of this type is an English case, *Jànvier v. Sweeney* 2 K.B. 316 (1919), in which a private detective posing as a police officer threatened to charge the plaintiff with espionage unless she surrendered some private papers. Recent cases involving abuses by collection agencies have been based on this theory of liability.

Just as tort law protects against certain interferences with another's life, property, or reputation, it also provides privileges and immunities used to defend against tort actions.

For example, consent of the plaintiff or the existence of a recognized privilege on the part of the defendant absolves the defendant from liability for an act that might otherwise be considered a tort. To be considered favorably, the consent may be express or implied. Privileges that can exonerate a defendant include self-defense, defense of others, defense of property, recovery of property, and necessity. For example, a lawsuit alleging battery can be countered by claiming the defendant was privileged, under the circumstances, to use reasonable force to effect an arrest.

VICARIOUS LIABILITY

Security officers who engage in tortious conduct are personally liable for the damages caused by their action. Because the security officer usually is employed by an entity more solvent than he is, the plaintiff typically sues the employer as well as the employee. The plaintiff then attempts to establish the employer's liability under the doctrine of "respondeat superior," which is also called vicarious or imputed liability.

---

[22]Belair, R. R., "Awareness of Privacy Rules Is Crucial For Security Pros." *Security Management,* Vol. 23, No. 3, March, 1979, p. 14.

Respondeat superior is a doctrine based on the principles of agency law. Agency law addresses situations where two persons agree that one is to act for the benefit of the other according to specific directions. An agency relationship arises where one individual, called the principal, has the right to control the action of this other individual, who is called his agent.

The term "principal" includes in its meaning the term "master." A "servant" is a species of "agent" and is normally one who gives personal service as a member of a business or domestic household, subject to the control of the master.

Respondeat superior applies in situations where a master (employer) is liable for the torts caused by the servant (employee) while in the service of the master. In other words, an employer is legally responsible for an employee's actions when the action occurs in the scope of employment. Therefore, an employer is liable for the negligence of his employee even though the employer did nothing to cause the plaintiff's injury. The employee's negligence is "imputed" to the employer, whose liability rests upon the master-servant relationship.

Numerous justifications have been advanced by legal scholars to explain this shared liability. Some have argued that the employer is liable because he controls the employee. Others believe the employer sets the events in motion by selecting the particular individual as an employee. The justification may be that vicarious liability attempts to allocate risk by allowing an injured person to sue the party most financially capable of compensating for the damages—the business employer.

Early decisions refused to hold an employer vicariously liable for the intentional acts of an employee because it was difficult to infer that the employer approved of such conduct. Today, "[I]t may be said, in general, that the master is held liable for any intentional tort committed by the servant where its purpose, however misguided, is wholly or in part to further the master's business."[23] Employers may also be liable for punitive as well as compensatory damages if the employer ratified, participated in, or authorized the employee's intentional act.[24]

In cases where an employee acts for strictly personal reasons and not as a result of his employment, an employer may still be liable. In these cases, though, the vicarious liability rationale is not applied if the employer's negligence was a substantial factor in causing the plaintiff's injury.

For example, assume that a guard was provided with a weapon by his employer. While at home and off-duty, the guard used the weapon to injure a neighbor. The neighbor might be able to bring action against not only the guard for the guard's intentional act, but also against the employer claiming the employer was negligent in entrusting a dangerous instrument to the

---

[23]Prosser, p. 464.
[24]*Dart Drug v. Linthicum,* 300 A.2d 442 (DC 1973).

employee, or negligent in hiring an individual with known dangerous propensities.[25]

Because vicarious liability depends on an employer-employee relationship, the doctrine does not apply in situations where an independent contractor is hired. Liability is not extended to the independent contractor because the "employer" has no right to control the way an independent contractor performs the work. However, the rule that an employer is not responsible for the acts of an independent contractor has so many exceptions that the exceptions are the rule. For example, an employer who hires an independent contractor may be liable because of the negligent selection of the contractor, or because of the "inherent dangerousness" of the work, or because he owed a non-delegable duty to the injured party.[26]

In the case of *Brien v. 18295 Collins Avenue Corp.,*[27] the plaintiff brought an action against a motel owner to recover damages for the death of her husband, who had been killed by a security guard at the motel. The guard was an employee of an independent contractor hired by the motel owner to provide protection for the motel. The plaintiff sued the guard, the guard agency, and the motel owner. Although the contract guard service and the guard were liable (the service was vicariously liable for the negligence of the guard/employee; and the guard was liable for his own negligence), the motel owner was dismissed from the case by the trial court. The Florida appellate court affirmed the dismissal on the basis of the general rule that an "owner is not ordinarily liable for the negligence of an independent contractor employed by the owner." The court rejected the plaintiff's contention that the owner was liable because the work of an armed security guard is inherently dangerous.

The *Brien* court noted that the owner might have retained liability if the plaintiff had alleged that the owner had actual or constructive notice of the dangerous propensities of the guard. Thus, the defendant could have been liable through negligence even though vicarious liability was not applicable under the facts.

The case also illustrates the point that a plaintiff in a civil case will use all theories of liability that could apply given the facts of the case, and will bring all potentially liable individuals into the case. Most cases, therefore, involve multiple theories (counts) of liability and multiple defendants. As a result, the torts and defenses discussed previously should not be considered in isolation, but rather as interacting components of a single liability system.

---

[25]See "Negligent Entrustment Revisited: Developments 1966–1976." 30 *Arkansas Law Review* 288 (1976) and *Bonsignore v. City of New York,* US District Court, SDNY. reported in 24 ATLA L. Rep. 262, Vol. 2;4, No. 6, August 1981, where jury awarded $425,000 in compensatory and punitive damages against the City of New York for negligent entrustment of firearm to a policeman who shot his wife.
[26]Prosser, 468–475.
[27]233 So. 2d 847 (FL App. 1970).

STRICT LIABILITY

Liability without "fault" is sometimes imposed where persons are engaged in particularly hazardous or dangerous activities, for example, dynamite blasting, oil drilling, or the ownership of a vicious animal such as a lion. The theory of strict liability holds that because of the danger involved and the difficulty in protecting against the possible risks, the liability rests with those who engage in such activities.

Strict liability is seldom applied to activities of security personnel. Perhaps such liability might apply in situations involving a "vicious" guard dog. However, cases involving vicious dogs have not applied strict liability against the owner if the dog attacked trespassers or tortfeasors—the most likely victims of a guard dog attack.

Strict liability can apply to security agencies as a result of statutory enactments that make holders of certificates of authority liable for the torts of agency employees committed while on the job.[28]

CRIMINAL LIABILITY

Many aspects of criminal liability are similar to the concepts of tort liability. Much of the discussion of tort law therefore applies to the criminal sanctions against security officers.

However, an exception to these shared concepts is that an employer is not vicariously liable for the criminal acts of his employees, although there are circumstances in which an employer will be held liable for an employee's violation of a "regulatory offense." In most jurisdictions, before liability is imposed, the prosecution must prove that the employer knowingly and intentionally aided, advised, or encouraged the employee's criminal conduct.[29]

As with tort law, criminal law is concerned with the enforcement of legal duties to act rather than moral duties to act. A legal duty may arise as the result of a contract (e.g., a lifeguard obligates himself to attempt to rescue the drowning swimmer); by virtue of a special relationship (e.g., a parent has a duty to provide for the welfare of his or her child); by statute (e.g., a hospital has a duty to provide emergency care); or by common law (e.g., one who places another in peril has a duty to make reasonable attempts to assist the one endangered).

Elements of criminal liability are:

---

[28]Illinois Revised Statutes, Chapter 111, Section 2622(10) states: "The holder of a certificate of authority who employs persons to assist him in the work of private detective and in the conduct of such business shall at all times during such employment be legally reponsible for the good conduct in the business of each and every person so employed."

[29]*Commonwealth v. Koczwara,* 155 A. 2d 825 (Pa. 1950). But contrast with *Ex parte Marley* 175 P.2d 832 (Calif. 1946), where the court imposed liability on an employer even though he did not know about or authorize the employee's violation.

- a voluntary act or omission (actus reus or "guilty act");
- a mental state (mens rea or "guilty mind"); and
- causation of the crime charged.

As previously noted, certain regulatory offenses impose liability by deleting the requirement of mens rea—the fact that the "regulatory offense" was committed is sufficient for criminal liability regardless of the intention of the actor.

Corporations as well as individuals can commit crimes. In contrast to the situation in which an employer is generally not responsible for the criminal acts of his employees, corporations may be liable for criminal offenses even where a mens rea is required for the crime. A corporation can only act through its agents. Thus, the mental state (mens rea) is supplied by the corporate officer when he acts on behalf of the corporation. A corporate officer who steals for a corporate purpose within the scope of employment can make the corporation criminally liable.[30] The corporation is punished by financial penalties and forfeitures and the stigma of being a corporation convicted of a criminal offense. In extreme cases of corporate officer criminality, corporations may have their corporate charter revoked—a form of capital punishment for the corporation.

Corporations must be aware of the following areas of business crime: securities fraud, Foreign Corrupt Practices Act, criminal antitrust, bank fraud, commercial bribery, tax fraud, commercial espionage, Hobbs Act, Travel Act, Racketeer Influenced and Corrupt Organizations Act (RICO), labor law violations, Occupational Health and Safety Act (OSHA), food and drug violations, environmental law, mail and wire fraud, as well as the "traditional" areas of criminal liability.[31]

Criminal liability is most frequently imposed on private security personnel in situations involving the use of force against another—assault, battery, manslaughter, and murder. Actions by security officers may also result in criminal liability for burglary, trespass, criminal defamation, false arrest, unlawful use of weapons, disorderly conduct, extortion, eavesdropping, theft, perjury, and kidnapping, among others.

An individual charged with a crime has various defenses available. The security officer might defend himself by demonstrating that he was privileged to use force in self-defense or that he made a reasonable mistake of fact negating criminal intent.[32] Other defenses include entrapment, compulsion or necessity, consent, intoxication, and insanity.

---

[30]See W. T. Grant Co. v. Superior Court, 23 Cal. App. 3d 284 (1972); New York Central and Hudson Railroad v. United States, 212 U.S. 481 (1908); and People v. Canadian Fur Trappers Corp., 161 N.E. 455 (NY 1928).
[31]Business crime has become an area of such concern that corporate counsel can now purchase a multivolume series called Business Crime: Criminal Liability of the Business Community, from Mathew Bender, Business, Legal and Tax Publishers, New York, NY.
[32]Bassiouni, op. cit., p. 64.

In general, a private citizen has no legal duty to report crime or to prevent it. Under the common law, citizens were liable for a failure to report felonies and could be charged with misprision of a felony. Early common law required the citizen to act affirmatively when a felony was committed within his presence. Some jurisdictions have retained the concept of misprision of felony:

> *Whoever, having knowledge of the actual commission of a felony cognizable by a court of the United States, conceals and does not as soon as possible make known the same to some judge or other person in civil or military authority under the United States, shall be fined not more than $500 or imprisoned not more than three years, or both.*18 USC 4[33]

The federal statute just quoted and most state "misprision" statutes have been interpreted to require the purposeful concealment of a major offense. The term "purposeful" requires some affirmative action on the part of an individual rather than simply a failure to report a crime about which one has knowledge. Some case precedents exist, however, for applying criminal liability for a mere failure to report a felony or to take obvious steps in prevention of violence. The rule in England, for instance, is that if one knows a felony has been committed and fails to report it, one is guilty of misprision of felony. In England and Australia concealment need not involve a positive act and a mere omission is sufficient for criminal liability.

In the United States federal system and most state systems, to be guilty of misprision the prosecution must prove beyond a reasonable doubt that: the principal committed and completed the felony alleged; the defendant had full knowledge of that fact; the defendant failed to notify the authorities; and the defendant took affirmative steps to conceal the crime of the principal.[34]

Although the security officer who fails to report a crime occurring in his presence on property he has agreed by contract to protect may not be guilty of misprision, there may be liability as a result of his failure to perform a duty he was physically capable of performing. For instance, assume a guard has been employed to protect tenants in an apartment building. As he is making his rounds, he comes upon an apartment with smoke pouring out the window and a tenant inside screaming for help. If the guard fails to act in this situation, the case law suggests he could be criminally liable for his omission to perform a duty arising out of his contract.[35] The law of

---

[33]See *Sykes v. Director of Public Prosecution,* 3 All. Engl. L. R. 33 (1961), discussed in F. E. Inbau, U. R. Thompson, and A. A. Moenssens, *Criminal Law,* 2nd ed. (Mineola, NY: The Foundation Press, 1979), p. 642.

[34]*United States v. Stuard,* 566 F. 2d 1 (CA 6, 1977), quoting *Neal v. United States,* 102 F. 2d 643 (CA 8, 1939).

[35]See C. N. Guthrie and B. C. Bridgman, *Security Guard Powers to Arrest,* Harcourt Brace Jovanovich Legal and Professional Publications, Inc., distributed by Law Distributors (Gardena CA), 1978, pp. 3–4, discussing *Perrine v. Pacific Gas and Electric Company,* 186 Cal. App. 2d 442; and *Powell v. U.S.,* 2 F.2d 47 (CA 4, 1924) discussed in Bilek et al., op. cit., p. 153.

criminal liability in this area is unclear, however. Certainly the guard would have tort liability and liability for breach of contract. Whether he would also be criminally liable cannot be stated with any degree of certainty. As a minimum one would have to show a duty, that the guard's action was a gross violation of his duty, and that his breach of duty was the cause of the resulting injury.

An offense similar to misprision because it hinders criminal prosecution is the compounding of a felony. Illinois law states:

> A person compounds a crime when he receives or offers to another any consideration for a promise not to prosecute or aid in the prosecution of an offender. Ill. Rev. Stat. chp. 38 § 32-1[36]

The common law defined compounding a crime as "the making by one directly injured by the commission of a crime of an agreement not to inform against or prosecute the offender in return for a reward, bribe, or reparation for the injury."[37] The elements of the crime are knowledge of the commission of the original crime, an agreement not to report or prosecute that crime, and the receipt of consideration.

Compounding a crime is an unlawful agreement to accept something of value (consideration) in exchange for a promise to curtail criminal prosecution. Because prosecutors have a discretionary charging function, a presecutorial agreement to drop charges in exchange for a release from liability for the arrest is considered a lawful agreement, which does not give rise to the compounding offense.[38] But when a security officer, for example, agrees to let an individual he apprehended go in exchange for money or some other form of compensation to which he is not legally entitled, he has compounded a crime and is subject to criminal prosecution. Depending on the exact circumstances of the case, he may be guilty of theft, extortion, or blackmail as well.

A problem faced by private security officers, especially those involved in undercover investigations, is the allegation that they solicited a crime by encouraging another to commit a crime. The criminal offense of solicitation is committed when one requests, commands, entices, or induces another to commit a crime with the intent that the other person engage in criminal conduct.[39] The security officer acting without such an intent has not committed solicitation nor has he committed the offense of conspiracy, which is a combination of two or more people for the purpose of committing a criminal act.[40]

Where the security officer intends that a crime be committed, he could

---

[36]See also California Penal Code, Section 153 and the Nevada Revised Statutes, Sections 178.564, 178.566 and 178.568, as well as the Comment, "Compounding Crimes: Time for Enforcement," 27 *Hastings Law Journal,* 175 (1975).

[37]15A Am. Jur. 2d, Compounding Crimes, Section 1, p. 767.

[38]*Haines v. Barney's Club Inc.,* California Supreme Court, 80 Daily Journal D.A.R. 3337 (1981), overruling 166 Cal. Rptr. 577.

[39]*People v. Lubor,* 272 N.E. 2d 331 (NY 1971).

[40]J. Sigler, *Understanding Criminal Law* (Boston: Little, Brown and Company, 1981), p. 253.

be charged with solicitation or conspiracy. Whereas public law enforcement officers are usually protected by statute for "crimes" they commit in the performance of their official duties,[41] private persons are not similarly protected. Therefore, the intent of the private person may become an important jury question upon which the individual's liability will depend.

An issue related to the preceding discussion involves the matter of entrapment. Entrapment is an affirmative defense that completely exonerates a criminal defendant if his crime was incited or induced by a public officer or agent.

The defense of entrapment is not constitutionally required, but is a judicially[42] or statutorily[43] created defense. Entrapment is applied in many jurisdictions when a private person works in concert with public officials.

In general, entrapment does not apply to private conduct. Particular fact situations and local law can cloud the otherwise clear "rule" that entrapment does not apply to private citizens. Consider the following case of *United States v. Maddox,*[44] which is frequently cited for the proposition that the entrapment defense does not extend to inducement by private citizens.

In *Maddox,* Alatex, Incorporated, a shirt manufacturer, was experiencing severe inventory shortages and, suspecting theft, obtained the investigative services of its parent corporation, Cluett-Peabody, Incorporated. Investigation by these private officers eventually led to the arrest of the defendants in Atlanta, GA. The case was tried in federal court and the defendants raised the entrapment defense. The trial judge submitted the entrapment issue to the jury, which found against the defendants who appealed the conviction to the United States Court of Appeals for the Fifth Circuit. The Court of Appeals affirmed the conviction and said:

> *The defendants argue that the company's deep involvement in the conspiracy, to the extent of suggesting and arranging for the transportation, amounts to complicity and precludes their conviction because of entrapment as a matter of law. The argument overlooks the fact that private investigators, rather than governmental agents, participated in the arrangements. The entrapment defense*

---

[41]See Iowa Code Annotated, Section 704.11 Police Activity: "A peace officer or person employed by any police agency who joins in the participation of a crime by another person solely for the purpose of gathering evidence leading to the prosecution of such other person shall not be guilty of that crime, provided that all of the following are true: (1) He or she is not the instigator of the criminal activity. (2) He or she does not intentionally injure a nonparticipant in the crime. (3) He or she acts with the consent of his or her superiors or the necessity of immediate action precludes his or her obtaining such consent. (4) His or her actions are reasonable under the circumstances."

[42]The United States Supreme Court recognized and applied entrapment in *Sorrels v. United States,* 287 U.S. 435 (1932). See a discussion of entrapment in federal cases in D. A. Jones, *The Law of Criminal Procedure* (Boston: Little, Brown and Company, 1981), p. 111–113.

[43]Illinois Revised Statutes, Chapter 38, Section 7-12 states: "A person is not guilty of an offense if his conduct is incited or induced by a public officer or employee or agent of either for the purpose of obtaining evidence for the proseuction of such person. However, this Section is inapplicable if a public officer or employee, or agent of either, merely affords to such person the opportunity or facility for committing an offense in furtherance of a criminal purpose which such person has originated."

[44]492 F.2d 104 (CA 5, 1974).

does not extend to inducement by private citizens. Moreover, the defendants received the benefit of the defense when the District Court submitted the issue of entrapment to the jury for factual determination. The jury found against the defendants. In any event, the conduct of the private investigators merely afforded opportunities and facilities for the commission of the offense, a continuing illegal enterprise, without initiating the criminal design in the defendants' minds.[45]

The specific rationale for the *Maddox* decision is unclear. In the paragraph quoted above the appellate court indicated: the entrapment defense does not apply; the defense might apply but the jury decided the issue against the defendants as a matter of fact; and even if entrapment applies, the investigators did not put the criminal design in the mind of any defendant and therefore there is no entrapment as a matter of law.[46] Because the court covered all the bases in its decision, there is no single rationale for the decision. The case provides scant authority for an unequivocal statement that entrapment does not apply to private citizens. Furthermore, the *Maddox* court applied the federal rule of entrapment. Some states have extended their state entrapment rule to private persons acting in concert or support of the police. One draft of the proposed Federal Code would apply entrapment to persons acting in expectation of reward, pecuniary or otherwise, for assisting public officials.

The law is far from settled on the entrapment question and various state approaches will have to be examined in the future—particularly the developing security law in California. Even where the law is clear that entrapment does not apply to the conduct of private citizens, local prosecutors, judges, and juries may individually apply the entrapment defense "unofficially" because they do not agree with an investigative technique used by private personnel in a particular case.

Security officers employing undercover operatives who are also on the payroll of local police, security officers coordinating a "private" investigation with local police, and security personnel working in a jurisdiction that applies an ad hoc entrapment rule to private citizens must be aware of the entrapment issue and investigative techniques that can successfully avoid this defense.

CIVIL RIGHTS ACT

Actions by private citizens are not regulated by the Civil Rights Act. However, security officers who have been commissioned and are therefore acting "under color of state law" are potentially liable under the Civil Rights Act when they deprive another of a right, privilege, or immunity secured by the

---

[45]*Ibid.*
[46]The federal courts and the majority of states use the subjective approach to entrapment, which concentrates on the predisposition of the defendant to commit the crime. A minority of states use an objective approach to determine if entrapment exists, focusing on the conduct of the government officials.

Constitution.[47] An off-duty police officer working as a private security guard has been held to be acting under color of law for jurisdictional purposes under the Civil Rights Act.[48] However, other cases have held that off-duty officers are not acting under color of law when they perform private duties.[49]

The United States Supreme Court held in *Williams v. United States*[50] that the Federal Civil Rights Act applied to the actions of a commissioned private detective. Because of his commission by the City of Miami, the private detective had special police powers, which created the necessary nexus to government action that subjected him to liability under the federal statute.

To come within the provisions of the Civil Rights Act, the plaintiff must show that his constitutional rights were violated and that the violation was accomplished under color of a statute, ordinance, regulation, custom, or usage of a state or territory.

One of the few cases to date where a private party has been found to come within the language of the Civil Rights Act is *Smith v. Brookshire Brothers, Inc.*[51] In this case, two store managers detained two shoppers, and a police officer summoned by the managers arrested a shopper and took her to the police station. The police officer's action was pursuant to an agreement with the store management. The law enforcement officer did not independently investigate the incident. Subsequently, the charges were dismissed, but the Civil Rights action commenced in federal court, which found jurisdiction on the basis of a customary plan by which store officials could have

---

[47]Federal Civil Rights law, Section 1983 of Title 42 of the United States Code is based on the Civil Rights Acts of 1871 and states: "Every person who, under color of any statute, ordinance, regulation, custom, or usage, of any State or Territory, subjects, or causes to be subjected, any citizen of the United States or other person within the jurisdiction thereof to the deprivation of any rights, privileges, or immunities secured by the Constitution and laws, shall be liable to the party injured in an action at law, suit in equity, or other proper proceeding for redress." 42 U.S.C. § 1983.

The major federal civil rights laws of a criminal nature which remain on the federal statute books are sections 241 and 242 of Title 18 of the United States Code. Section 242, Title 18, of the United States Code states: "Whoever, under color of any law, statute, ordinance, regulation, or custom willfully subjects any inhabitant of any State, Territory, or District to the deprivation of any rights, privileges, or immunities secured or protected by the Constitution or laws of the United States, or to different punishments, pains, or penalties, on account of such inhabitant being an alien, or by reason of his color, or race, than are prescribed for the punishment of citizens, shall be fined not more than $1,000 or imprisoned not more than one year, or both." 18 U.S.C. § 242.

Section 241, Title 18, United States Code is a conspiracy statute and states: "If two or more persons conspire to injure, oppress, threaten, or intimidate any citizen in the free exercise or enjoyment of any right or privilege secured to him by the Constitution or laws of the United States, or because of his having so exercised the same; or if two or more persons go in disguise on the highway, or on the premises of another, with intent to prevent or hinder his free exercise or enjoyment of any right or privilege so secured, they shall be fined not more than $5,000 or imprisoned not more than ten years, or both." 18 U.S.C. § 241.

[48]*David v. Murphy*, 559 F. 2d 1098 (CA 7, 1977), later appealed 587 F. 2d 362 (1978).
[49]J. A. Vroman, "The Potential Liability of Private Police Under Section 1983 of the Civil Rights Act," 4 *Law Forum*, 1185 (1976).
[50]341 U.S. 97 (1951).
[51]519 F. 2d 93 (CA 5, 1975).

persons detained merely by telephoning local officials and designating the subject to be arrested.

As a general rule, non-commissioned security officers, even if acting pursuant to a state licensing law or mercantile shoplifting law, are not liable for actions under the Civil Rights Act. As the court said in *Weyandt v. Mason Stores, Inc.,* "[T]he fallacy of plaintiff's argument appears to be in equating acting under license of state law with acting under authority of state law."[52]

SUMMARY

Though there are many similiarities in function and dress between public law enforcement officers and private security personnel, the legal authority of each group differs in many significant respects. Generally, private security personnel possess no more authority than the average private citizen. Exceptions to this general rule occur when the security officer is specially commissioned or when he is a public law enforcement officer working in an off-duty security position. The private citizen as private security officer has been the focus of this article.

The security officer derives his authority from tort, contract, criminal, constitutional, and administrative law.

A tort is a civil wrong arising out of conduct that affects some legally protected interest and causes damage. Tort law is the primary source for the authority of security personnel. Rather than authorizing their activity, however, it sets limits on their conduct.

A crime is any act or failure to act that injures the public at large and that is prohibited and punishable by law. Like tort law, criminal law restricts the activity of the security officer.

A contract is an agreement between two or more competent persons and consists of a promise or set of promises the law will enforce or the performance of which the law recognizes as a duty.

The United States Constitution establishes the basic rights of all individuals and sets limits on the conduct of government officers. In general, these limitations do not apply to private persons.

Administrative law is the area of civil law that deals with the creation and activities of federal and state independent agencies and executive departments. Private security is frequently regulated by state and local laws. The commissioning of private security officers does not confer the authority of the public law enforcement officer, but does subject the commissioned security officer to the constitutional restrictions and obligations placed on the public officer.

Private security personnel have the authority to arrest, perform limited searches and seizures, interrogate, and use force.

---

[52]See footnote 8.

A citizen has arrested another when, with lawful authority, he has deprived another of personal liberty. In general, a private person may make a warrantless arrest where a felony has actually been committed and there is reasonable cause to suspect the person committed the crime. A private citizen may only make a warrantless misdemeanor arrest where the misdemeanor was committed in the arrestor's presence.

At common law, there was a limited right for a person to arrest and detain but the arrestor acted at his peril. Probable cause to believe another had committed a crime was not sufficient if the arrestor was mistaken. This is still the rule with regard to private citizens in the overwhelming majority of states. The rule has been modified by some state courts and statutes to allow a merchant to arrest and detain on the basis of probable cause in order to protect his merchandise. The acts of the merchant or his agent must be reasonable. Furthermore, the shoplifting statutes only provide protection for certain types of liability.

Private searches have been judicially approved on the basis of search incident to a valid arrest and pursuant to consent of the party searched. Where possible, private security personnel should obtain a search warrant to be executed by a public official.

A private citizen acting under citizen's arrest authority is not required to inform a suspect of his constitutional rights. However, some jurisdictions by local custom require private security personnel to give *Miranda* warnings. Statements must be voluntarily made to be admissible in court.

Citizens are privileged to use reasonable force in defense of self or others, to protect property, to arrest, and to prevent crime. Excessive or unreasonable force will result in criminal and civil liability.

Persons are liable for the tort of negligence when they fail to act as a reasonably prudent individual would have acted under the same or similar circumstances and this failure caused injury to a person to whom they owed a duty. A plaintiff injured as a result of another's negligence will be awarded compensatory damages and may be awarded punitive damages in some states for a defendant's gross negligence.

Intentional torts occur when one acts in a manner designed to bring about a certain result. Intentional torts include assault, battery, false arrest, defamation, malicious prosecution, invasion of privacy, trespass, and infliction of mental distress.

Punitive damages can be obtained for intentional torts and are designed to punish and deter the tortfeasor.

Employers are vicariously liable for the negligence of an employee that occurs within the scope of employment. An employer may also be liable for an employee's intentional act if is can be shown that the employer's negligence was a substantial factor in bringing about the harm, or where the employer ratified, authorized, or approved the employee's intentional act.

Criminal liability is based on a voluntary act or failure to act, performed with a culpable mental state, that results in conduct proscribed by society.

A security officer most frequently incurs criminal liability as a result of the use of force. However, criminal charges of compounding a crime, theft, extortion, solicitation, and conspiracy, among others, may arise from his conduct. As a general rule, the Civil Rights Act and the entrapment defense do not apply to private security personnel.

The law as it applies to security personnel is in a period of transition and development. Some issues raised in this article have not been addressed by the courts or legislatures in many jurisdictions. Thus, there is not single body of law to which the private officer can presently turn. In order to determine the legal limits of a security officer's authority in a particular jurisdiction, a local prosecutor or private counsel should be consulted.

CHAPTER 32

Know Who Is Liable
Roger L. Fritze, CPP
Security Coordinator
Florida Power & Light Company

When using an outside security service, a security director should be aware of the complications and liabilities that could result from this contractual relationship. For example, if a corporation uses a contract security force seeking union representation, who does the union negotiate with? The corporation probably believes this is an issue the subcontractor must face, but this conclusion may not be accurate. If the corporation has exercised too much control and/or influence over the contractor's security force in the terms of the contract, the corporation may find itself directly involved in labor negotiations or lawsuits resulting from the actions of the contract officers.

The issue that leads to this potential difficulty is the legal interpretations of a joint employer situation. According to *Words and Phrases,* a legal reference found in most law libraries, joint employment exists when two employers hire the same employee to perform work simultaneously for both under the control of both.

To further define joint employment, the court in *Wirtz vs. Lone Star Steel Co.* (C.A. 5th, 1968, 405 F2d, 668, 669) ruled that five circumstances of employment should be considered when deciding if an employee is working simultaneously for two employers: "(1) whether or not the employment takes place on the premises of the company; (2) how much control the company exerts over the employees; (3) whether the company has the power to fire, hire, or modify the employment conditions of the employees; (4) whether employees perform a 'specialty job' within the production line; and (5) whether the employee can refuse to work for the company or others."[1]

The parameters of control were also used as the basis for defining joint

---

Reprinted with permission of the American Society for Industrial Security, from *Security Management,* May 1982, pp. 43.
[1]Wex S. Malone, Marcus L. Plant, and Joseph W. Little, *The Employment Relation* (St. Paul, MN: West Publishing Company, 1974), pp. 674, 675.

employment in a decision rendered by the National Labor Relations Board (NLRB). Manpower, Inc. supplied Avis Rent-A-Car Systems with employees under a contractual agreement. When these employees sought union representation, Manpower contended they were the sole employer. The NLRB ruled, however, that Avis was a joint employer because Avis hired, directed, disciplined, and discharged the Manpower employees.[2] This ruling, then, placed Avis directly in the negotiating process.

Legally binding decisions involving contractual situations seem to conclude, then, that a joint employer relationship depends on the degree to which companies choose to involve themselves in the personnel administration of the contractor's employees.

Another case involving security related duties seems to contradict this conclusion, however. In *Bowman vs. Pace Co.* (C.C.C.A. 5th, 1961, 119 F. 2d, 858), the employee in question was hired by a security agency to perform guard duties at the warehouse of a grocery company. The court decided that the mere fact that the guard occasionally assisted warehouse and trucking employees of the grocery company did not make the grocery company his employer.

The implications of joint employment can also touch the disposition of workmen's compensation. In its definition of joint employment, *Words and Phrases* also states that "there must be some harmonious action with reference to wages paid by each employer, hours of employment, or terms of service."[3]

A case example is *Hunt vs. Regent Development Corp.* (143 N.E. 2d, 892, 893, 3 N.Y., 2d 1333). A night watchman was employed by two different employers whose properties were located a block or so apart. The employee was paid thirty dollars a week by one company and fifty dollars a week by the other. The watchman was injured as a result of a fight that occurred on one employer's property. The court ruled that the watchman was a joint employee and, therefore, both employers were liable for workmen's compensation in proportion to the wages they paid the watchman.

Determining liability in employment situations also calls for a review of the circumstances surrounding the employment relationship. While every case presents different facts, the usual test of liability when two employers are involved is whether the actions of an employee that caused the liability claim were subject to the direction and control of his original employer or of the person or company that requested his services.

A joint employer relationship also places an employer within the legal definitions of employee/employer, called master-servant or respondeat-superior. Several case examples can add further insight into the question of liability in joint employer situations. Consider the master-servant relation-

---

[2]National Labor Relations Board, Vol. 226, No. 1.
[3]"Joint Employment," *Words and Phrases,* Permanent Edition (St. Paul, MN: West Publishing Company, 1966), Vol. 23, p. 125.

ship defined in *Stewart vs. Reutler, et al.* (32 Cal. App. 2d 195, 89 P. 2d 402, 1939). Reutler owned and managed a roadhouse where a bouncer/floor manager was employed. Stewart was a guest. While leaving the roadhouse, Stewart removed a number of firecrackers from his pocket and lit them. He was between the entrance to the roadhouse and the curb when he lit the firecrackers. The bouncer/floor manager approached Stewart and told him to stop. When Stewart tried to light more firecrackers, the bouncer hit him in the face and knocked him out. Stewart subsequently sued Reutler, the owner, and others. Upon appeal by Reutler, the court again ruled for the plaintiff Stewart, stating that the bouncer's actions were within the scope of his job duties and therefore Reutler was liable. The following reasons were cited:

- The bouncer was employed to use force on guests whenever he thought it was necessary to keep peace and preserve order.
- Sufficient evidence supported the claim that the bouncer was acting within the scope of his authority and employment.
- The bouncer was directly involved in the duties he was employed to perform when the incident occurred. Clearly, the bouncer's duties included a duty to preserve order not only on the floor of the roadhouse, but also on the approaches to the roadhouse.

A clear parallel can be drawn between this case and instances in which a contract security officer is responsible for protecting an employer's property and is authorized to use force to protect that property. If an employer is going to be held liable for all actions of a contract employee performed as part of his job, the company may decide to exercise complete control and make the security staff proprietary.

Also, for a company (employer) to be held liable for injuries inflicted by an employee under the doctrine of respondeat-superior, the employee/employer (master-servant) relationship must exist at the time of the injury and cause the circumstances that resulted in injury.

For example, in *Lawrence v. Crescent Amusement Co.* (8 TENN. App. 216), the owner of a theater had been robbed and requested special police protection. The owner gave the police officer a key to the theater so the officer could enter the premises when necessary. On one such occasion, the officer found a person on the premises and, subsequently, the person was killed by the police officer's actions. When the case came to court, the owner was not held liable because the police officer was not directly employed by the theater owner when the incident occurred.

The liability of an employer who hires police officers as security personnel is a special case. Unless otherwise provided by statute, a private person or company employing a police officer is not responsible for the acts of the officer if the acts are performed in carrying out the officer's sworn public duties, even if the officer is employed by a private company at the time of the act. However, if the officer is performing duties for which he is employed, such as the protection of property, the employer may be liable for the officer's acts. The company's liability, then, is subject to the legal interpretation of the actions of the police officer, and whether or not they were directed by the employer.[4]

From another side of the liability question, can a company protect itself or even prepare a defensible position when a contract security officer is injured as a result of possible negligence on the part of the company?

Generally, whether or not a particular act constitutes negligence is a question based on an interpretation of the law by the court and then an interpretation of the facts by a jury. The court must first consider three elements of the law before concluding that negligence has occurred: (1) the existence of a duty on the part of the defendant to protect the plaintiff from injury or damage; (2) the failure of the defendant to perform that duty; and (3) that injury or damage to the plaintiff arose from such failure.[5] If the court rules that these three factors did indeed occur, the case then goes to a jury who makes a punitive or actual award based on the facts of the case.

Like all employees, a contract security officer is considered an invitee on the corporation's premises. The legal reference *American Jurisprudence* states that "an owner or occupant of lands or buildings who directly or indirectly invites other to enter for some purpose of interest or advantage has a duty to use ordinary care to have the premises in a reasonably safe condition."[6] The owner must also give the invitee "adequate and timely notice and warning of latent or concealed perils which are known to the owner but may not be known to the invitee."[7]

The first recorded case specifically concerning the liability of a company caused by negligence that resulted in injury to a contract security officer was *Lincoln vs. Appalachian Corporation* (Louisiana Supreme Court, Nov. 3, 1919, 83 So. 364). The plaintiff, Lincoln, appealed a judgment rejecting his demands for damages because of personal injuries received through the fault and negligence of the defendant, Appalachian Corporation. The company, in its defense, generally denied the allegation, stating that Lincoln contributed to the factors that caused the accident.

Lincoln was employed by a guard agency that had contracted with Appalachian Corporation for guard services in their building. Lincoln's duties were similar to making clock rounds as he passed through the premises.

One night, Lincoln started on his rounds and came upon a closed door that was normally open. Lincoln attempted to pull open the door, and it

---

[4]"Master and Servant," *Corpus Juris Secundum* (Brooklyn, NY: American Law Book Company, 1948), Vol. 57, p. 284.
[5]"Negligence," *Florida Jurisprudence* (San Francisco, CA: Bancroft-Whitney Company, 1959), Vol. 23, p. 264.
[6]"Negligence," *American Jurisprudence*. 2nd Edition (Rochester, NY: Lawyers Cooperative Publishing Company, and San Francisco, CA: Bancroft-Whitney Company, 1972), Vol. 62, p. 309.
[7]*Ibid.*

eventually came off its track and fell, pinning him to the floor. He was freed by passersby and taken to a hospital.

The facts in the case proved that the door was normally open. On the day of the accident, an employee of the company had been ordered to close the door. Incidents where similar doors had come off their tracks were on record, but Appalachian had made no effort to correct the situation. While some evidence indicated that Lincoln had been rough and careless when handling doors on previous occasions, this fact only proved further that the company needed to install safety rails.

In the appeal, the courts ruled that while Lincoln was not an employee of the company in the strict sense, he was an employee of the company's guard agency. Therefore, the company, in fulfilling its duties to the guard agency, was obligated to provide a safe place for Lincoln to perform his job.

In contract negotiations, both the company and the contractor make tradeoffs when determining the amount of control and the potential liability each will assume. The more control, the greater the liability and the more likely the arrangement will be ruled a joint employer relationship. The tradeoffs can be plotted in graph form to determine where maintaining control but limiting liability is most economical, but this point should not be considered a stable indicator, since rulings by the courts change with circumstances.

A corporation should consider all the potential liabilities when writing security procedures and specifications for obtaining contract security services. The legal questions raised by joint employer relationships as they relate to workmen's compensation laws and the potential for union representation have underlying effects. Since security contracts are not usually signed for short periods, a company has to decide prior to the onset of a contract what type of control it wishes to assume.

The time to prepare for the amount of control is in the performance specifications and in the final bid review with the contractor. At that time, the decision can be made whether to withdraw completely from administrative control, or to accept the responsibilities of a joint employer relationship.

CHAPTER 33

Awareness of Privacy Rules Is Crucial for Security Pros

Robert R. Belair
Attorney

Privacy standards expressed in federal and state statutes, in proposed legislation, and in judicial decisions increasingly need to be taken into consideration by security professionals. In the last five years the pace of privacy activity has quickened dramatically: the Congress enacted two major privacy statutes; ten states adopted comprehensive privacy legislation; and half a dozen special commissions were at work. During the past year alone, dozens of bills were introduced in state legislatures and countless court decisions, including several Supreme Court opinions, grappled with the subject.

Because of efforts by the ASIS Privacy and Security Committee chaired by Don Duckworth, the private security industry is becoming more aware of the importance of these new and strengthened privacy rules. The following discussion gives the security professional a thumbnail sketch of the types of activity that may be affected by current and proposed standards.

An analysis of privacy law suggests that security departments and organizations should review at least six types of practices in order to evaluate the extent to which their operations may be affected by privacy standards:

- practices that result in physical interference with individuals;
- truth detection devices;
- electronic surveillance practices;
- visual surveillance practices;
- procedures for the collection of personal information; and
- procedures for the disclosure of personal information.

Security professionals are sometimes called upon to detain or search employees or customers. The risks associated with such practices are high and growing higher. The law concerning physical interference differs in each

Reprinted with permission of the American Society for Industrial Security, from *Security Management,* March 1979, pp. 14.
Based in part on a presentation Mr. Belair made to an ASIS workshop on privacy held in Washington, D.C. March 13–14, 1977.

state; however, generally speaking, any touching or physical contact with an individual against that individual's will can result in a civil action against the security professional and his organization for battery. Furthermore, any interference with a person's freedom of movement and liberty, even if no physical contact is involved, can lead to a civil action for assault and/or false imprisonment, and arrest. Most states, either by statute or judicial decree (common law), recognize a limited exception for shopkeepers, their security personnel and certain other persons or organizations to detain or even search employees or customers. However this exception is narrow and should not be relied upon except in circumstances where the theft or other illegal act was actually observed. Even then, liability for the employer or business organization may result if physical force or verbal intimidation is used.

The outcome of recent lawsuits suggests that the courts are increasingly receptive to damage actions for detentions and other types of physical interference. For example, in *Black v. Kroger Company*[1] a grocery store checkout clerk was accused of stealing money from her cash register. Although she was never touched by her employer, the jury found that she was sufficiently intimidated to be put in fear of her life, property, or reputation. The court found that the employee felt that she could not leave a room where she was being interviewed by security personnel and further had to accompany security personnel at their request to her bank. In the court's opinion, the employee never asked to leave or affirmatively indicated a desire to terminate the interview. She sued for false imprisonment and was awarded $25,700.

In a similar suit, *General Motors Corporation v. Piskor,*[2] security guards detained an auto worker leaving the plant because they suspected that he was carrying auto parts. The court found that the guards yelled at the employee and "nudged and shoved him." Eventually, the employee won $25,000 in punitive damages in a successful action for defamation, assault, and false imprisonment.[3]

Attacks on the use of the polygraph and newer "truth detection" devices such as the voice analyzer are increasing. Security professionals should review carefully the nature and extent of their use of such devices. On the legislative front, congressional observers believe that within the next couple of years Congress will enact S. 1845, a bill that would prohibit the use of truth detection devices by non-governmental organizations for most employment purposes. The federal government already has regulations that bar the use of the polygraph in employment decisions for most federal jobs.

About one-third of the states currently have statutes that prohibit or restrict private use of the polygraph. Another third regulate the use of these

---

[1]527 S.W. 2nd 794 (Ct. of Civ. App. Tex. 1975).
[2]340 A.2d 767 (Md. App. 1975).
[3]Security personnel and their counsel who are interested in reviewing other physical interference cases are referred to the *Legal Liability Reporter,* published by Americans for Effective Law Enforcement, May 1976.

devices—typically by setting operator licensing requirements. The remaining third of the states do not have statutory restrictions.

The issue of whether the polygraph violates privacy has seldom been litigated for the simple reason that the subject must consent to a polygraph test before it can be administered. This consent generally has the effect of barring the subject from bringing an action later on for invasion of privacy. This standard is not expected to change.

On the other hand, the use of potentially covert truth testing devices such as the voice analyzer does raise the possibility that a court would find that covert and thus nonconsensual use of the device would violate a subject's expectation of privacy. Members of the security industry that still use truth detection devices should at least begin to plan for the possibility of their future prohibition.

Federal law prohibits the use of electronic devices to intercept conversations transmitted by wire or wireless means (18 U.S.C. § 2510 *et seq.*). The sole exception permits the interception of communications if one party to the conversation consents to the interception provided that the interception is not done for criminal or tortious purposes.[4]

Despite this exception, security professionals should be extremely wary of engaging in wiretapping and eavesdropping. In the first place, some states have enacted statutes that prohibit all electronic surveillance by private parties. Secondly, in some cases security professionals may have trouble demonstrating knowing and intelligent consent by one of the parties to the conversation. Proving this consent can be especially difficult in companies where employers monitor their employees' business calls at random and without specific advance notice. For example, in *United States v. Perkins,*[5] a federal district court found that a radio station manager's practice of surreptitious monitoring of the telephone conversations of employees could not be excused by the theory that the employees had implicitly consented to the surveillance.

Third, and perhaps most importantly, the courts are increasingly receptive to claims of wiretapping violations. In one recent decision, the Eighth Circuit Court of Appeals reiterated the Supreme Court's admonition that wiretapping is "dirty business."[6] In that case, the court held a private detective firm liable for participating in the wiretapping of a husband's telephone calls although the wife authorized the tap and installed the device. The detective agency had supplied the device and instructed the wife in its installation.

Visual surveillance can lead to lawsuits in at least two circumstances. First, if the surveillance involves shadowing and trailing that is obvious, unreasonable or likely to embarrass a person of ordinary sensibilities, courts

---

[4]See, *Smith v. Wunker,* 356 F. Supp. 44 (S.D. Ohio, 1972)
[5]383 F. Supp. 922 (N.D. Ohio 1974)
[6]*White v. Weiss,* 535 F.2d 1067 (8th Cir. 1976)

may find that the subject's right of privacy has been violated. Secondly, if the visual surveillance exposes an area where the subject reasonably expected that his actions would be hidden from view, a court may also find that his privacy has been invaded. Visual surveillance of rest rooms, fitting rooms, hotel rooms, or other locations where individuals normally expect privacy come within this category.

Security professionals should also be wary of visual surveillance practices that involve the use of covert cameras, telephoto lenses, night lights, and other sophisticated devices. Given the direction of privacy and search and seizure law, courts may begin to compensate subjects who are the target of visual surveillance that is made possible or more effective through the use of the new generation of advanced visual surveillance aides.

In fact, recovery may be possible someday for advanced technology visual surveillance even when the subject is not in a private or hidden location. Predictions indicate that the corporate use of cameras to photograph employees in the work place will become a more frequent subject of litigation.

For example, several years ago employees at General Electric brought suit for use of cameras to photograph work sites. The federal district court's opinion denied the employees' privacy claim but left unanswered most questions about the extent and nature of permissible employer visual surveillance.[7] And just last year a labor union sued the Michigan Liquor Control Commission for conducting camera surveillance of employees doing stock work in warehouses.[8] Although the local court once again dismissed the privacy claim, security professionals and their counsel should review visual surveillance practices—especially advanced technology surveillance—in light of potential privacy claims. Covert surveillance of public areas as opposed to the use of highly visible cameras or signs warning of surveillance may present the more substantial privacy claim.

Each of the practices discussed thus far has its own unique legal and policy considerations, but all three are used typically to collect information. Legal issues surrounding these information collection practices should logically be separated from two legal issues related to collection practices: the subject matter of the information, and the use of third parties as sources of information.

The general rule, until now at least, has been that security professionals could assemble as much information about an individual as they pleased—provided they used legal means to collect the data. This rule may be changing. For example, a recent decision by a federal district court in Baltimore suggests that an applicant's right of privacy may be violated by the amount or type of personal information that a *public* employer collects when making an employment decision. In that case, an applicant for a social worker po-

---

[7]*Thomas v. General Electric*, 207 F. Supp. 792 (W.D. Kent., 1962)
[8]*Local 1342 v. Michigan Liquor Control Commission* (Cir. Ct. of Wayne County 1977)

sition charged Montgomery County with sex discrimination and invasion of privacy for denying her a job when she refused to complete an employment application that included questions about "vaginal discharges" and other intimate "women's questions."[9]

Security professionals, whether acting as employers or as agents for employers, should review collection practices to eliminate or at least minimize the gathering of personal information that is not directly related to qualifications for employment. This task is especially difficult in light of information collection responsibilities imposed by state investigator and private police licensing statutes, and by more general employer requirements found in the *Equal Employment Opportunity Act*, the *Employees Retirement and Income Security Act*, and the *Occupational Safety and Health Act of 1970*.

In addition to concern about the extent and nature of the data collected, security professionals need to be concerned about soliciting personal information from third parties. The *Fair Credit Reporting Act* (15 U.S.C. § 1681 *et seq.*) governs the use of reports that contain information about a person's credit record, character, and personal living habits. Although the *Fair Credit Reporting Act (FCRA)* has been criticized as insufficient protection for privacy interests, the Act does contain some limits on the use of this information and significant penalties for violations.

Several factors need to be kept in mind about this statute. First, FCRA may soon be strengthened as a result of the recommendations of a two-year federal commission, the Privacy Protection Study Commission, and the work of Senator Proxmire's Committee on Banking and Finance. Second, the Federal Trade Commission, which enforces the federal act, shows signs of new vigor in its prosecutions. Third, many states have adopted their own fair credit reporting acts, some of which differ in content from the federal act or have a different enforcement history.

Security professionals should determine whether they are functioning under the FCRA as a "consumer reporting agency" in preparing investigative reports or as a user of such reports. In both cases, the security professional has responsibilities under the Act, which should be reviewed periodically with counsel.

Another third party data collection issue that deserves special attention is the use of "pretext interviews." The procedure of misrepresenting, either explicitly or by implication, the identity or purpose of an investigator has drawn fire from the Privacy Protection Study Commission, legislators and a bevy of state prosecutors. Those engaging in such practices run a high risk of civil and perhaps even criminal liability.

One last note about the collection of personal information. Over the last few years, more and more federal and state agencies must operate under statutes or regulations that greatly limit a private corporation's access to

---

[9] *Cox v. Montgomery County* (U.S. Dist. Ct. of Md., Civ. No. B-75-1086, June 13, 1977)

personal information held by these agencies. These restrictions especially affect the release of arrest and conviction records. Assuming, as some indications suggest, that this development will continue, security professionals would be well advised to review their need for and use of personal information held by divisions of the government.

Disclosure of personal information about an organization's employees and customers involves severe risks. Most employees and customers consider their personal information confidential and the courts are likely to agree. Indeed, a 1978 survey of employee attitudes toward privacy conducted by the Center for Study of Privacy Issues at Purdue University found that most employees are far more concerned about the disclosure to outside agencies of personal information held by their employer than any other privacy issue.

Security professionals and other corporate officers should not disclose personal information, either orally or in writing, without first obtaining the subject's consent. (Be careful that the consent measures up to standards proposed by the Privacy Commission and meets the requirements of federal agencies such as the FTC and the Department of the Treasury. The consent or authorization should be in writing and should include specifics about the information to be disclosed, the party authorized to disclose, the party authorized to receive, and a reasonably short expiration date.)

When requests for information must be filled without the subject's consent, security professionals should first identify the precise information being sought, the party receiving the information, and the purpose of the disclosure. Then, security professionals can, with the advice of counsel asses whether a disclosure of that type or for that reason is proper.

Increasingly, non-consensual disclosures of personal information expose corporations to legal liability. In most states, courts can award a subject damages for improper disclosure on either a defamation (libel and slander) theory or an invasion of privacy theory. An action for defamation can be maintained in most states if evidence can be produced to show that a party disclosed information about an individual to a third party, either in writing (libel) or orally (slander), that had the effect of damaging the reputation of the individual. Disclosure of derogatory information about an individual's honesty, morality, and business or employment performance is especially open to liability.

In most states, two defenses are ordinarily available to businessmen in defamation actions. First, if the information disclosed is true the defamation action cannot be maintained. Second, groups with common interests, including employers, credit grantors, and other business and professional organizations, can exchange personal data provided that disclosure is made in good faith for a legitimate business purpose even if the information turns out to be untrue or damaging to the individual's reputation.

This defense of "privilege" has been incorporated into FCRA and in most state fair credit reporting acts. These acts permit parties to disclose personal information to consumer reporting agencies and in turn permit consumer reporting agencies to pass the information along to their customers without fear of defamation or invasion of privacy suits. The exceptions are cases where the information is false *and* is disclosed with malice or willful intent to injure the consumer.[10]

However, security professionals should be wary of relying upon these various privilege doctrines. For example, a 1976 decision by a Florida State Court of Appeals ruled that a corporation does not have an absolute right to tell its employees or anyone else why it fired someone. In that case the Westinghouse Corporation discharged an employee for allegedly taking scrap iron rods from its plant without authorization. At a subsequent meeting a company spokesman was asked why the employee was discharged and the spokesman replied, "for misappropriating company property." The discharged employee sued for slander and the court suggested that if a corporation impugns an employee's honesty it must be able to prove, as a legal matter, that the employee is guilty of theft.[11]

In all but a handful of states, employees and customers can also bring suits for improper disclosures on an invasion of privacy theory. Privacy liability can result from public disclosure of private facts (even true facts), disclosures that put the individual in a "false light," or from appropriation of the individual's personal information for the corporation's own commercial or other purposes.

For instance, in a 1977 case, the Michigan Supreme Court found that an employee could bring action for invasion of privacy based on public disclosure of "embarrassing private facts." The court found that the employer gratuitously and unnecessarily made derogatory remarks about the employee's job performance in a letter to the US Army Reserves sent by the employer to verify his military duties. The letter accused the employee of being "disloyal and insubordinate" and informed the reserve unit that the employee used his reserve status in an "abusive and manipulative manner."[12]

Security professionals need to be in the forefront of efforts by the private sector to review practices for the collection and disclosure of personal information. When reviewing information gathering and investigative practices, security professionals should keep a few points in mind: do not permit security personnel to use force or verbal intimidation or abuse in investigations of employees and customers; collect and disclose personal information only to the extent necessary; inform the subject of disclosures to the greatest extent possible; avoid the use of pretext interviews; avoid the use of advanced technology surveillance devices whenever possible; know the standards adhered to by the consumer reporting agencies and other parties with whom you exchange personal information; train your employees in privacy safeguards; and periodically review your information practices with appropriate personnel and counsel.

---

[10]See, *Peller v. Retail Credit Co.*, 359 F. Supp. 1235 (N.D. Ga. 1973)
[11]See, *Drennen v. Westinghouse Electric Corp.*, 328 So.2d 52 (Dist. Ct. App. Fla. 1976)
[12]*Beaumont v. Brown*, 96 L.W. 1051 (Oct. 4, 1977, Michigan Supreme Court)

CHAPTER 34

Private Security in the Courtroom: The Exclusionary Rule Applies

Steven Euller
Attorney at Law

The way you investigate a case may have to change as a result of two court cases decided last year—one in California and one in Washington, DC. So far no one seems to be talking about them, but *People v. Zelinski* and *United States v. Lima* are likely to affect the investigative practices of private security professionals across the country.

This article will give you a brief summary of what the judges said in those cases and what changes you can expect as a result. Finally, it tells you why security professionals must act in unison to shape those changes, or live with the dismal consequences of leaving the job for someone else to do.

In *Zelinski* and *Lima* the judges held that the exclusionary rule applies to *private* security officers. If a security officer obtains physical evidence or confessions during an investigation and violates the suspect's constitutional rights in the process, the judge will suppress the tainted evidence, excluding it from the trial.

This ruling is entirely new. Several writers have proposed such a rule, and many security professionals and prosecutors have already adjusted their practices in anticipation of such a development. However, these are the first reported decisions that have actually enforced the exclusionary rule against purely private security actions.

The Fourth Amendment (no unreasonable searches) and Fifth Amendment (no forced self-incrimination) only restrict the acts of the government—the so-called "state action" requirement. In the past judges have refused to suppress evidence seized illegally by *private* citizens (including security personnel). The exclusionary rule applied in private security cases

Reprinted with permission of the American Society for Industrial Security, from *Security Management*, March 1980, pp. 38.
[1]155 California Reporter 595
[2]47 U.S. Law Week 2696

only if the security officer had been deputized, or if the police were somehow involved.

The state action rule still holds. What is new is that now, for the first time, judges have ruled that when private security officers investigate crimes, their acts are "government actions." Government action is state action, so the full force of the Constitution must govern those acts.

In *Zelinski,* two detectives in Zody's Department Store observed a suspect who took a blouse from a rack and placed it in her purse. They stopped Virginia Zelinski outside the store and led her back to the security office. There they opened her purse and retrieved the blouse. They searched further and found a vial which was later determined to contain heroin.

During her trial on the charge of possession of narcotics, Zelinski asked the judge to suppress the heroin because it had been seized in an illegal search. The trial judge allowed the evidence to come in because, he said, store detectives aren't governed by the prohibition against unreasonable searches. On appeal, the Supreme Court of California disagreed. They said the search was illegal, the State Constitution's prohibition against unreasonable searches applies, and the evidence must be suppressed.

Lima was a routine shoplifting case. A Lord & Taylor's detective watched Adelaide Lima take a blouse into a fitting room. Looking through the louvers on the fitting room door, the security officer was able to see Lima put the blouse in her purse. She arrested Lima outside the store and recovered the blouse. The trial judge ordered the blouse excluded from evidence on the motion of the defendant. He ruled that Lima had an expectation of privacy in that fitting room, and therefore that the store detective's observation of her through the slats constituted an illegal search. The blouse, a fruit of the illegal search, was suppressed.

In both cases, store detectives conducted searches that, although not particularly offensive, they were not authorized to make. Heretofore, the courts allowed such evidence to be presented since the search was not considered to involve state action. In these two cases, the judges viewed the actions differently and disallowed the evidence.

The reasoning behind both decisions can be set out in a few short steps. First, when store detectives make arrests, investigate crimes, and gather evidence by search and interrogation, they perform what is commonly regarded as police work. Second, police work is a public function. That is to say, such duties are a service normally provided by public employees—the police—on behalf of the public. Third, the police are subject to Constitutional restrictions when they act.

When private security officers substitute for the police by doing police work, thus performing a public function, they, too, act for the state. Since state action is being performed, the same Constitutional restrictions apply to those officers as would apply to the police.

These cases, especially *Zelinski,* establish a precedent. For now, they are the law only in California and perhaps the District of Columbia, but their rulings are almost certain to be adopted elsewhere. You could speculate that in the past many judges who were accustomed to applying Constitutional standards to police actions also wanted to apply them to questionable private security actions. They were stopped from doing so only because no existing law justified such an action. Those same judges will now be able to cite a decision of the influential California Supreme Court as persuasive grounds for their decisions to suppress evidence.

Some states will probably reject the *Zelinski* rule. Security officers who ignore *Zelinski,* however, may be unlucky enough to find that their own cases are the occasion for the adoption of the new rule in their home state. Until your state's highest court decides the issue, it would be wise to assume that the *Zelinski* rule might end up governing your actions.

You cannot safely ignore the *Zelinski* rule when you investigate. Every time you, the security professional, take the stand at a trial and offer evidence against a defendant, the first issue raised will be how you obtained that evidence. Your investigative practices will be on trial. If your practices don't measure up, your evidence will be refused, and at best you will suffer embarrassment and frustration.

The better way to proceed is to review your current methods and, if necessary, change the way you gather evidence to comply with the law. In an effort to comply you will probably search only after obtaining the suspect's clear consent, or in certain emergencies when you are justified in suspecting that the person is hiding a weapon or contraband. You will probably require Miranda warnings and waivers before you interrogate anyone. No doubt you will also avoid using threats, tricks, and other tactics which are sometimes taken as evidence that a confession wasn't voluntary: extended questioning, denial of opportunities to contact outsiders, failure to provide food and drink, and so on.

Like it or not, the *Zelinski* rule is coming. There are good reasons why security professionals should welcome it. The *Zelinski* court recognized that private security personnel play an important role in law enforcement and often act on the public's behalf. Part of the reason some people are concerned about abuses is simply because security professionals have at times demonstrated their impressive investigative skills and sophistication. The new rules will encourage the private security industry to upgrade its level of professionalism, to discipline itself, to erase the image of the lawless private eye.

Most important, these cases offer a challenge and opportunity to security professionals that will be ignored only at great cost. Since only *legally* obtained evidence will be admissible, courts must now determine what security methods are legal. One way or another, new rules are about to be written that will govern the conduct of security personnel. The courts will establish some, legislatures may write others. If security professionals don't take the initiative and help to write guidelines they can live with, they may be stuck with a disastrous set of laws. Once established, such laws are undone only with great difficulty.

If the courts are left to write the rules, they are not likely to develop a comprehensive and consistent set of laws. Courts decide only what they have to—the issues presented in the cases before them. The process is both slow and unpredictable.

Legislators, by the nature of the legal system, have a better chance to write a comprehensive, logical set of rules. The risk is that legislative bodies may write laws that are either too strict or too broad in scope. They need persuasive, informative input from security experts. They need to be educated about different functions and levels of expertise within the security industry, so they do not try to apply the exclusionary rule where it will be totally ineffective for deterrence purposes. (Right now both judges and legislators tend to lump together all security personnel—from the corporate security directors down to the gatekeeper—into one catch-all category. They are all viewed essentially as guards.)

Security managers have both an interest in and an obligation to take charge of the rule-making. An industry that governs itself and corrects its own abuses can more reasonably expect cooperation from the lawmakers. The time for fighting to avoid any rules or restrictions at all has passed.

Security professionals should agree that they do work in the public interest and that they are part of the law enforcement team. In that role, they should agree to respect the constitutional rights of suspects and to be bound by the same restrictions that bind the public police.

At the same time that security professionals accept greater responsibility for their actions, they should be given expanded powers to enable them to perform their law enforcement role effectively. Their expertise and interest in criminal investigation, the same factors that justify the application of the exclusionary rule, should also qualify them for the exercise of greater discretion than the lay citizen. This greater authority could take many forms. The most apparent needs are for the power to arrest upon probable cause and powers of search comparable to these held by a police officer.

Legislation that separates the security professional for special treatment is not hard to envision. Accordingly, higher standards ought to accompany greater authority. The numerous shoplifter detention and deputization statutes are meager beginnings in this direction. The eventual form of such legislation is unclear—it might be tied to the CPP program, licensing, deputization, and so on—but the potential is there.

Security professionals need to take the lead now. The opportunity is at hand. *Zelinski* and *Lima* in the courts are paralleled by legislative developments in the areas of credit investigation, polygraph, and employee privacy. The new rules will be written. The security industry cannot afford not to participate in the process.

CHAPTER 35

You've Caught a Thief— Now What?

B. Dustin Ball
Director of Loss Prevention
Davidson's Foodtown Supermarkets

Frequently, members of a retail company's management team attend seminars and workshops on loss prevention and security. They come away from these meetings eager to make use of the new material digested. Many seminar programs are geared toward arming the attendee with the ammunition to effect an apprehension. Thus, the store manager, front end manager, or other attendee returns to his or her operation, and lo and behold, apprehends a dishonest employee. But, *now what?*

This is often a difficult question for that particular manager to answer, and it is at this point that the success of the apprehension is most in question. It is also at this point that this manager will become successful at loss prevention or give up on the process because of his or her insecurity about following through with the apprehension.

These problems are illustrated by the following case histories:

Store A. The store manager, aware of the policies of the company, observed a cashier waiting on what was obviously one of his friends. Curious, the manager positioned himself so he could see three dollars cash tendered for what he felt sure was at least ten dollars worth of products. The manager approached the cashier and customer while the cashier was giving change, looked at the receipt, and discovered that his suspicion of dishonesty was well-founded.

At this point, the manger totaled the order and found its value to be $11.96, while the receipt showed the purchase price to be $2.80, a discount of $9.16. The store manager had apprehended an employee and detained a customer—now what?

The store manager collected the $9.16 from the customer and had the cashier ring it up. Then he allowed the customer to leave and take the

Reprinted with permission of the American Society for Industrial Security, from *Security Management*, January 1982, pp. 35.

purchases. The cashier was told to close down and count out. At this point, the manager telephoned his loss prevention supervisor to tell him what had occurred.

The manager was completely surprised when the loss prevention supervisor was critical of the manager's actions. The manager had apprehended a dishonest employee and recovered a potential loss. What else could have been done?

Store B. In Store B, the assistant store manager observed a cashier via camera and with the monitor function of his electronic cash register system (the manager's suspicion was based on a tip from another employee). The cashier rang out a $42.10 order for $23.57.

The manager approached the cashier with the copy of the receipt generated by the ECR system and detained the customer and the cashier. The manager then retotaled the purchase, which came to $42.10. The cashier had rung it up at almost a fifty percent discount. Because of the obvious difference between the amount registered and the actual value of the products, the manager asked the customer to accompany him to the back room. He placed a female employee in the room with the customer, who was also female.

The manager then closed out the cash register and detained the cashier in a separate room. He secured the the detail tape, the customer tape, the ECR duplicate tape, and the items in question. He then telephoned his loss prevention supervisor for further direction.

In the case of Store A, the manager had the company's interest at heart when he began his course of action. Because of several procedural errors, however, he placed the success of the apprehension in jeopardy. When the Store A manager allowed the customer to pay for the product and then remove the evidence, the case became a nightmare to prosecute. Physical evidence and its control strengthens the case against an employee in a union hearing and is essential for a criminal prosecution. The manager effectively ruled out any option to prosecute the employee. By not isolating the cashier in question, he allowed that cashier to formulate excuses for his actions with other employees, or to decide that silence would be an effective defense.

In Store B, the assistant manager not only secured the physical evidence of the case, but he isolated the parties involved in the offense. Most important, he timed his call to his loss prevention supervisor so that all options of procedure were left open.

In Store A, the loss prevention supervisor was able to salvage the case by getting a written statement of a violation of company policy from the cashier, resulting in termination of the employee. In Store B, the loss prevention supervisor was provided with evidence that allowed for a successful prosecution of both the cashier and the customer. In addition, the loss prevention supervisor was able to obtain information about other dishonest activities in that store from another employee apprehended later.

The management personnel in both these examples were motivated to protect the assets of the company. Both cases had positive results in terms of product recovery, but by properly securing the evidence, Store B was able to control the outcome of the incident with greater success.

In examining both cases, it is evident that certain criteria are essential for apprehension:

- Observation of the violation.
- Preservation of the physical evidence, such as customer receipts, detail tape, and the merchandise involved.
- Isolation of the parties.
- A call to the loss prevention supervisor for further direction.

Several factors affected the outcome of both these cases. Both occurred in New Jersey, where discounting by cashiers is included in the shoplifting statute. In each case, the customer who was arrested could not claim innocence of the cashier's action because of the wide discrepancy between the price paid and the actual value. Had the discount been four dollars on a forty dollar order, the court might justly have felt the customer was unaware of the discount.

What if the situation in Store B had occurred in a company without a loss prevention department? What additional steps could that assistant manager have taken to ensure a positive outcome from the apprehension?

If the manager intended solely to terminate his employee, he should have started his investigation by speaking with the customer. The discussion with the customer should have included getting a written statement of what had just occurred. Should a similar situation occur in your store, keep the following procedural tips in mind. The customer should be asked to write down facts such as how long he or she has known the cashier involved, their relationship, whether or not he or she expected to get the discount in advance, and whether he or she is willing to pay the full price. The customer should not be allowed to pay the full price of the item at this point; instead, the manager should refund the portion already paid.

The customer's statement should be signed and dated by the customer, with another employee as a witness. The person's full name, address, and driver's license number or other identification should be noted. The manager should also obtain a statement in the customer's own writing to the effect that no duress was applied in obtaining the statement.

At this point, the customer should be released. Detaining the customer beyond this point without calling police to press charges could cause severe civil complications.

The manager should interview the cashier once the customer has been released. The cashier should not be admonished for his or her behavior, but the situation should be discussed calmly and positively. A statement of the cashier's involvement should be obtained. Again, this statement should be written by the cashier, not by the manager. *Once the statement from the cashier is complete,* the manager is free to discuss past incidents in which the cashier has discounted, stolen merchandise, or committed other violations with the cashier. The manager is also free to discuss other employees and their involvement in theft, being careful to let the cashier bring up names of individuals involved, so it doesn't appear as if the manager is singling out other employees he may already suspect.

When the manager feels he has completed the investigation, he should then advise the employee that he is terminating him for violating company policy, *not* for stealing. This is a critical step, because unless the employee has been convicted in court of theft, he or she is still innocent of the crime of theft. However, no such restrictions apply to stating that the termination is for violation of company policy in register procedure.

Let's consider several ways of handling these two cases. If the cashier in Store B had refused to give a written statement and the manager had elected not to prosecute, for example, a termination could still have been sustained. To build a strong case for termination of an employee in a situation like this, the manager can take several steps. Photographs should be taken and witnessed by another employee, the customer tape should be saved, and a detailed report should be made of the incident, including the customer's statement.

If, on the other hand, the manager of Store B *did* want to prosecute the customer and the employee, he should call the police (with the evidence already secured). A long investigation before telephoning the police is not encouraged. To obtain a statement from the customer is desirable, but not necessary; in court the customer may enter a plea of guilty if he or she knows a statement exists. However, the court usually will not accept a statement made to a store manager, requiring instead that the prosecution proceed on evidence and witnesses' statements.

The same is true of the cashier's statement. If the employee is bonded by Fidelity Insurance, however, previous acts of dishonesty detailed by the cashier in a statement may have significant value. Depending on the state in which the violation occurs and the amount of admissions a cashier makes, civil proceedings may accept the statement as a basis for civil recovery.

Managers are generally neither trained investigators nor skilled interviewers. Therefore, they should not actively continue the investigation past the four-point procedure previously described. Rather, their situations should be turned over to a trained loss prevention supervisor.

The loss prevention professional should be the first to conduct interviews with the violators. Where no loss prevention or security department exists, the store manager must proceed with the basics outlined.

Few things are as frustrating as having a dishonest employee reinstated because the procedures used in apprehending him or her were mishandled. Worse yet is seeing a dishonest employee succeed in a civil proceeding because of a poorly executed investigation. Store managers should be properly trained so they will know what to do after they apprehend a dishonest employee.

CHAPTER 36

Coping with Legal Restraints
E. Gary Baker
President
Baker and Associates, Inc.

During the past several years, instances of violence occurring during labor disputes have been increasing. In response, management requests for special security services, from awareness programs to undercover agents, are frequently seen in industry publications. Security managers are also called on to provide additional services during labor disputes. If, in these cases, security managers and contractors are unfamiliar with labor law and the consequences of violations, the services provided could easily constitute unfair labor practices on the part of management.

While it is important to plan for a labor dispute, documenting improper worker activity on the picket line and providing evidence of illegal acts, these security activities cannot precede an actual dispute, thereby possibly intimidating or coercing workers in their legitimate union activities—a thin line, obviously. If precautions are not taken, union officials can charge that management did not bargain in good faith, since the company geared up for the strike by improving physical security, hiring contract guards, and briefing supervisors on security awareness.

Security activities must be designed to prevent security employees from committing any act that could produce allegations of unfair labor practices. Particular attention should be paid to surveillance of employee activities and security investigations.

Employer surveillance of employee union activities has met with unmitigated hostility from the National Labor Relations Board (NLRB) since its inception. The United States Supreme Court in *Consolidated Edison Co. v. NLRB*[1] affirmed the enforcement of an order from the NLRB to require the company to cease and desist from:

Employing detectives to investigate the activities of their employees on behalf of

Reprinted with permission of the American Society for Industrial Security, from *Security Management,* March 1982, pp. 41.
[1]*Consolidated Edison Co. v. NLRB,* (305 U.S. 197, 230 (1938)).

*[an organizing union] or any other labor organization of their employees or
employing any other form or manner of espionage for such purposes.*

In this case, the NLRB had found that the company employed detectives as "industrial spies" in order to investigate several union meetings and
conventions, as well as activities of individual employees. The company
denied the allegation, but the manager of the detective agency testified about
the nature of the investigation, providing the evidence necessary to support
the claim.

The primary development of the law regarding surveillance has focused
on organizational activities. Unlawful surveillance has, however, consistently
been analyzed as a violation of the National Labor Relations Act,[2] which
makes it an unfair labor practice "to interfere with, restrain, or coerce
employees in the exercise of the rights guaranteed by section 7" of the act,
which reads:

*Employees shall have the right to self-organization, to form, join, or assist labor
organizations, to bargain collectively through representatives of their own choosing, and to engage in other concerted activities for the purpose of collective
bargaining or other mutual aid or protection. . . .*

Even a purely economic strike has been held to be a concerted activity
for mutual aid and protection, and therefore covered under section 7.

The NLRB, supported in general by the courts, has not shown the
slightest hesitation in applying these principles, particularly in cases that
include photographing picket lines. The following is a representative statement of the NLRB's view of strike photography:

*Few propositions are more firmly embedded in the law of labor relations than
that an employer who spies upon the union activities of his employees engages
in a flagrant violation of [Section 7]. Such conduct has been condemned by the
Board and the Courts since the earliest days of the Act, for experience has shown
that employers resort to labor espionage or surveillance for the purpose of
obstructing or destroying employees' self-organizational rights and activities. If
such first steps leading to discriminatory practices are outlawed, the commission
of other unfair labor practices may be thwarted [citing Wallace Press, Inc., 146
NLRB 1236, 1238 (1964)].*
    *Surveillance is unlawful regardless of the employer's good faith [citing
Kingwood Mining Co., 166 NLRB 957 (1967), enf'd 404 F. 2d 348 (4th Cir.
1968)], or whether there is proof that any employees were intimidated or coerced
thereby [citing Premier Worsted Mills, 85 NLRB, 985, 986 (1949)]. Thus,
photographing the activities of striking employees constitutes unlawful surveillance absent any legitimate purpose for taking the pictures [citing Russell Sports-
wear Corp., 197 NLRB 1116 (1972)].*

---

[2]National Labor Relations Act, S 8(a)(1).

There is no basis, then, for presuming that surveillance is inherently more acceptable in the context of a strike than in a union organizational campaign. Rather, the critical question is whether surveillance of employee activities serves a legitimate purpose.

In certain situations, the status of the one who performs, or who is requested to perform, the surveillance is relevant. An employer that asks an employee to attend a union meeting and report back violates the act, regardless of whether the employee actually performs the surveillance.[3] Similarly, statements by managerial or supervisory personnel implying that management is engaged in surveillance of union activity can be a violation; the actual occurrence of the surveillance is irrelevant. It has been held that "creating the impression" of surveillance can coerce employees as effectively as the surveillance itself since the fear of future reprisals will result from such an impression.[4] In this case, though, the existence of an established bargaining relationship may give the supervisor more latitude in discussions with employees than in instances where the union is organizing.[5]

The concept of creating an impression is not limited to management statements, and is often used as a ground for liability in situations involving surveillance devices. For example, the NLRB found that training closed-circuit security cameras on the company building in which a union meeting was held created the impression of surveillance, despite the evidence that the security guards were not monitoring the meeting or those who entered the building.[6] The Tenth Circuit Court, however, has explicitly adopted the comparatively narrow standard requiring the union to demonstrate that the employer has created an impression of surveillance by showing a "willful conduct and a justifiable impression."[7]

Employers have hired detective or security agencies to perform various functions in connection with strikes or organizational campaigns, such as hiring uniformed guards for plant protection. Clearly, such employment practices will come under scrutiny. The deciding factor will be "whether, under all the facts and circumstances of a particular case, surveillance of employees [in the form of patrolling guards] is for the lawful purpose of plant protection, or for the prohibited purpose of employee restraint and intimidation. . . ."[8]

Even if the need for plant protection can be proved, statements by the employer about the reason for employing the guards can constitute a violation. The Third Circuit Court enforced an NLRB decision finding a violation by an employer who indicated that it was using guards to patrol its

---

[3]*Suburban Transit Corp. v. NLRB*, 499 F.2d 78, 87 (3rd Cir.), *cert. denied.* 419 U.S. 1089 (1974).
[4]*NLRB v. Dayton Tire & Rubber Co.* 503 F.2d 759 (10th Cir. 1974).
[5]*NLRB v. International Typographical Union*, 452 F.2d 976, 978 (10th Cir. 1971).
[6]*CBS Records Division*, 223 NLRB 709 (1976).
[7]*NLRB v. Simplex Time Recorder Co.*, 401 F.2d 547, 549 (1st Cir. 1968).
[8]*NLRB v. National Paper Co.*, 216 F.2d 859, 866 (5th Cir. 1954).

property because "the union is coming in."[9] Of course, even when the use of the guards is not unlawful in itself, the guards themselves can commit individual acts of surveillance that are illegal. Explicit training is necessary to avoid this possibility.

Hiring detectives to investigate the activities of employees away from the workplace has invoked the following comment from the NLRB:

> *Such surveillance of an employee has long been held to be a flagrant violation of the rights guaranteed by section 7 of the Act. The Board and the Courts have condemned such spying since the early days of the Act.* Consolidated Edison Company v. NLRB, 305 US 197, 230 (1938). . . .[10]

Both *Consolidated Edison* and *Manuel San Juan* involved "tailing" individual employees believed to be union activists. However, other types of surveillance by detectives have been held to be unlawful. The activities of security guards observing who was going in and out of a union meeting were held to be a violation,[11] despite the fact that, at the time of the observation, they were performing duties as police officers. Similarly, the activities of a supervisor who noted the names of those entering and leaving a union meeting during an economic strike were held to be coercive.[12]

Surveillance of employees in public bars by management representatives has also been scrutinized by the NLRB. The board indicated that if a supervisor goes to a public bar with the intent of overhearing employee discussions related to union activity, such conduct would constitute unlawful surveillance.[13] In that specific case, however, it was established that the supervisor had been a frequent patron of the bar for years, and had often associated with employees. The NLRB found no violation since the supervisor was not deviating from his normal routine. An intentional increase in contacts with employees by a supervisor on and off work encouraged by the employer, was found to be a violation.[14]

The use of undercover agents disguised as employees has also been condemned, even if the evidence discloses that some of the agents' activities involved normal company problems such as wasted time and thefts.[15] The court found that a security agency hired during a union organizing drive had "placed undercover agents in the plant who masqueraded as ordinary employees. The procedures employed by the agency displayed cloak and dagger techniques worthy of the CIA."

---

[9]*NLRB v. Treasure Lake, Inc.*, 453 F.2d 202 (3rd Cir. 1971).
[10]*Manuel San Juan Company, Inc.*, 224 NLRB 653, 655-56 (1976).
[11]*Clark's Stores*, 168 NLRB 273 (1967).
[12]*United Steelworkers of America v. NLRB*, 405 F.2d 1373, 1376 (DC Cir. 1968). *Accord, NLRB v. Standard Forge & Axle Co.*, 420 F.2d 508 (5th Cir. 1969), *cert. denied* 400 U.S. 903 (1970).
[13]*Vicent's Steak House, Inc.*, 216 NLRB 647, 649 (1975).
[14]*Russell Stover Candies, Inc.*, 551 F.2d 204, 206 (8th Cir. 1977).
[15]*NLRB v. Southwire Company*, 429 F.2d 1050 (5th Cir. 1970), *Cert. denied* 401 US 939 (1971).

Of particular interest is the manner in which the court disposed of the employer's objection that there had been no detection of the operations, and therefore no coercion:

> *The Company correctly states that not all surveillance is prohibited by the Act; that the only surveillance prohibited is that which interferes with, restrains, or coerces union activities. The Company submits that the Master did not make a finding of interference, coercion, or restraint and the surveillance here was not violative of the Act. The Company also argues rather futilely that the purpose of the security program was to spot theft, safety violations and inefficiency and hence that any ancillary or by-product spying on union activities was de minimus. But the record convincingly shows that while union surveillance was not the sole or perhaps even the chief function of [the security agency], it was by no means* de minimus.
>
> *The Company's basic argument is that since its undercover work was undetected the employees could not have felt coerced by the surveillance. It would be a surprising result if the law were such that an employer could engage in any devious spying technique it desired so long as the program was not detected by employees. Surreptitious surveillance has been disapproved as unlawful surveillance. Cf.* NLRB v. Tidelands Marine Service, Inc., *5 Cir. 1964, 339 F.2d 291;* Olsen Rug Co. v. NLRB, *7 Cir. 1962, 304 F.2d 710, 714-715;* NLRB v. Collins and Aikman Corp., *4 Cir. 1944, 146 F.2d 454, 455.*
>
> *It is true that the Master made no specific finding that a specific employee's rights were interfered with, restrained, or coerced. However, it is a reasonable inference that such information received from its agents provided the Company with a knowledge of the union leaders' activities and facilitated the Company's subsequent harsh reprisals.* (429 F.2d, at 1054, 1055.)

One employer made a rather expansive argument that it had employed security agents to pose as production workers in order to "detect theft and disposition of stolen goods, prostitution, dope peddling, gambling, and the unauthorized sale of liquor."[16] The NLRB held that the operatives acted as labor spies, reporting the identity of pro-union sympathizers.[17]

Nothing in the cited opinions indicates that it is necessarily improper to use undercover agents who do, in fact, provide information on an endemic problem, such as theft. However, if the agents are brought in for a period coincident with major union organizational drives or strikes, the propriety of such surveillance will be highly suspect.

In addition, the NLRB general counsel is not required to build his case concerning the employment of security agents based only upon the files of the employer. In both *Consolidated Edison Company, supra,* (4 NLRB, at 94-95), and *Manuel San Juan, supra,* (224 NLRB, at 654), the heads of the respective security agencies were the "star" witnesses for the general counsel.

---

[16]*Harvey Aluminum,* 139 NLRB 151 (1962).

[17]The Board's order was not enforced, however, based on the failure of the NLRB general counsel to produce statements by witnesses which were in the possession of the Department of Labor and the FBI. *Harvey Aluminum v. NLRB,* 335 F.2d 749 (9th Cir. 1964).

In addition, the agency in *Manuel San Juan* was required, pursuant to a *subpoena duces tecum,* to produce its files on the case. The files were used to show the extent of the investigation and its methodology, as well as communications with the company. In each of the cases cited, the testimony of the heads of the security agencies directly contradicted employer claims denying labor surveillance.

Decisions concerning photography and electronic devices primarily deal with two situations: photographs (or motion pictures, videotapes, etc.) showing the activities of strikers on picket lines; and recordings repeating conversations of employees or union agents through the use of "bugs."

An employer normally attempts to justify the photographing of pickets as a necessary step in collecting evidence of unlawful conduct. On the other hand, the union and the employees will normally argue that the photography serves no legitimate purpose and is "calculated to coerce and restrain the striking employees by creating a fear among them that the record of their concerted activities might be used for some future reprisals."[18]

In general terms, the NLRB, supported by the courts, has found continuous photographing of picket lines to be unlawful, without a reasonable basis for anticipating violence or mass picketing.[19,20,21] In a recent decision, the board found that photographing pickets was a violation, concluding that no unlawful conduct by the pickets took place nor was there a basis for anticipating such conduct; no injunction proceedings were instituted; inconsistent explanations for the photos were given by management; and the photography occurred in conjunction with discharges motivated by anti-union prejudice.

The court further indicated that it was the "tendency to interfere or coerce," as opposed to coercion in actual fact, that determines a section 8(a)(1) of the National Labor Relations Act violation. Once it had been established that the photographing was "anticipatory," in the sense that it predated any incidence of violence, the burden shifted to the employer to "provide a solid justification for its resort to photography." Significantly, however, it held that "the efficient gathering of evidence is a legitimate endeavor. . . . Photographing of pickets does not violate Section 8(a)(1) of the Act where the photographs are taken to establish for purposes of an injunction suit that pickets engaged in violence."[22] Further, the court refused to be swayed, as had the *Larand* Court, by the argument that the photographs were not, in fact, used in state court injunction proceedings.

The use of electronic eavesdropping or bugging devices has been uniformly condemned, regardless of whether the surveillance occurs on or off

---

[18]*NLRB v. Colonial Haven Nursing Home, Inc.,* 542 F.2d 691, 701 (7th Cir. 1976).
[19]*Larand Leisurelies, Inc.,* 213 NLRB 197, 199 (1974). enf'd 523 F.2d 814, 819 (6th Cir. 1975).
[20]*International Union, etc. v. NLRB,* 455 F.2d 1357, 1367, 1368, (D.C. Cir. 1971).
[21]*Flambeau Plastics Corp. v. NLRB,* 401 F.2d 128, 136, 137 (7th Cir. 1968), *cert. denied,* 393 U.S. 1019 (1969).
[22]Citing *Larand Leisurelies, Inc., v. NLRB, supra,* 523 F.2d at 819. (542 F. 2d, at 701).

the employer's premises. An employer was found to have engaged in unlawful surveillance by placing a tape recorder next to the employee dining room. Another employer was found to have violated Section 8(a)(1) by bugging various plant locations to ascertain the identities of union supervisors.

Electronic eavesdropping outside the plant is assumed to be illegal. Instead of debating this question, the courts have focused on the conduct of the employer. One decision indicated that bugging the hotel rooms or offices of union members would be "reprehensible" and an unfair labor practice if the employer specifically intended to obtain information useful in strike negotiations. However, in that case it was found that the security agency hired to protect the plant had initiated the surveillance without the employer's knowledge. Since the agency had been trying to ascertain the source of threats to the president of the security agency, no unfair labor practice was found.[23]

Lack of knowledge or explicit approval by top management is not always a determining factor, however. The activities of middle management personnel who placed the motel rooms of union organizers under electronic surveillance were found to be in violation.[24] Noting that the acts benefited only the company, and that the personnel acted in a "realistic expectation" that surveillance was desired by the company, the court attributed the unlawful conduct to the employer.

The decisions cited indicate that the NLRB has consistently denounced all forms of employee surveillance. Further, the courts have generally enforced NLRB orders based on this viewpoint. Perhaps even more importantly, unlawful surveillance has been seen in the courts as an element contributing to the "unlawful prolongation" of a strike, turning an economic strike to an unfair labor practice strike.[25]

Surveillance of the employee union activities can be accomplished with impunity only within a rather narrow spectrum of legitimate purposes. Although it would appear that the spectrum has been broadened somewhat, especially with regard to photographing pickets, the rules governing the use of undercover operatives and detectives, as well as electronic surveillance equipment, remain quite restrictive.

Proper training of the security team, along with explicit written instructions and special orders for the officers and all other working employees, is required to reduce possible exposure to violations of the National Labor Relations Act. Documentation of picket line misconduct and other strike

---

[23]*Street Railway Employees v. NLRB,* 294 F.2d 264, 266-68 (DC Cir. 1961).
[24]*NLRB v. JP Stevens & Co., Inc.,* 563 F.2d 8, 18 (2nd Cir. 1977) *cert. denied.* 434 US 1064 (1978).
[25](*See Kohler Co.,* 128 NLRB 1062, 1100 (1960), *enf'd* in this respect, 300 F.2d 699, 701 DC Cir. 1962), *cert. denied* 382 US 836 (1965) (dealing with surveillance by detectives); *c.f., Flambeau Plastics Corp. v. NLRB, supra, enforcing* 167 NLRB 735 (1967) (photographing pickets).

related investigations should be accomplished only by trained, experienced specialists who are familiar with labor law and who work closely with corporate management, the security director, and the labor relations department.

INDEX